GOD, MAN, & EPIC POETRY

VOLUME I
CLASSICAL

CAMBRIDGE
UNIVERSITY PRESS
LONDON: Fetter Lane

NEW YORK
The Macmillan Co.

BOMBAY, CALCUTTA and
MADRAS
Macmillan and Co., Ltd.

TORONTO
The Macmillan Co. of
Canada, Ltd.

TOKYO
Maruzen-Kabushiki-Kaisha

GOD, MAN, & EPIC POETRY

A STUDY
IN COMPARATIVE LITERATURE

BY

H. V. ROUTH, M.A.

*University Reader in English Language
and Literature, London*

VOLUME I
CLASSICAL

CAMPION
COLLEGE

A | M
D | G

REGINA

CAMBRIDGE
AT THE UNIVERSITY PRESS
MCMXXVII

PREFACE

A PREFACE is an author's last words, so it usually resembles a vote of thanks to collaborators or the last appeal from the dock why sentence should not be passed. I have, unfortunately, very little occasion to speak in the former capacity, and I know, even more unfortunately, how useless it is to employ a preface for the latter purpose. So it is enough to say that I am haunted with the fear of having sometimes used authorities without the proper acknowledgment. Such oversights became inevitable because this book was begun years ago without any definite aim, and it gradually developed into an effort to justify the study of literature, at any rate to myself. Gradually a dominating idea emerged and gave point to my investigations, but by that time I had lost track of many books which I had absorbed merely as an impressionist. I have not appended a "Bibliography," because all, or nearly all, the standard works on this wide province can be found in more specialised treatises, and I should merely be copying lists from books as well known to the reader as to myself. On several occasions I have arrived independently at conclusions which were to appear in other people's books long before my own was ready for press. This also was inevitable. My scheme grew so gradually and automatically that I could not publish any part of it, till the whole was more or less developed. The division into two volumes was an after-thought. It was found that the first eight chapters dealt almost exclusively with Greek or Roman civilisation, and so might be useful to readers who had not the time or the inclination to look further. But of course they are only parts of a larger scheme.

The composition of the book as a whole has been prolonged amid interruptions and disappointments, till I am
only too glad to dismiss it from my thoughts—even the
title does not satisfy me, but I can find no better—and
I have for long understood that the ideal at which I first
aimed is unattainable.

H. V. R.

WYLDEWAYS

HAMPSTEAD

July 1926

CONTENTS

CHAPTER I

THE SCOPE AND METHOD OF THE PRESENT WORK

THE following chapters are the result of many years' work, not so much in collecting material as in finding a way to use it. Nor has the spread of academic culture rendered the quest less difficult. In fact, the methods and means of research have improved so vastly during the last few decades, that it is now easy to acquire knowledge without having in view any very definite purpose whatever. The more deeply you bookworm your way into a subject, the further does the object of this facile but minute labour recede into the distance, and as material multiplies, it becomes less easy to keep the direction in sight. The writer does not claim to have solved this difficulty to everyone's satisfaction, not even completely to his own. But when, some years ago, he let himself be absorbed, almost completely, by the study of English literature, he soon found that every waggon road ended for him in a trackless moor. This book is an attempt to erect a signpost over the waste.

It is not that specialisation is ever in itself irksome. There is always a secret pleasure in identifying oneself with a subject and gradually winning, inch by inch, a sense of confidence and intimacy among its labyrinths. Nor can anyone object that English literature is lacking in variety of interests. On the one hand it offers an admirable opportunity of watching national characteristics develop under the influence of culture, and on the other hand it is an unfailing source of inspiration and refinement. Yet many people find the study of English unsatisfying, though they do not all give the same reasons for their disillusionment. The older school used to condemn the academic study of English, because our native language and literature were (they considered) too easy to be used as a means of education. English literature might teach good taste and even morality, but cultivated people could safely be left to find these benefits for themselves, and its study was not a sufficiently exacting intellectual exercise. It did not develop the sense of fitness, the power to recognise distinctions, the capacity to differentiate thought from expression, the complete control of the reasoning powers, which every gentleman ought to possess.

Such may be, despite the efforts of teachers, the attendant disadvantages of an English education. But if these were the only or even principal drawbacks to studying our literature, the student would find all that he wanted in Greek and Latin. The classics are as unworldly, as inspiring and as full of humanity as is English literature, while the effort needed to master two such intricate and subtle languages involves the severest mental discipline. Yet it is quite useless to pretend that a specialised classical education satisfies the student of to-day. He or she may take a deep interest in Greek and Latin thought, or may even prefer these subjects to any other study, as offering the best examples of literary perfection, or again may find that the wisdom of the ancients is just as good a preparation for life as the confusion of political and economic ideas which are supposed to be an equipment for present-day problems. But the classical student will end with a feeling that he is still left on the frontiers of the promised land; he will be conscious that his study is merely a pursuit which, despite its linguistic difficulties, does not fully absorb his mental energy. It is not an integral part of his emotional and spiritual life. In fact Greek and Latin literatures fail to satisfy him, much as English literature would fail.

Let us look a little deeper into the claims of a classical education, because they will prove a test case. No other branch of learning has, within modern times, exercised so absorbing an influence for so long a period, and thus the causes of its present failure will stand out in relief on this background of popularity. Two hundred years ago, the relics of Greek and Roman civilisation satisfied the modern need for culture. The classics once stood for all that the spirit and intellect of man required. La Bruyère[1] declared that by his time the ancients and the few talented moderns had left nothing but gleanings for the moralists and poets of his own day; Swift went further and

---

[1] *Les Caractères*, chap. i.

denied that modern resembled ancient literature more than a spider resembled a bee[1]. The classics were considered to offer the complete and perfect type of literary culture. If they have now lost their hold on civilisation, it must be because the demands of civilisation are changed. We cannot be finding fault with the languages and literatures themselves, which so many generations have felt to be perfect. Our quarrel must be with something inherent in all forms of literary training. If we can lay our finger on the defect or inadequacy of classical education, we shall probably find what disappoints us in the study of English.

It is easy to see why Greek and Latin are now at a disadvantage. We know too much. We know too much, first of all, in the literal sense that history and archeology have restricted our imagination in the interpretation of the classics. In 1869 J. T. Wood began to excavate the site of the temple of Artemis at Ephesus, and in 1871 Schliemann began to dig on Hissarlik. From that period till the discoveries of Sir A. Evans in Crete, in the first decade of this century, we have not ceased to develop realism in the study of antiquity. These researches have opened a new field of intellectual endeavour. Following the sixteenth-century discovery of manuscripts and the eighteenth-century cult of statuary, they may prove to be the third renascence of the ancient world. But in the meantime they lessen the spiritual appeal of the classics. We cannot, any longer, accept so readily the great characters, whether real or legendary, as fulfilling our ideals. The great lord of Mykenai has become too materialised a monarch, the product of an ambiguous civilisation, and the romantic figure of Orpheus has evaporated into a mere abstraction, the ghost of animistic superstitions. The democratic principles which Thoukydides discussed can no longer be applied to our own political problems; Brutus is no longer the ideal of a perfect patriot whose hands are clean; nor Juvenal the type of righteous and withering scorn. Even the golden bough, which Aeneas sought at the bidding of the Sybil, has now been found by Sir James Frazer. If we stop to ask what remedies Sokrates or Plato or Marcus

[1] *Battle of the Books.*

Aurelius would suggest for our present-day difficulties, we shall only find that the question is useless, because the answer cannot be found. And then we know too much in a deeper and more philosophical sense. Who has not learnt, whatever the particular line of his studies, to discover in himself something infinite? The conviction comes to some people with overwhelming force in the presence of Alpine scenery, or on catching sight of a distant horizon, or by contrast, in the contemplation of something slight and almost commonplace, such as a streamlet, or a field of snow, rendered magical by some simple effect of colour. To others this whisper from eternity comes with the sound of music or, strangely enough, after witnessing some unexpected touch of human nature while passing in the street. In all such highly wrought moments the mind becomes praeternaturally clear, and realises its own familiar ideas so vividly and intensely that they seem to be inspirations. It is especially during the last century or so that the consciousness of infinity has been bred in all educated people, whether or no they are susceptible to the poetry of nature, and has altered their conception of man. Whoever is sufficiently developed to examine his own thoughts carefully, will find (in some cases to his surprise) that there is in him something boundless and undefined, such as no single figure or symbol can represent, and at the same time a curious impatience of his own egoism and even an occasional desire to escape from his own personality.

It may well be objected that this mood is not peculiar to the nineteenth and twentieth centuries, but must always have been present in human beings, not excluding those generations which found the most satisfying expression of themselves in the study of classical literature. But since the Augustan Age our mentality has come under the influence of science. For however exclusively we may devote ourselves to "letters" or to "the humanities," we all have scientific tendencies. By this I do not mean the "scientisme" which possessed the intellectuals of Bourget's youth as "un spécieux monisme intellectuel qui enveloppait inconscieusement un monisme métaphisique."[1]

---

[1] *Nouvelles Pages de Critique et de Doctrine*, Paris, Plon-Nourrit, 1922.

I mean the necessity of viewing life from a speculative and scientific point of view. For it is this attitude which makes us feel the new mystery outside of and yet part of ourselves. As far back as 1833 Carlyle had written "There is yearly growing up the strangest crabbed, one-sided persuasion, that art is but a reminiscence now; that for us in these days prophecy (well-understood) not poetry is the thing wanted. How can we sing and paint when we cannot believe and see." Carlyle found what he wanted in German transcendentalism, especially in Goethe. A little later we find Sainte-Beuve writing, "Je n'ai plus qu'un plaisir, j'analyse, j'herborise, je suis naturaliste des esprits,—ce que je voudrais constituer, c'est l'histoire naturelle littéraire." Then in 1871 Nietzsche, attributing his own nineteenth-century mentality to a Greek, wrote,

Mit dieser Begabung, mit aller Helligkeit und Behendigkeit seines kritischen Denkens hatte Euripides im Theater gesessen und sich angestrengt an den Meisterwerken seiner grossen Vorgänger wie an dunkel gewordenen Gemälden, Zug um Zug, Linie um Linie, wiederzuerkennen. Und hier nun war ihm begegnet, was dem in tieferen Geheimnisse der Aeschyleischen Tragödie Eingeweihten nicht unerwartet sein darf: er gewahrte etwas Incommensurables in jedem Zug, und in jeder Linie eine gewisse täuschende Bestimmtheit und zugleich eine räthselhafte Tiefe, ja Unendlichkeit des Hintergrundes[1].

Anton Chekhov in 1888[2] admitted that even poetry must be the product of universal and mysterious forces, and that younger writers of his generation were founding a "physiology of creative art" on natural laws. And lastly we have Ray Lankester's claim that "science commends itself to us as does honesty and great art and all fine thought and deed, because it satisfies man's soul." Science does not repress the imagination or the emotions. On the contrary it pushes back the boundaries of the invisible world to infinity and fills the intervening space with all kinds of energies and impulses which we cannot see, but try to understand. This present-day tendency has nothing

---

[1] *Die Geburt der Tragödie*, § 11.

[2] *To A. S. Souvorin*, Moscow, Nov. 1888. See *Letters on The Short Story, The Drama and other Literary Topics*, by Anton Chekhov, ed. L. S. Friedland, Geoffrey Bles, n.d.

to do with the positivism which dominated J. S. Mill and which has become associated with the teaching of Darwin. In fact some of our most modern writers, amongst them Synge, Yeats and De la Mare, in obedience to a scientific influence, have revolted against Victorian materialism and plunged into metaphysics and second sight. It is sometimes said that science teaches the insignificance of man. It rather teaches that man is not complete in himself, any more than the earth is isolated from the solar system. Man is a maze or network of cross influences and energies; his nature is bound up with all kinds of phenomena which were once considered to be no more than a background. Whatever may have been our training, we cannot help realising, however vaguely, that every human being is a channel through which tendencies flow; an enigma which can be understood solely in connection with world-wide forces. Thus most people who think are haunted by the consciousness that life is a mystery. So whoever devotes his mind to serious study, probably cannot help expecting this mystery to be recognised, and, if possible, explained. He does not necessarily turn to his books with such a question already formulated, in fact nothing may be further from his uppermost thought. But there is always some such curiosity lurking in his mind; he is never without a desire to recognise the hidden forces which make up human nature. If his chosen intellectual pursuit cannot become in any sense a means to this end it will become unsatisfying, a mere technical occupation, a matter of business; not a feast for both the intellect and the emotions. Science itself proves unsatisfactory whenever it obliterates this sense of background. Gibbon, after describing the wonders of St Sophia, exclaims, "Yet how dull is the artifice, how insignificant is the labour, if it be compared with the formation of the vilest insect that crawls upon the surface of the temple."[1] Who, in our own day, would echo this eighteenth-century sentiment when a student may write his M.A. thesis on the anatomy of some hemiptera? This is the real reason why Greek and Latin literatures have lost prestige. It matters little that they do not give the student preliminary experience

[1] *Decline and Fall*, chap. XL.

in the usages and practices of the modern world, for they offer his mental faculties an almost perfect training. They fail because, in and by themselves, they are too anthropomorphic. If made the subject of a specialised study, their general conception of man is disappointingly simple. They portray him too much as an isolated phenomenon, so complete in himself that even the supernatural powers were of much the same quality; and so they stop short where curiosity begins.

But it is not the purpose of this introduction to discuss ancient literature for its own sake. The present disadvantages of a classical education are quoted merely to show that as civilisation changes, our minds change in a certain fashion, and so our way of looking at literature must sooner or later change also. What is true of the classics is true in a certain degree of any single modern literature. Each will prove unsatisfying if studied as complete in itself. After fully appreciating the literary, linguistic or bibliographical interest of his author, most students will have to confess that their other mystifications are not illumined. The fault lies with ourselves. There are, no doubt, great poets and humanists gifted with such intuition and felicity of self-expression that, through their inspiration, we can penetrate to newly realised mysteries around us. And even if the older seers were not conscious of its presence, they exemplify its influence. Cannot then a youth, pleasurably undecided between the spiritual realities and possibilities of existence, be safely left to explore for himself the works of Goethe, Shelley, Browning, Senancour, Dante, or even Lucretius and Plato? I venture to suggest that in many cases the explorer will fail to make the discoveries which we hope for him, because his previous training has restricted his interests and has given him an inadequate idea of what literature really is.

So we come back to the question: "What is the best use to make of our knowledge, especially of our knowledge of literature?" The difficulty, and its solution, as they present themselves to me, can most easily be made clear by an allegory. In very ancient times, at least as far back as the neolithic age, the world was just as full of spirits and daemons as it is now, but they did not then lead a concealed and shadowed life. Their existence was fully recognised. Men did not always understand them and their power, and they did not always understand what man meant by his fantastic and often bloody rites. But the attitude of human beings was on the whole one of respect and so the spirits were able to play their part. But with the manufacture of bronze and with the earliest tribe migrations, new deities came into existence, and it has generally been supposed that each new group of divinities exterminated or subjugated the previous dynasty. In reality nothing of the kind happened. The Immortals may have personal animosities, like human beings, but as a class they hold together. No god will utterly abandon another in the struggle to survive in the memory and worship of men.

Now the anarchy of the spirit world arose because, with each change on earth, men kept bringing in deities who were less clearly defined as to locality but more clearly defined as to qualities. The ancient spirits were universal and all-pervasive, but they picked up their worship here and there, in different places, according as groups of human beings recognised in them the power which gave life and character to the surroundings of men. So the spirits had enjoyed their existence in herbs, trees, corn, or even in some particular stream or crag. But there was now a demand for gods and goddesses with definite attributes, such as war, love, wisdom, fertility or revenge. So the more ancient spirits had to efface themselves. But they did not disappear. They generally managed to cling to the younger deities who gave them shelter and allowed them, anonymously, to enjoy a share of man's worship. Finally, nearly all of them were cultivated under the names of their protectors. Even when Christianity began to supersede all other religions, the ancient universal spirits continued to enjoy attention. Amongst others the spirit of the desert found his way into the hearts of the anchorites and the spirit of strife was equally at home with the followers of Mahomet, and the crusaders.

But there was one spirit which, ever since the age of primitive animism, had never again found its proper place, because it could not contract its influence to one sphere, or function, or quality. It was not a spirit of the wild, nor a virtue peculiar to civilised man, nor does it possess in itself any unique or even outstanding quality. It is the spirit common to all humanity; the feeling of mental or emotional contact which most men experience when they think of their fellow-creatures. This spirit came into existence as soon as ever men became aware of their own egoism, and began to feel that their individuality was a burden, and that they ought to escape from themselves. It was then that they became conscious of a spirit common to all men but peculiar to none; a power which took them out of themselves and merged them in some all-embracing sentiment and ideal. But now, when men expected each deity to represent one special province of mental or social activity, this spirit was left unrecognised. It could not command worshippers under the name of Hope, nor Enthusiasm, nor Progress, though it partook of all these virtues, because such qualities are apt to drive the thoughts of men upon themselves, and to make them self-centred, while this nameless spirit, as we have said, is potent chiefly in helping men to lose their personal considerations in fellow-feeling. So this dispossessed deity addressed itself to the soul of Wisdom, which was already becoming famous among the Pelasgians and was soon to be known as Athene, and asked by what means it might regain the worship of men. Wisdom replied:

"I will do anything that I can to aid your restoration, for—as I can clearly see—humans have more need of your influence than they are themselves aware. As soon as a man's thoughts become concentrated on himself, he grows either spiritually or physically diseased. Just as people who are bodily sick talk and think too much about themselves, so the mentally self-centred become law-breakers, revolutionaries, or, what is worse, those who think out and sow errors. Besides, human beings have always suffered from fear. I do not mean fear of each other in war time, but fear of themselves—of their own weakness and folly—and of disease, famine and tempest. Just as they need the presence of their comrades when facing an enemy, so they need the sense of kinship and common humanity when afflicted by despair or dread of the immortal gods. You must do as all other deities have done: you must seek out human beings and make them feel your power."

"But," replied the nameless spirit, "that is already done. A human being has only to gaze on the silent majesty of a mountain range, or on the broken sheen of a rivulet caught by the setting sun, and he will forget himself utterly and yet feel something which is a source of common joy to all his fellows."

"I see well," replied Wisdom, "that you have by now grown unfamiliar with the ways of men. You have forgotten that though they remain at heart the same, yet they change their manners and thoughts from generation to generation. So although they will need you just as much ten thousand years hence as now, they will continually be thinking of you as something which changes from age to age. No doubt there will always be human beings who recognise you in the grandeur or beauty of nature, for there will always be somewhere in every age a generation which is discovering for the first time the joy which scenery can inspire. But races and nations will not for long be content with the same enthusiasms. They will always be inventing for themselves new sources of happiness and sorrow. If you would regain your empire, you must keep pace with these changes. You must reflect these moods, you must embody these fashions." Hereupon the nameless spirit was silent for a while, plunged in thought, so Wisdom continued, "Besides, you can appeal to human beings only by appearing in their likeness. All deities have had to adopt this guise; even Othin and Apollo will be constrained to resemble human beings when they commune with men. So although you are the most universal of all spirits, you must yet disguise your true nature under the form of a mortal as often as you wish to rescue men from carking thoughts of self and to remind them of their common humanity."

The nameless spirit was not slow to follow this advice. Almost without ceasing, from that time forward, it has exercised its influence on men, but always under some such disguise as the goddess suggested. In fact it has followed these counsels

so thoroughly that it does not even send its intimations direct
from itself. It first enters some human being and through him
delivers to the world the dreams and imaginings which look
like the mere thoughts of a man and seem to be pictures or
reflections of men, but are really embodiments of a universal
spirit. Each manifestation is conceived and created to suit
the atmosphere of some particular age, but they are only
messengers, emissaries or intermediaries. They stand for something else more universal and less earth-bound. Their function
is to give eloquence and precision to deeper tendencies and to
bring order into what would otherwise be a tangle of half-
realised ideas. If they are properly to be understood they must
be received as symbols or mouthpieces, first of some age and
then of the immemorial spirit of humanity. They are means
and not an end. To study literature as an end in itself seems
almost as unsatisfactory as listening to a voice without com-
prehending the words or the thought behind the words.

It is for all these reasons, I believe, that specialisation in one
period and much more in one group of authors so often proves
inadequate as a liberal education. Such concentration need
not, of course, necessarily be disappointing; it all depends on
the sympathy and insight with which the thought is studied.
Provided that the investigator uses his material as a means
towards contact with the Human Spirit, there is no reason
why the minute examination of a single work should not
broaden his mind and refine his emotions. Besides, research,
even into the most recondite and accidental fragments, is
indispensable to the pursuit of truth. We never know when
the discovery of some apparently insignificant fact is going to
shed unexpected light on the history of this same Human Spirit.
But academic methods are accompanied by this disadvantage.
They not only multiply and facilitate the approaches to knowledge; for that very reason, and by that same process, they
emphasise the difficulties of drawing near to Truth. Every
new effort in criticism and exegesis is like discovering some
unexpected fortification, which must be captured before the
castle itself can be reached. The beginner who sets out to
cultivate some admired poet or humanist, generally finds

himself confronted by an intervening series of problems concerning archeology, literary transmission or textual criticism. The bibliographies of a subject become its defences, not its avenues of approach. Such are, no doubt, the inevitable conditions of intellectual progress, nor, perhaps, would one wish it otherwise. But it sometimes happens that these researches are prosecuted with such zeal and consummated with such ingenuity, that one cannot help valuing the discovered obstacle for its own sake. One thinks more of the new field to be traversed than of the objective which lies beyond it. For these reasons the methods of modern scholarship, in some cases, are likely to leave the investigator still gazing at the form and type of his author, or the sources of his material, as if there was nothing behind. He runs the risk of missing the point of view which brings every author into touch with some tendency of the Human Spirit. At the worst he may lose interest in anything more humanistic than these technical details, and so contribute towards rendering higher literary education nothing but a preparation for teachers.

These disadvantages may not be ineradicable though they certainly are prevalent, and, in any case, no one would be so over-confident as to insist on one single remedy as sovereign. But literary study will certainly be benefited by a more comprehensive and philosophical spirit. We need a method which puts several poets, or dramatists, or moralists together, regardless of differences in epoch or nationality, in order to understand their common source of inspiration. It is, I am convinced, by such means that one can best pierce the erudite superficialities of specialisation and, while developing our sense of human infinity, train the mind to appreciate thought and imagination at its highest value. We must compare these authors in order to understand their idea. It is only when we have discovered the same spirit beneath the transformations and idiosyncrasies of different epochs and interpreters, that we come into contact with its essence.

For instance, our typical student takes up a dramatic poet. Before long he becomes conscious, with his twentieth-century intelligence, that a profound human tendency underlies this literary art; what may be called, for want of a better term, the tragic spirit. To revert to our allegory, the Human Spirit is trying to bring its influence to bear, under this guise. The reader feels, perhaps only half consciously, a deep curiosity in the tragic spirit, but he will be an exception if he finds any one dramatist who, apart from the others, can satisfy this curiosity. In fact literature is so profoundly influenced by conventionality and example, that probably all the best dramatists of any one nation will still leave him with a sense of incompleteness. Besides, his attention will be distracted by an infinity of bio-graphical and textual problems. If his author is Shakespeare, he will hardly have room for the disputed text on his reading table. He needs to compare, not the different authors of one nation among themselves, but the most representative authors of different nations, all the more if they have lived and thought in widely different ages. Or suppose that the student is reading Shelley. Shelley will completely satisfy certain of his moods and will moreover fill his leisure hours with joy. But if Shelley is also to satisfy his desire for culture, he must give him insight into the lyric spirit. Now Shelley was himself possessed and permeated by this spirit, but the reader will not be prepared to receive his lyricism in its fullness and universality, until the same impulses and idealisms have been felt through the great lyric poets of other nations.

To sum up. As each author, and generally each school, gives an incomplete picture, obscured by details and perplexed by inconsistencies, the kindred authors or schools must be compared and the different streams of inspiration must be brought together. When these various masterpieces show a true fellowship of mood, however much opposed in age and nationality, the student will find himself able, out of these glimpses, to construct a complete story of some great emotion. Whenever the documents display a fundamental variance, however similar in subject or treatment, the student will com-plete and clarify his ideas by contrast. Such is the service that can be rendered to culture by the study of Comparative Literature.

There need be nothing slipshod or unprofessional about this

method. Its pursuit can be just as scholarly and make just as exacting demands on intelligence and accuracy as does the most specialised and academic researches into origins, influences or evolutions. In fact the two points of view are not opposed, they supplement each other. It is hoped, however, that the scheme here outlined will lead to those larger and more universal issues which transcend the mechanism of the intellect and become a part of one's spiritual life.

But it is a waste of words to advocate a system, when for better or for worse two volumes follow to demonstrate its principles. I have chosen the epic because such poetry reveals the impulses and promptings of the human spirit in perhaps their intensest forms; because in English literature this field of study is particularly in need of illustration from other literatures; but also because all kinds of scholarly and scientific interests, such as questions of communal origin, aetiological interpretation, euhemerism, national objectivity and individual subjectivity, are specially likely to obscure the issues which they are so urgently needed to illuminate.

CHAPTER II

THE HEROES OF THE *ILIAD*

1. *Difficulties in the way of appreciating Homer.*

SUPPOSE, then, some curious reader who wishes to come into contact with the epic spirit and to broaden his mind and refine his emotions by discovering and enjoying the power of this inspiration. Where should he begin? He will find at his disposal a large number of narrative poems, many of them dealing with legendary subjects and cast in the traditional form which, yielding to the systematising influence of universities, we have found it convenient to call epics. But among these many and varied specimens, he will find the greatest diversity of spirit and inspiration. Some will declare themselves to be anything but epics, except in the merest superficialities of form. Some others will seem to be on the borderline, to have some share of the grandeur, intensity and heroism, and what W. P. Ker called "the possibilities of mental conflict and tragic contradiction"[1] which we feel instinctively, even at the outset of the inquiry, ought to be the virtue of an epic. But if the student confines himself to English literature he will not find a single poem which exhibits these qualities in their fullest and most convincing forms. He will not even find unanimity of opinion about the claims of any particular English poem to the title of epic. As soon as he looks beyond his own country, he will find a few supreme compositions, standing in a class by themselves, filled with a fuller measure of enthusiasm and emotion, and universally recognised as epics of the purest type. He must begin by reading these, if only by way of introduction. Thus only will his mind acquire the breadth and insight to understand this great human impulse and to recognise its strivings in other less felicitously developed forms. Such a course of research starts with a good omen, for there is no doubt whatever that the greatest and the most complete type of epic will be found in the two poems attributed to Homer.

---

[1] *Epic and Romance*, chap. II, § I.

Thus any idea of epic poetry should be based on the *Iliad* and the *Odyssey*. But the eminence which renders Homer indispensable to the student, makes his poetry all the more difficult to appreciate. Like all poets who "belong to the ages," he has been detached from his own. Alexander the Great, according to Onesikritos, declared Homer to be the best and most reliable source of military science[1]; Horace found in him a moralist plainer and better than Chrysippos and Krantor[2]; in the third century A.D., Porphyrios saw in the cave of the nymphs a neo-Platonic allegory[3]; Montaigne declared that all rulers, administrators, generals, artists, philosophers and religious controversialists had consulted the pages of Homer as "une pépinière de toute espèce de suffisance"[4]; Pope felt that the fire which is discerned in Vergil, flashes in Lucan and Statius, glows in Milton and surprises us in Shakespeare, is found at its best only in Homer, "in him only it burns everywhere clearly and everywhere irresistibly."[5] Goethe went so far as to speak of "Die Ilias" which "das Interesse der Völker, der Welttheile, der Erde und des Himmels umschliesst." Like Vergil, Dante, Shakespeare and the Bible, Homer has been haunted by a reputation which possesses his readers' enthusiasm and persuades them to realise in his pages their own aspirations. At some epochs he has almost entirely ceased to express himself in order to inspire self-expression in others. And so the modern student, who wishes literature to teach him more a knowledge of men than of commentators, must begin by forgetting an immense body of laudatory criticism.

The reader who approaches the *Iliad* in this spirit has something more difficult to forget. Even when he has cleared his mind of all that a less critical if more appreciative age has attributed to his author, he has still his own literary training to reckon with. We come to Homer, after more than twenty centuries of poetic experiments, during which time every successive generation has learnt more and more to recognise the limitations of literary expression, and to search in the words for

---

[1] Plut. *Vit. Alex.* VIII.   [2] *Ep.* I, 2.
[3] Περὶ τοῦ ἐν ᾿Οδυσσείᾳ τῶν Νυμφῶν ἄντρου.   [4] Livre II, ch. XXXVI.
[5] Pref. to *Iliad*.

what their author feels but cannot say. Since modern times, and the triumph of lyric poetry, this attitude has become almost second nature. Lovers of verse now expect to dissociate the purest and most felicitous poetry from any story of men's earthly pursuits, such as are portrayed in dramas and satires, and to look for it in glimpses of the poet's own soul. Any incident, such as the song of a bird, the fall of a leaf, may serve the artist as a parable or symbol of his passion and the reader is thus prepared for a thrill of joy as he divines the emotion which faintly colours the picture but throbs and swells in the rhythm.

> *Füllest wieder Busch und Thal*
> *Still mit Nebelglanz,*
> *Lösest endlich auch einmal*
> *Meine Seele ganz*[1].

Students who have grown accustomed to the kind of appeal suggested by these lines are apt to expect the inwardness and aloofness of modern lyricism in any verse which has the touch of inspiration.

The most modern and exclusively intellectual type of reader, who has escaped these prepossessions, often achieves his freedom by exposing himself to another danger. He believes that the object of the critic is to appreciate the poet's expressiveness —his style, form, originality and indebtedness. With this end in view he is accustomed to begin, as we saw in the last chapter, by familiarising himself with his author's mentality, environment, predecessors and method of composition. But Homer allows no such secrets to be wrung from him, as we shall see later, and so, when the commentators have looked in vain for their usual data, they seek to replace the defects by conjecture and analogy. Thus poetry becomes an incentive to deductions based on archeological, paleographical and even anthropological researches. No one would grudge this new field opened to the exercise of scholarly ingenuity and penetration, nor the training in accurate thought which is thereby acquired. We shall have to follow that same road more than once in this volume. But the taste for such speculations is apt to obscure

[1] Goethe, *An den Mond.*

what may really be found in Homer, and to leave a sense of dis-
satisfaction because of what one fails to discover.

So when the reader begins an ancient poem like the *Iliad*,
his first feeling is one of disappointment. Despite the enthusiasm
and simplicity of the descriptions, he finds whole passages, if
not books, unsatisfying. So he betakes himself to the famous
passages—the death of Hektor, the last talk with Andromache,
Sarpedon's exhortation, or the weeping of the horses for
Patroklos—because he finds in these episodes something which
gives satisfaction to his own state of mind: the "roominess of
great literature." And yet it may eventually be found that these
and such other celebrated scenes give a wrong impression unless they are read as mere incidents of the poem. If isolated,
or detached from what we now consider to be the background, they encourage the reader to become too conscious
of himself. His attention is diverted from the real spirit
of the poem. He fails to discover that the men who fought
round Ilion and who afterwards shared the adventures of
Odysseus were not of the same clay as the men who have
inspired or produced literature within historical times.

II. *The peculiar greatness of Homer is not to be found in the*
subject nor in the style, but in the first place in the character
of the heroes: their self-confidence and their enthusiasm for all
they achieved and possessed. Their love of horses.

To appreciate the Homeric character, it is necessary to remember that the glory of the Trojan war arises neither from
its occasion nor its conduct. Agamemnon sailed from Greece
with his tributary forces to bring back his brother's wife.
According to one legend, the Greeks were the aggressors.
Telamon had ravished Hesione from Troy, and Paris, having
already been promised the aid of Aphrodite, carried off Helen
as a reprisal[1]. However slight his justification, Troy would have
fallen after the first assault, if Agamemnon had been able to
concentrate his whole army on the fortress. But as Proklos[2]
tells us and as is obvious from the poem itself, his forces dissipated their strength in raiding expeditions, so the neigh-

---

[1] Dares Phrygius, *De Excidio Trojae Historia*, IV–IX.   [2] *Chrestomathy*, I.

bouring settlements rallied round Priam and the war dragged
on for ten years. During these tedious and desultory operations,
both sides seem to have grown thoroughly weary of warfare,
and only the personal pride or ambition of Agamemnon on one
side and of Paris on the other prevented a settlement. According
to one legend, Priam and his sons were dazzled by the wealth
which Helen brought, and Hektor opposed her surrender
because she had come as a suppliant[1]. Dissensions fermented
in the Achean camp and during some phases of the struggle
there was probably no attempt at maintaining a siege. Besides,
it seems likely that Troy was not a city. The fortress excavated
by Schliemann is quite small, and may have contained only
the palaces of Priam and of his sons, and some magazines and
shops and barracks and other institutions necessary to the
government of the domain. The ordinary people may very well
have lived in open villages scattered here and there about the
countryside, and so the war possibly resembled a desultory
invasion rather than a siege. At any rate the Trojans frequently
gave battle in the plain and we must imagine two straggling
lines of combatants, full of dust and clamour, more often than
not standing off from each other, dodging the stones and
arrows[2], while the chariots of the chieftains manœuvred in
their immediate rear or dashed forward to an encounter. Often
opposing chiefs seem to have shouted challenges to each other,
lauding their own ancestry and vilifying that of their opponent.
If a serious duel was to hand, the warriors dismounted and met
on foot, but they kept their chariots well within hail, in case
the enemy proved too formidable; sometimes a furious battle
arose round a fallen comrade, not only to recover his corpse
for the funeral pyre, but also because his armour was too rare
and valuable to be lost[3]. The equipment which Hektor stripped
off Patroklos had been given by the gods to Peleus, and he in
his old age had bequeathed it to his son Achilles[4]. In these
hand-to-hand struggles, the most hideous wounds were sometimes inflicted, but the general effect must have been very
different from what Wiertz imagined. As often as not these

[1] Dictys Cretensis, *De Bello Trojano*, II, 25.   [2] Cf. *Il.* XVII, 370–5.
[3] Chadwick, *The Heroic Age.*   [4] *Il.* XVII, 194–7.

puny bronze weapons broke or bent, or their armour burst its fastenings, and the heroes were feign to hurl stones, like their followers. Archers and javelin throwers again and again missed their aim. The corslets of which they were so proud rarely if ever resisted an arrow or a spear, unless the impetus of the missile had been weakened by piercing the shield. The courage of these warriors was hardly more reliable than their skill and their equipment. When their opponents' resistance slackened, they became possessed with overweening confidence, but in the supreme hour of trial their hearts often failed them. Achilles, Odysseus and Aias are the only chieftains who never took counsel in flight and of these Achilles never takes the field except in moments of fanatical hatred, and Odysseus never takes the lead but once. The whole action covers only a few days' fighting which did indeed involve the Acheans in innumerable woes, but achieved nothing more decisive than the death of Hektor. Moreover the whole episode was brought about by the caprice of a deity to humour a mortal.

What then is the charm of this ancient collection of poems, which delighted Horace, inspired Bossuet and educated Pope? If the field and scope of Homeric activities are so infinitely limited in comparison with modern ideas, and if the warriors who are held up to admiration appear to be of an order so different from ourselves, why is the poem claimed to be the most perfect type of an epic? In the first place the *Iliad* is delightful for its felicity and completeness of expression. It is difficult to think of any other author, ancient or modern, who can surprise the reader with such vivid glimpses into life. As Voltaire was forced to admit, he is "un peintre sublime."[1] And then the Homeric poets have achieved, more completely than any latter-day writer, the art of telling a story. But though these qualities are conspicuous in the *Iliad*, they are peculiar neither to the poem itself nor to the type. The essential excellence of this epic is found neither in its style nor in its theme but in something which inspires them both. As the reader turns the pages and the swift full rhythm seems to grow into distinct figures of men or animals full of passion and energy in a world

[1] *Essai sur la Poésie épique*, chap. II.

of bright colours and tints, he becomes conscious of one dominating theme: the glory and pride which surround human beings. The object of all bards of the Heroic Age was to exalt the achievements of some warrior, but the Homeric poets have succeeded, from their point of view, in exalting human nature, and have inspired their imagery and diction with this enthusiasm. The Achean warrior survives as the most consistent and successful attempt yet made by man to realise his own grandeur and freedom.

If a modern poet had accompanied Helen on the walls of Troy[1] when she met Priam and his elders and pointed out to them the Achean chieftains marshalling their contingents on the plain in front, he would vaguely have been conscious of a ghost hovering behind each warrior—the unattainable ideal which haunts the civilised man. He would have felt that Agamemnon, or Aias, or Odysseus, after fighting the Trojans, would have to fight himself; and this conviction would have rendered illusory and unsatisfying all that they did against other men. The first and most obvious characteristic of the Homeric warriors is that they have no such bad dreams. We can never know what these rovers and marauders were truly like, but their poets depict them as men who found comfort and assurance in the external world, because they were at peace with themselves. A later minstrel realised this trait when he represented Homer as saying that the thing most worth praying for was εὔνουν εἶναι ἑαυτῷ[2]. Schelling[3], possibly influenced by Herder[4], must have had the same quality in view when he dwelt on the serenity of the epic poet and pictured him composing in an unhurried absolute world, indifferent to the fate of his heroes, presiding over the scene like some detached being beyond the reach of pity or fear. The character of Agamemnon is a curious illustration of the Homeric conception. Andrew Lang compares his portraiture to that of Charlemagne by the French minstrels of the later Middle Ages. For the most part the trouvères represent the medieval monarch as fat, lazy and

[1] *Il.* III, 146 ff.   [2] ΠΕΡΙ ΟΜΗΡΟΥ ΚΑΙ ΗΣΙΟΔΟΥ, 320.
[3] *Sämmtliche Werke*, Stuttgart, 1856–61, Abt. I, Bd. v, *Philosophie der Kunst*.
[4] *Briefen zur Beförderung der Humanität*, 1794.

demoralised. That is to say, the feudal princes hated a king and so the poet degraded the type to please them[1]. Dares[2] represents Agamemnon as holding his position by no power of his own but by the election of his peers, until Palamedes succeeds him in their favour. But in Homer, the king of Mykenai has all the inevitable characteristics of an overlord. He takes the lion's share of the spoil; he is domineering, censorious, and to our modern minds contemptibly vacillating; on two occasions he is actually treacherous. Yet Homer has not lost faith in him. He is not humiliated or traduced. He accomplishes an ἀριστεία[3]; he maintains his right to upbraid the chieftains; he has no fear for the anger of Achilles; he enjoys the reputation of being one of the most formidable of the warriors; he is devoted to his brother and even his two lapses into poltroonery seem to be the result of his brooding on the responsibilities and difficulties of his position. In a word he is an epic character.

None the less, the *Iliad* displays an unmistakeable tendency to revolt against centralised authority and to look for the splendour of life in the character and surroundings of the irresponsible individual. Agamemnon's position as a responsible administrator receives only grudging recognition, while according to another legend, the army as a whole placed the fullest confidence in his forethought and wisdom—*eum quippe optimum consultorem suum, non secus quam parentem miles omnis percolebat*[4]. The Homeric warriors cared for other things. Their equipment was so dearly prized, that its strength or beauty seemed to become a part of themselves. Their helmets shone like a star; compared with such brightness, their horsehair plumes cast a shadow and appeared to partake of the warrior's grimness; Aias's oblong shield gave him the strength and firmness of a tower. Their greaves were of beaten tin; their shields had a layer of copper, which was riveted to the layers of hide with studs of gold, so their armour lent them dignity through its costly workmanship, as well as imagined safety through its

---

[1] *E.g. Chevalerie Ogier* and *Gui de Bourgoyne*. See A. Lang, *Homer and His Age*.
[2] *De Excidio Trojae Historia*, xx, xxv, xxix.   [3] *Il*. xi.
[4] *De Bello Trojano*, i, 23.

strength. Hektor is twice described as holding a spear whose
shaft was ringed with gold, while the bronze point glittered
before his face[1]. The breastplate which Kinyras gave as a
ξεινήιον to Agamemnon was made of three rare metals and
engraved or inlaid[2]. The sceptres which symbolised their kingship and even the golden cups reserved for libations are not
alluded to as ordinary insignia or possessions. They have a
history and a grandeur of their own which ennobles their possessors. Idomeneus, newly armed, is compared to the lightning
which flashes far and wide from Olympos[3]. This enthusiasm
was stimulated by something more than the "antique zest, the
animal happiness, the naïveté of blessed children."[4] As we shall
see later, the Homeric poems are not the involuntary expression
of a primitive civilisation. They are part of a mature effort to
realise the grandeur of man. Indeed, it seems likely that this
effort was nourished by contrast with other races, if not by a
sense of novelty. The warriors on the fragment of the "siege
vase" and on the "dagger with lion-hunters" have no body
armour and it is doubtful whether the men on the vase of
Aristonothos are accustomed to other defences than a shield.
Now and then a warrior in the *Iliad* is described, apparently
through inadvertence, as though he was covered only by a
huge shield of hide, instead of a round targe with breastplate
and greaves[5]. So whether the designs represent Pelasgians or
Acheans before the period of the Trojan war, the possession
of armour may well have been something of a privilege and a
distinction. Their weapons may also have been immensely improved within memory. J. A. K. Thomson points out that the
bow seems once to have been the almost universal weapon and
whereas the Homeric chariot-wheel had eight spokes and iron
tyres, the Lybians had only four[6].

Nothing is more characteristic of the Homeric warrior than

---

[1] *Il.* VI, 320; VIII, 495.   [2] *Ibid.* XI, 25 ff.
[3] *Ibid.* XIII, 242.
[4] E. C. Stedman, *The Nature and Elements of Poetry*, Boston, 1892.
[5] *E.g.* the unforgettable glimpse of Hektor leaving the battle with his
shield of black bull's hide curving round his body and reaching down from
his neck to his ankles. *Il.* VI, 117–18.
[6] See the chariot once at the necropolis of Thebes and now at the Archeological Museum at Florence.

his admiration of horses. It seems almost certain that little, dun-coloured creatures, too small to ride, had for many generations been familiar to both Acheans and Trojans, and had long ago been domesticated as draft animals[1]. But it also seems likely that in the Homeric period, the Acheans were beginning to become acquainted with a new and much finer strain, and it is typical of the epic spirit that this discovery fills them or rather their poets with enthusiasm. When Rhesos joined the Trojans, it will be remembered how he at once gained epic importance, though his life was so futile, because he possessed wonderful horses of a pure white breed[2]. As Achilles is the greatest warrior of the whole war, he is imagined to have the finest horses and it is worth noting that they come from afar. They were born of the harpy Podarge as she grazed by the stream Okeanos; their sire was Zephyros, and they were given by Poseidon. The horses of Aeneas were even more famous. King Erichthonios had three thousand mares, twelve of whom were crossed by Boreas. His son Tros inherited these, but Zeus gave him a yet finer breed, and Anchises eventually stole this blood from Laomedon[3]. In the chariot race at Patroklos's funeral these animals easily surpassed all others. Prof. Sir W. Ridgeway[4] has shown how these fascinating stories point to the introduction of two new breeds, one from Libya, as exemplified by Achilles's steeds, and one from Thrace, as we see from the steeds of Rhesos and of Aeneas. But in the present connection it is to be noted how the poet speaks of horses as a theme in which man's highest aspirations can find their scope. A comparison with the celebrated chapter in the *Book of Job*[5] will make clear the quality of epic enthusiasm. An introspective and devotional poet sings of the strange cunning and power of wild animals and ends with a magnificent eulogy of the horse. No passage in Homer can compare with this chapter for lyrical fervour and sheer wonder. But though the Hebrew poet surpasses the Greek in enthusiasm and imagination, his description is really quite unepic. The voice which spoke out

---

[1] See Prof. Sir W. Ridgeway, *The Prehistoric Horse*.
[2] *Il.* x, 436–7, 543–51.   [3] *Ibid.* xx, 221.
[4] *The Prehistoric Horse*.   [5] xxxix.

of the whirlwind is condemning the arrogance and self-sufficiency of man, and is reminding him of the inexplicable wonders of the brute creation, and of their vigour and sagacity, so far above human ken. One leaves the passage with a sense of the greatness of God and of the littleness of man. But the lions and boars and especially the horses of the heroic age are not the superiors of man, but only his fellow-creatures, in a certain sense his comrades in courage and energy. The latter are as mettlesome and as haughty as their high-born masters. The best would not listen to any voice but that of their own charioteer and were capable of the nobler of human emotions. Xanthos and Balios, the two far-famed steeds of Achilles, felt so keenly their comradeship with the greatest warriors that they wept over the corpse of Patroklos[1]. The most prized were, like the very best of their royal masters, of immortal strain. One steed was granted the power of speech and the knowledge to prophesy[2], and the famous pair descended from Podarge claimed more pity from the Father of gods and men than was ever accorded to human beings[3]. But these superhuman associations do not dwarf men, as they do in the *Book of Job*. It is proof that both Acheans and Trojans were free to view their animals not only as friends but as equals, though of a different breed. Their ancestry, just as much as their bearing and gait, could be as noble as that of a warrior. So in all the suspense of an approaching battle, or when night interrupted some conflict at its crisis, they did not feel it unepic to remember that the steeds were tended and fed with white barley and given wine to drink[4], and one of the proudest titles of these men of war was "Tamer of Horses."

These pretentious descriptions should not be dismissed as "epic exaggeration." There were indeed good reasons why an Homeric warrior should be so proud of his equipment. The weapons and appliances of those days constantly reminded a hero of his own manhood. It must be remembered that with each advance in efficiency, war loses something of its grandeur.

---

[1] *Il.* xvii, 426 ff.   [2] *Ibid*. xix, 407 ff.   [3] *Ibid*. xvii, 441.
[4] A. Lang reminds us that "'Dictator' always had his bottle of port before a race," *Homer and the Epic*.

If any modern man could suddenly see an Homeric warrior, he would at first be tempted to smile. The little two-wheeled chariot would be drawn by a yoke of horses more tiny than Shetland ponies; the spear head, whose glitter the owner admired so much, would probably fall off the shaft before the day's fighting was over; the armour, perhaps inlaid with gold, was liable to break its laces and his silver-hilted sword was often broken or bent. But on the other hand the warrior himself was not belittled by his weapons, much less was his personality subordinated to the requirements of machinery or tactics. The Sarmatians were according to Pausanias the most remote of all barbarian peoples, and did not even understand the use of iron, and yet produced spears and arrows and even shirts of mail which proved them the equals of the Greeks in skill and inventiveness[1]. So with the Homeric warrior, when he found that his sword or spear, however futile to our judgment, could cut deeper than those of other soldiers and that his armour often rendered their missiles impotent, above all, when he remembered that the spirit of his followers depended on his own bearing and stout-heartedness, he was filled with an exhilaration and sense of glory such as we rarely, if ever, have an opportunity of enjoying. Bouchardin the sculptor used to declare, "Lorsque j'ai lu Homère, j'ai cru avoir 20 pieds de haut."[2] This sense of pride and of mastery has disappeared from the human race and can be recovered only by reading the old epics, because our modern inventions convince us of our own littleness. Let the reader consider what is perhaps the grandest sensation accorded to a man of the twentieth century; the moment in which for the first time he rises from the earth in an aeroplane. To see the landscape expand and unfold

---

[1] Paus. I, xxi, 5.

[2] Voltaire, *Du Poème Épique*; and it must have been this same influence which caused Hesiod to write:

> εἰ γάρ τις καὶ πένθος ἔχων νεοκηδέι θυμῷ
> ἄζηται κραδίην ἀκαχήμενος, αὐτὰρ ἀοιδὸς
> Μουσάων θεράπων κλέεα προτέρων ἀνθρώπων
> ὑμνήσῃ μάκαράς τε θεούς, οἳ Ὄλυμπον ἔχουσιν,
> αἶψ᾽ ὅ γε δυσφροσυνέων ἐπιλήθεται, οὐδέ τι κηδέων
> μέμνηται, ταχέως δὲ παρέτραπε δῶρα θεάων.

Theog. 98–103.

beneath him in all its varied hues and undulations, to enjoy
the sense of perfect steadiness and solidity though hung
thousands of feet high in space; to be conscious, at the most,
of slow and majestic movement, though in every minute he
covers two miles or perhaps more—surely this is the epic of
our own time. And yet the experimenter will find that his
second flight will seem to be a little less ecstatic, the next even
less so, till at last a voyage by air, though no doubt retaining
all its mechanical or topographical interests, has lost all suggestion of the sublime. This gradual abatement of enthusiasm is not
due solely to familiarity—mountain climbing does not become
less exhilarating the more it is practised—but rather to the
gradual and unconscious discovery that it is the machine and
not the man that is great. At the end of a war, compared to
which the siege of Troy would rank as a minor operation,
those who review their experiences will find that however
much they admire isolated acts of self-sacrifice, the predominant
impression is one of human littleness. It is not merely that
the numbers engaged were too vast to allow any single person,
whatever his rank, to play a conspicuous part. It was rather
that the science of destruction has developed to such a degree
of ingenuity that human beings are left with nothing but a
sense of annihilation. When the strongest and bravest warriors
are either crushed and smashed to atoms, or suddenly felled
by something which they can neither hear nor see, it is impossible to discover any grandeur in a modern battle and for
that reason an epic can never be composed on the Great War.
But when the Acheans settled in Greece, the arts of war created
just the opposite impression. Every movement of the game
reminded the warrior of his own skill and strength and of the
glory of his equipment.

III. *The spirit of the* Iliad *expressed in its similes.*

Men who could flatter and stimulate their sense of power
by such possessions, were likely to find their own greatness
reflected in everything they touched or saw. Their ideal was
not, like that of the modern hero, so elusive that its glamour
might be tarnished by everyday concerns. If even their cookery

and ideas of feasting, which seem to us so surprisingly rudimentary and unimaginative, had for them a poetic appeal, is it not natural that they should discover copies of their own energy and vigour in all the common experience of life? Here we touch one of the most characteristic and significant features of the *Iliad*: its similes. It is probable that this figure of speech was first employed to supplement and intensify the usual word at a time when the language was not sufficiently rich to provide a specialised verb. If there were no such expressions as "to hurtle" or "to crash" we should need a simile to intensify the verb "to fall." In fact one of Dante's most celebrated lines simply intensifies and specialises this same verb *cadere*:

E caddi, come corpo morto cade[1].

There is no single word to produce this effect, so he uses a simile. As a language develops its synonyms and variants, the tendency is for a long simile to be condensed into a metaphor as one word can now do the work of several. Thus the famous likening of Here's flight to a man's thought[2] became in later poetry something like ὠκύδρομός θ' ὥστε νόημα[3]. Or else the simile becomes a *genre* of its own, a kind of poetical inset, an excuse for gratifying the poet's sense of beauty or his interest in activities which have nothing to do with his avowed theme. The *Iliad* is by no means free from such artificialities. Patroklos weeps like a streamlet frothing in cloudy spray over a rock[4]; Aias defends the ships, jumping from one prow to another and thrusting at the Trojans with his pole, as a professional *desultor* jumps from the back of one horse to another[5]; Skamandros, swooping down on Achilles, is compared to a streamlet threading its way through the tiny channel dug through a kitchen garden[6]. But for the most part the Homeric similes are drawn from hunting scenes or from the more strenuous labours of men, or from the aggressive instincts of animals and insects, or from the violence of the wind and the sea, or the sudden

[1] *Inf.* v, 142.
[2] *Il.* xv, 80-3.
[3] Orph. *Hymn.* p. 166.
[4] *Il.* xvi, 3-4.
  Ibid. xv, 674-88.
[6] *Ibid.* xxi, 257-62.

movements of clouds or the influence of the stars. Even among these primitive scenes we sometimes feel the touch of a later age, as when Achilles declares that there can be no truce between wolves and sheep[1], thus using the same illustration as Shakespeare was afterwards to put into the mouth of Antonio[2]. Yet others are undoubtedly prehistoric. Sir Arthur Evans[3] has pointed out that a number of Minoan entaglios, executed perhaps five centuries before the Homeric poems took their present shape, seem strikingly similar to episodes described in the *Iliad*, especially hunting scenes. Some of the Homeric similes may well be as old as the signet rings or even older. At any rate they are free from the spirit of more modern and studied literature. For the emotions and actions of men are not only compared to what we now think to be imposing or beautiful, but also to flies round a milk pail[4], or hornets attacking an intruder[5], or even the disdainful obstinacy of an ass[6]. Such descriptions have been quoted as proof of the "homeliness" of the Greek epic, in reality they are signs of its primitive origin. As will be shown again and again in the course of this inquiry, primitive and warlike peoples, almost up to the dawn of history, have believed that animals were possessed of certain qualities of wisdom, swiftness or ferocity which needy mortals could gradually acquire by means of worship and ritual. Hunters after killing a wild beast would eat its heart or drink its blood in order to absorb its nature. Even mice and serpents were worshipped as well as the fiercer and more active brutes. As late as the *Gylfaginning*, to which Snorri gave final shape in the first half of the thirteenth century, the epic wonder for the wind is retained: its power to stir the sea and swell the fire, and despite all this strength it is so wonderful that it cannot be seen[7]. The Acheans also were filled with emulous admiration for this *mana*—the energy, impetuosity, power or terror—which earlier ages worshipped in creation, but, except for some half recognisable and wholly

---

[1] *Il.* xxii, 263. [2] *Merchant of Venice*, iv, i.
[3] "Minoan and Mycenean Element in Hellenic Life," *J.H.S.* vol. xxxii, pp. 291 ff.
[4] *Il.* xvi, 641–3. [5] *Ibid.* xii, 167–72; xvi, 259–65.
[6] *Ibid.* xi, 558–62; xvii, 742–5. [7] *Gylf.* xviii.

debateable traces, totemism had passed out of their civilisation.
It is characteristic of epic pride and confidence that they did
not need to pray for these qualities. They already possessed
them. They sought encouragement and exaltation by recognising in themselves what was once believed to be divine in
animals or insects, the wind, the sea or the clouds. When some
one or other of their heroes was doggedly giving way against
great odds, they were reminded of a lion or a boar at bay and
when Hektor or Paris was returning to battle with renewed
vigour, they pictured him as a well-fed horse who has escaped
from the stable and is galloping to the pastures. What they
recognised in fire was its ruthlessness ($\mu\acute{\epsilon}\nu\sigma\varsigma$ $\sigma\iota\delta\acute{\eta}\rho\epsilon\sigma\nu$)[1]. The
original Homeric similes are surely those which contain this
idea of energy, whatever the kind of creature which exemplifies
it, and suggest the completeness, adequacy and satisfying reality
of something perfectly fitted for what it does. Such a principle
is familiar to all students of art. Famous examples are to be
found on the Vaphio gold cups, embossed centuries before
the Homeric poems took their present shape. Examples nearest
Homer in later classical art are the bull in the Keramicos and
the relief of the boar in the Roman forum. This conception
of artistic fitness can always be recognised. The poet who gave
Menelaos the courage of a fly[2], which loves the sweet blood
of man, was possessed by the very soul of Greek epic. But the
minstrel who described the two goddesses marching forth to
war like timid doves[3] in the way they stepped, belongs to
another age with different ideals.

IV. *Homeric sense of beauty not inconsistent with their interest in*
battle wounds.

Quite apart from their choice of similes, the Homeric sense
of beauty was rather different from ours. They liked to imagine
that what was most evanescent among the joys of life and had
proved to be the most perishable quality of human greatness
need not be so inevitably lost or might be miraculously restored.
Thus among all the manifold misadventures and disasters of
the two long narrative poems, the prominent chieftains retain

[1] *Il.* xxiii, 177.   [2] *Ibid.* xvii, 569-72.   [3] *Ibid.* v, 778.

their personal dignity and prestige. We never hear of a king
that is crippled, or mutilated, or shorn of one of his senses or
broken in spirit. Above all, the worst mischance does not rob
a hero of his youth and beauty. It is one of the charms of the
Homeric poems that they show so marked a sense of the human
form. We should expect Briseis, Andromache and Helen to be
admired in an epic designed for men, but it is a distinguishing
feature of the most redoubtable warriors that they are young
and endowed with a certain comeliness and masculine grace.
This epic sense of beauty is quite distinct from modern
aestheticism. Though no prominent chieftain suffers disfigure-
ment, the lesser warriors, many of them mere names in the
story, are slaughtered in the most gruesome fashion[1]. We cannot imagine the same poet—or even similar poets—in modern
times describing the beauty of a warrior revived by a god, and
then revelling in such ghastly details. Herein, again, lies the
difference between our own ideal and that of the Heroic Age.
We need not imagine that the description of battle wounds
had no painful associations for an Homeric poet or audience,
but their centre of interest was not the same as ours is. Whereas
we, even involuntarily, associate ourselves, to some extent,
with those who receive the thrust, they felt for the warrior who
gave it. They rejoiced in the stout arm and accurate aim,
which could shatter a human body so terribly. The most
hideous wounds are those inflicted at the height of some ἀριστεία,
either by Diomed, Hektor, Patroklos or Achilles, and redound
to their glory. Even the weapons themselves partake of the
wielder's ferocity. According to Vedic notions, a sword or a
spear was actually endowed with a soul[2]. Homer still believes
that this spirit was like a man's. The bronze point which reaches
its mark is pitiless, the point which misses thirsts for death.

v. *The defects of these qualities. Homeric egoism. The wrath of
Achilles. Indifference to rebuke. Confession of fear.*

But however confident of his own worth, no man would
face danger or even engage in any prolonged effort, without
some other powerful motive. We can only guess at what grim

[1] *E.g.* v, 65–83; xvi, 401–10, 740–50.   [2] H. Oldenberg, *Die Religion des Veda.*

necessity or other powerful emotion really drove the Achean
and Pelasgian tribes to arms, but in the poet's eyes, fame is
the ruling passion. The admiration of their fellows, but, above
all, of posterity, was the last and greatest joy that could be
won from life, and in the attainment of this prize a warrior was
prepared to risk all others. Students of literature have now
for so many generations delighted themselves with the spectacle
of self-sacrifice on the field of honour, that it comes almost as
a shock when we realise how self-centred the heroism of the
Homeric warriors really was. By the time that Herodotos wrote
his history, men had cultivated a more impersonal ideal. When
Gobryas, one of the seven Persians engaged in the assassination
of the pseudo-Smerdis, was wrestling in the darkness with one
of the Magians, he called out to Darios to thrust with his sword
into the gloom, gladly risking his own life, if one of their
adversaries might be killed[1]. Zopyros, even more daring and
devoted than Sinon, cut off his own nose and ears, and
scourged the skin off his back, in order to gain an entrance
into Babylon and so betray it to his master[2]. We shall look in
vain for such acts of self-devotion among all the glorious deeds
of the Trojan war. One of the most notable and mysterious
figures in the whole of the poem is Sarpedon, the Lykian son
of Zeus. He was almost certainly well known to the audiences
of the *Iliad* as the protagonist of some other epic now lost, and,
throughout Homer, he is graced with more than a mortal's
share of divine nobility[3]. In one of the finest passages of this
or of any poem, this paragon of men describes the reward for
which he and his friend Glaukos are content to face so many
dangers and exertions in a land so far from home. It is the
wealth, the honour and the privileges of kingship, which men,
during this short life, will accord only to those who surpass
them in valour[4]. In order to appreciate the peculiar temperament and mentality of an age which could be satisfied with
such an ideal, the words of Sarpedon should be compared with

[1] Herod. viii, 78.   [2] *Ibid*. iii, 154–8.
[3] Cf. the heat with which the question of his death is debated in Olympos,
and the honour which the Father of the gods pays to his corpse. *Il.* xvi,
431–57.
[4] *Il.* xii, 310–28.

the attitude of the last representative of classical civilisation.
St Augustine, before his conversion, puts to himself the same
question as the Lykian demi-god puts to Glaukos. Suppose that
we were immortal and left in full possession of bodily enjoy-
ments and were freed from all sense of insecurity—should we
not then be happy? The future Christian replies, no. He feels
that any of us would be harassed with the sense of an indefinable void, would yearn for the *lumen honestatis et gratis am-
plectendae pulchritudinis, quam non videt oculus carnis et videtur ex
intimo*[1]. It is particularly characteristic of Homeric idealism
that it lacks any inkling of this "beyondness." The warriors
do not seem to have understood any purpose in life outside
the realisation of their own manhood and ascendancy. Unlike
Beowulf, Roland, Aeneas, or even Satan, they had no great
mission to perform or service to render.

It will readily be understood that an enterprise such as the
Achean invasion could not have been put on foot and maintained without considerable organisation applied somewhere,
and from many sources we gather hints of the management
and administration which lay behind that protracted war. For
instance, Dictys Cretensis preserves the legend that the Acheans
brought under cultivation a part of the Trojan plain which
was unsuitable as a battle ground[2]. But in Homer the responsibilities of generalship are passed over as if the theme were
uncongenial. It cannot be that the Muse regarded these considerations as beneath her dignity, for the poem abounds in local
touches and picturesque details. We know where the women
washed their linen[3], where a ruined column[4] stood on the plain,
how Iason's son Euneus sold wine from Lemnos to the troops[5],
and that young Lykaon was cutting twigs to make a chariot rail
when he was caught in Priam's orchard[6]. The reason must be
partly that the *Iliad*, contrary to the opinion of Montaigne, is
not a manual of warfare but a roll of honour. The poets are
recording how great and magnificent certain men became in
the course of that long adventure. But the reason must also be

---

[1] *Confess.* VI, 16.   [2] *De Bello Trojano*, II, 41.
[3] *Il.* XXII, 153.   [4] *Ibid.* XI, 371.
[5] *Ibid.* VII, 467–75.   [6] *Ibid.* XXI, 37.

partly that all subordination to the requirements of sustained
warfare, all the give-and-take of co-operation, were repugnant
to the Homeric ideal. Thus whenever we are vouchsafed
glimpses of administration and of generalship, it is always
with a suggestion of revolt. A chieftain's only care in Homer
was to gather round him a band of followers as fearless and
predatory as himself, like the *comitatus* which Tacitus noticed
among the German chieftains[1]. As long as he could overawe
them by his own imperious personality and lead them by his
superior prowess to the booty which follows victory, his position
was secure and he was free to delight his soul with the possession of cunning metal work, costly fabrics and swift horses,
to drink sweet wine and feast on roasted sheep or stuffed pigs'
stomachs and to fortify his sense of worth with the homage
of his fellows. His son had probably the chance of succeeding
to his position, if like Pyrrhos he could show the same mettle
as his father and unlike Telemachos, at the beginning of the
Odyssey, was old enough to match his rivals. But the chieftain's
eminence depended on his personal prestige; one of Achilles's
most pressing anxieties in Hades is to know whether his father
Peleus is still able to command respect[2].

In a word, the ideals of the Homeric warrior, as portrayed
by their poets, were confidence, pride and self-sufficiency. So
much so that what we consider to be defects, they believed to
be qualities. It is an anachronism even to accuse Achilles of
unknightly conduct because he allowed his compatriots to
suffer till his own honour was satisfied. Neither Odysseus,
Aias, nor Phoinix appeals to his sense of patriotism. They go
no further than to urge an ideal of large-hearted forgiveness
(φιλοφροσύνη, ἵλαος θυμός)[3]. He was not expected to serve the
Acheans further than his own fame required[4]. According to
Dictys Cretensis he planned a treacherous attack on the
Acheans[5]. According to Dares he abstained from the war in
order to induce Hekabe to give him Polyxena to wife[6]. Homer's

---

[1] *Germania*, XIII; Chadwick, *The Heroic Age*, chap. XVI, p. 348. Chadwick
believes "that the system of the *comitatus* was not so highly developed as in the
North of Europe" (p. 363). *Post*, vol. II, chap. I, § 2.   [2] *Od.* XI, 494–503.
[3] *Il.* IX, 256, 496–7, 639.   [4] *Ibid.* 257–8, 300–6, 630–2.
[5] *De Bello Trojano*, II, 37.   [6] *De Excidio*, XXVII.

portrait is no satire but an idealisation. Suppose that he had
followed Phoinix's[1] advice and had accepted the gifts of atonement, which Agamemnon had sent, according to epic usage,
not for their own value, but as tokens that the king recognised
himself to be in the wrong. It would in that case never have
been proved how utterly the Acheans depended on Achilles,
nor how completely he could rout the Trojans in the very
hour of victory[2]. Besides, "the return of the avenger" seems
to have been a favourite theme in all old epics. On the other
hand, as the poems retain a conservative tone and are opposed
to the newer obligations of allegiance, they still lay enormous
importance on the older and more individual claims of kinship.
Personal friendship and family ties are amongst the strongest
motives in the epic age. We shall soon[3] have occasion to note
that Hektor thought more of protecting his wife and child than
of defending the whole city of Troy. So now it was perfectly
natural that Achilles should be more deeply moved by the
death of his friend than by the defeat of the whole Achean
host. Nor must we imagine that his paroxysms of grief were
regarded as a sign of weakness. Nowadays self-restraint is so
much an obligation, that any abandonment to passion is
ascribed, generally with good reason, to neurasthenia. The
modern man takes pride in controlling his feelings and regards
it as a humiliation to give way to them. Dante is considered to
have touched the height of intensity, when Ugolino mutters:

Io non piangeva, sì dentro impietrai[4].

Such an ideal of endurance and self-control had developed by
the fourth century B.C. and Herodotos records with admiration
how Hegesistratos cut off part of his foot to escape from his
bonds in Sparta and hobbled for three days and nights to
Tegea[5]. But the prehistoric Acheans must not be credited with
such an ideal of restraint and good breeding. They did, indeed,
recognise an amazingly high standard of courtesy and refinement. One has only to recall the ceremonial with which the
envoys from Agamemnon were received by Achilles[6], though

---

[1] *Il.* IX, 434 ff.   [2] See *Il.* XVIII, 121 ff.
[3] *Post*, § 8.   [4] *Inf.* XXXIII, 49.
[5] IX, 37.   [6] *Il.* IX, 196 ff.

still fuming with resentment, or the perfect good taste with
which the same impetuous warrior greeted the old man involved in the blood feud over the slaying of Patroklos[1], to
understand how subtle their perceptions had become. At the
same time passion was admired by them as being uncontrolled
strength, nor is this attitude inconsistent with a high degree of
civilisation. Modern science has discovered that wrath is a
great *energiser*, which prepares and disposes the body for
strenuous action, and Mr Stratton shows how the religions
can be grouped according to their use of the impulse of anger[2].
So it was not without some reason that warriors utterly
abandoned themselves to their feelings; nor could we expect
them to distinguish between the significance of wrath and of grief.
Even hardened warriors were not ashamed to burst into tears,
when they lost an athletic contest. The violence of Achilles's
grief is a sign of his fury; a kind of prelude to the slaughter
which he is to inflict on the Trojans. The Acheans looked
with much the same feelings on the power to shout. Tacitus
records that the German battle line advanced with a menacing
roar, to sustain the warriors' courage[3]. In Homer something
like this united shout of valour (*virtutis concentus*) is still heard[4],
but it is nearly always individuals who shout. At the height
of a crisis the warrior can still strike terror or inspire courage
by his cry[5], but at other times the capacity to yell is simply a
sign of superhuman strength, as when Ares roared[6], till βοὴν
ἀγαθός becomes a regular epithet of a nobly born warrior.

So we come back to warfare as the ultimate criterion; at
once the source and the proof of Homeric greatness. Could
we expect any other standard, when we realise how far the
chieftain's personality was a matter of life and death to all
who were associated with him? When the Achean ships first
touched the Trojan beach, Kyknos was conspicuous, opposing
their landing at the head of his force. Achilles slew him with
a stone and "when the Barbarians saw him dead, they turned

---

[1] *Il.* xxiv, 507.
[2] G. M. Stratton, *Anger, Its religious and moral significance.*
[3] *Germ.* iii.   [4] *Il.* xv, 312.
[5] *E.g. ibid.* xv, 321; xviii, 228; xx, 48–53.   [6] *Ibid.* v, 859.

and fled to the city."[1] If such were the responsibilities of the
individual warrior, if the steadfastness of his followers depended
so completely on his leadership, it was necessary for him to
develop and retain (at least in the ideal realm of poetry) a
complete independence of spirit, a sense of superiority to the
restrictions under which humbler folk laboured.

Thus the greatness of the Homeric character lies not so
much in their hardihood, or their alleged "loftiness of thought,"
as in their freedom from self-reproach, their intense appreciation of life and their pride in the glory of man. As a consequence
of this superb self-confidence they felt free, like their northern
brethren many centuries later, to pledge themselves to the per-
formance of the most extravagant feats[2]. Another consequence
was their comparative indifference to rebuke. This characteristic may easily be misconstrued, because so much depends
on the reader's interpretation of certain speeches. For instance,
Dr Leaf[3] remarks that Diomed accepts rebuke patiently and
suggests as an explanation that "he is essentially a retainer
with no status of his own," and he then draws our attention to
the way Sthenelos "fires up at the insolent and unjust accusa-
tions." Others may feel that Diomed does not appear in the
rest of the poem as a character of secondary importance nor is
he so represented in the Catalogue, and may feel inclined to
construe the words of Sthenelos as a moderate and reasoned
remonstrance. In any case it should be remembered that other
chieftains of unquestionable position are singularly unruffled
when a slur is cast on their characters. Paris twice submits to
rebuke[4] and so does Hektor[5]. Even the great Agamemnon himself remains unmoved by the outrageous insults of Achilles,
and accepts the censures of Odysseus[6]. It is not of course
suggested that these warriors were completely insensible to any
disparagement, but they are surprisingly self-possessed and
tolerant. One could not imagine such reprimands passing unchallenged among the characters of medieval romances or

---

[1] Apollodorus, *Epitome*, III, 34.
[2] *Il.* VIII, 228 ff.; XX, 83–5. For the boastfulness of the Teutonic warrior
see *post*, chap. IX, § 2.
[3] *Homer and History*, 1915, chap. VI.   [4] *Il.* III, 438 ff.; VI, 332 ff.
[5] *Ibid.* V, 493 ff.; XVII, 170 ff.   [6] *Ibid.* XIV, 103 ff.

Shakespeare's historical plays. Those more modern warriors
would have flamed with anger because, whatever the occasion
of the reproof, each one of them would have been reminded of
the unworthiness which he concealed but could not forget.
As soon as civilisation has reached a certain stage, it begins
to whisper in the ear of every man and reminds him of his
failures to respond to the requirements of the time, till the
nobler spirits, already conscious of their backslidings, become
morbidly sensitive to any form of detraction. In the ancient
world, this vulnerability is noticed by Gelon when he replied
to the Lakedaimonian envoys that ὀνείδεα κατιόντα ἀνθρώπῳ
φιλέει ἐπανάγειν τὸν θυμόν[1]. In the medieval world we have
Dante's exclamation:

> O dignitosa coscienza e netta,
> Come t' è picciol fullo amaro morsa[2].

Such treacherous thoughts did not creep into the Homeric
mind, at least not to any depth or extent. Their pleasures, their
wealth, and above all the necessities of their position excluded
misgivings of this kind.

In fact Homer is so convinced of his heroes' worth and
magnanimity that he can afford to describe their fear. Not
only Paris but well-tried warriors such as Hektor and Menelaos
have moments of timidity, and sometimes give way to positive
terror. Such attacks of moral exhaustion are perfectly true to
life. During the Great War, soldiers of approved gallantry
showed traces of alarm, and only new-comers to the firing-line
were surprised at these lapses or were ashamed to confess to
them. But medieval and modern war poetry shrinks from
showing sympathy with human weakness. Our admiration is
fixed on too high a dream of self-abnegation and moral
heroism, and we know how easily the ideal may be shattered.
It needs the Homeric sense of sureness and perfection to confess, even in moments of poetic exaltation, that we sometimes
fall short of what is required of us.

[1] *Herod.* VII, 160.   [2] *Purg.* III, 8

VI. *Homeric melancholy. Due in the first place to the origin and evolution of epic poetry.*

If then the Homeric warriors are such splendid examples of human impetuosity and self-confidence, we should expect the story in which they figure to be a protracted song of triumph, at any rate for one of the two opposing hosts. We find on the contrary that suffering and despair predominate, that melancholy seems to have overclouded the spirit of the poet, and that both mortals and immortals regard man as a being destined to unhappiness. Besides, Homer does not dwell only on the warrior's feats of strength and moments of victory; he appears more often to linger over the pathos of the conquered. The modern world, since the romantic movement, has been profoundly impressed by these pictures of the victims and losers in the struggle round Troy. Probably two out of every three readers are on the side of the Trojans and hail Hektor as the most magnificent champion of a losing cause. Herder, for instance, was particularly impressed by the sympathy which Homer seemed to show for the fallen, and believed that all the misfortunes of that war were to be assigned to the follies and passions of men or gods[1]. For many students there seems to be a contradiction between the shouts of victory and the cries of despair. Some hold that the fluctuating battle is merely the surface of the poem, while its true beauty is to be felt in the undertones of mourning and lamentation.

> *The finer ear discerned a secret strain,*
> *A vision pierced to the diviner eye;*
> *The far-off echo of a woman's sigh,*
> *Weakness made perfect unto strength in Pain*[2].

How far is this view the right one? How far does pity or pathos really inspire the poem?

In answering this question it must be borne in mind that the epic bards of all nations probably inherited a tradition expressive of sorrow and defeat. To begin with, poetry would naturally even in the earliest times be employed to express emotions, and most of these, if capable of expression, are

[1] *Briefen zur Beförderung der Humanität*, 1794.
[2] W. Leaf, *The Iliad of Homer*.

associated with suffering. In the earliest folklore, prose was probably employed for the narration of what was new, and verse for what was known but worth repeating. We know that Skalds rode round funeral pyres giving expression in song to their grief and admiration for the dead, and Achilles pronounced a dirge over Patroklos, describing by what deeds he was honouring his memory[1]. Besides, the conditions under which poetry was sung or performed would naturally lead a minstrel to choose some highly wrought scene with which his audiences could sympathise, and we are not surprised to find that so much of old Norse poetry was made up of tragic episodes couched in dialogue, not in narrative. Sometimes we can trace the unmistakeable influence of "laments" in later narrative poetry. The lament of Sigurth's wife, for instance, may have assumed lyric form as early as the seventh century: and has left its mark on *Guthrunarkvitha*, I and II, has influenced *Aventiure XVII* of *Nibelungenlied*, and by the tenth and eleventh centuries had inspired other Norse poems[2]. One cannot help suspecting, though there is no proof, that certain scenes in the *Iliad*, for instance the two Andromache episodes[3], are reminiscent of "laments" of this kind. Besides, there can be little doubt that the original impulse to compose epic poetry often came from the recollections of disaster. In the past history of most nations there seems to have arisen a golden age, that is to say a period untroubled by serious dissensions or invaders, during which monarchies were established and dynasties formed, and civilisation reached a height long remembered in tradition. One imagines that the elaborate but perhaps unfortified palace of Knossos, with its oil presses, treasure chambers, storehouses, baths, throne and sanitary arrangements, must have been the product of this epoch in Crete. Then came an age of migrations and of civil war and these centres of civilisation fell, and so it comes about that the ruined stones of Knossos are scorched by fire. The rumours of these overthrows must have spread far and lasted for many

[1] *Il.* XVIII, 324 ff.; XXIII, 12 ff.

[2] See H. A. Bellows's introductory notes to *The Poetic Edda* (Scandinavian Classics, vols. XXI and XXII), 1923.

[3] *Il.* VI, 392 ff.; XXII, 460 ff.

generations, and the poetry which afterwards developed into epics must, in the first place, have arisen partly to explain and celebrate the disasters and to hand on the sad story to those who should come after. So it happens that many epics deal with a downfall, whether of a hero or a fortress or a dynasty. There is the fall of Troy[1], involving not only the deaths of Sarpedon, Patroklos and Hektor, with the sorrows of Hekabe, Andromache and Priam[2]; but later the fall of Achilles himself[3], Palamedes[4], Antilochos and Memnon[5], Paris[6], Penthesileia[7]. Then there are the misfortunes which attended the warriors on their homeward way[8], especially Menelaos, Lokrian Aias, and Odysseus, and the foul play which awaited others in their own kingdoms, when, like Agamemnon, they had survived every other danger. In fact the ill fate of Troy seems to have passed on to its victors, bringing with it the weakening, if not the collapse, of the Achean power, and so perhaps preparing the way for the Return of the Herakleidai. Apart from the disastrous expedition to the Troad, other legends told how powerful families, like the descendants of Pelops and Labdakos, were afflicted, if not ruined, by internal feuds and crimes. Nor should it be forgotten that the poet who celebrated the long postponed triumph of Odysseus, may perhaps have adapted to his own purposes another dark story of slaughter. Some hundred and six chieftains are entrapped and killed. The original number (Dictys gives thirty[9]) may have been increased, as Prof. Bérard[10] suggests, by a process of epic exaggeration and compromise, but some at any rate of the victims have the status and connections of established characters, as if they had been brought into the *Odyssey* from some other story. Besides, though the exploit is skilfully reshaped into the greatest achievement of Odysseus, yet the poet does not succeed in justifying so indiscriminate a massacre, nor does he conceal

---

[1] *Ilias Mikra, Iliou Persis.* [2] *Iliad.* [3] Quintus of Smyrna and *Aithiopis.*
[4] *Cypria.* [5] Quint. and *Aeth.* [6] *Ilias Mikra* and Quint. [7] Quint.
[8] *Nostoi*, Quint. XIV; *Od.* III and IV. Dictys (*De Bello Trojano*) and Dares (*De Excidio Trojae*) cover nearly the whole field, though they vary in many details from other sources. [9] *De Bello Trojano*, VI, 6.
[10] *Introduction à l'Odyssée*, t. I, chap. VI, 1924.

the consternation which the deed caused in the town[1], nor the importance which they seemed to enjoy in Hades[2].

This suggestion of mourning is not peculiar to Greek epics. We have the death of Roland, Olivier and Turpin and the annihilation of Charlemagne's rearguard at Roncesvaux; there is the slaughter of the Franks in the *Waltharius* and the extirpation of the Nibelungs and the *Njalssaga* and the *Laxdaelassaga*; the burning of Leire[3] and the murder of Hrolf, whose reign had shed so much glory over the fame of the castle. Even in *Beowulf* we do not lose sight of the dangers which threatened[4] nor the misfortunes which actually befell Hrothgar[5]; and *Gudrun* ends with the storming of a castle. Such lyrics as *Seafarer*, *Wanderer*, *The Ruined City* and *Deor's Lament* ought probably to be taken as the rudimentary material for an epic.

So the succession of bards who contributed towards creating the narrative poems of the Heroic Ages, must have been rather like some ancient family which inherits a feud and hands on the grievance from generation to generation. It became traditional to regard Zeus as a deceiver and destroyer[6]. In an age of warfare men were perhaps disinclined to revere a god unless they recognised his power to hurt. Of course these were not the only purposes which poets and minstrels had to serve. As victories were achieved and the invading races settled down to develop their conquests and to establish their supremacy, other and less gloomy memories suggested themselves. The glory of chieftains had to be celebrated and feats of skill and daring had to be recorded. But it is important to remember that the original sources of epic poetry must have been twofold. They consisted of θρῆνοι as well as of παιᾶνες; of the *Song of the Bow* as well as of the *Song of Deborah*; of the *Battle of Maldon* as well as of the *Battle of Brunanburh*. It is not

[1] *Od.* XXIII, 111–51; XXIV, 327–437. All through the *Od.* there are special allusions to the outrages of the suitors, as if to supply Odysseus with motives, which could not be tacitly assumed. *E.g.* speech of Halitherses, XXIV, 450–62.
[2] *Ibid.* 98–190. The *Telegony* apparently began by describing the burial of the suitors by their kinsfolk. See Proklos, *Chrestomathy*.
[3] *Biarkamal.* See A. Olrik, *Danmarks Heltedigtning*, vol. I, chap. VI, § 3 (Transl. in Scandinavian Monographs, vol. IV).
[4] *E.g.* Beowulf's report to *Hygelac*, 2026 ff.
[5] *E.g.* the lament over Aeschere, ll. 1321 ff.   [6] *Il.* II, 116–18.

surprising, therefore, that when Telemachos visited Menelaos, their talk of the Trojan war was overcast with sadness, till Helen poured into their wine some of her Nepenthe[1]; nor that Hrothgar's minstrel at the rejoicings over Grendel's death, sings of Hnaef's ending and of the mourning and lamentation which accompanied his funeral pyre[2].

VII. *Epic melancholy brilliantly adapted by Homer to war weariness and horror of death. Ares as a god of death.*

Homer, being the descendant of a long tradition and the inheritor of a certain strain of inspiration, probably could not have escaped these influences, even if he would. But at the same time he was essentially, in the words of his epitaph, a ἡρώων κοσμήτωρ[3], a poet who made warriors seem glorious, and his epic genius rose to its height in combining melancholy with admiration, while making both intensely real. In the first place he seems to have understood, more clearly than any poet since, what a chieftain of the Heroic Age actually was like and might become. As has been explained[4], warriors maintained their lordship by prowess in war, and we may well believe that the descendants of migratory hordes still cherished a restless spirit of adventure and yearned for the excitement of an expedition. It is also possible that succession to the kingship was still in some places preserved through the female line, or had been so maintained till recently, and that while the daughters were kept at home to propagate the royal descendants, the sons were sent forth to marry princesses and reign among their wives' peoples, and thus we find Teukros, Peleus, Achilles and Neoptolemos successively seeking new kingdoms, though all descendants of Aiakos of Aigina[5]. We know, too, that some of the warriors had been guilty of homicide and had turned soldiers of fortune, either as fugitives from some blood feud or to perform their years of purification. It was famed that Herakles and even Apollo had undergone such a fate and so at a later time did Telamon, Peleus,

[1] *Od.* IV, 219-34.   [2] *Beowulf*, 1110-24.
[3] See end of *Contest of Homer and Hesiod.*   [4] *Ante*, § 5.
[5] See Frazer, *Lectures on the Early History of the Kingship*, chap. VIII.

Amphitryon, the husband of Alkmene, and then Phoinix and Patroklos. This custom would certainly help perforce to keep alive the instinct of the explorer and freebooter, nor is Homer blind to such an elemental fact of human nature. But at the same time, the poet is well aware that other influences were shaping the genuinely heroic character in a very different mould. The Acheans had come under the influence of a high civilisation, whether or no derived from the Pelasgians, and had begun to enjoy the arts of peace. Sir James Frazer[1] has collected many examples of the readiness of primitive peoples to face death, but the invaders had now certainly passed that stage and had reached the next altitude in which human beings learn to prize life. They had become lords who had tasted of the sweets of domestic life and conjugal love, who took pride in their children and in their wonderful palaces[2]. They had begun to feel keenly how war was likely to rob them of all these joys. Their instincts and their position were constantly forcing them into battle, and yet every encounter threatened to take from them all that they valued in their position. The arguments used by Kineas[3], when he catechised Pyrrhos on his motives for invading Italy, are already implied in the *Iliad*. This attitude is well illustrated by the atmosphere which gathered round the figure of Achilles. Apparently a god of healing was worshipped under this name in Phthia, Brasiai, Miletos and Byzantium, and the cult was probably introduced into Troy by Euboic and Boiotian settlers[4]. His temple was still standing in the town of Achilleion at the time of Julian. When the Thessalian invaders were occupying the Troad they must have noticed this centre of worship and it may have been natural that they should take it for a tomb. But in all likelihood they went much further, they assumed that this earth spirit was the same as their own legendary chieftain, who is repre-sented in a very different light by Dictys and Dares, and they jumped to the conclusion that their hero was fated to die at

---

[1] *The Dying God*, chap. IV.
[2] *E.g. Il.* IX, 365–7; XIII, 636, 730; XVIII, 288.
[3] Plut. *Vit. Pyrrh.* 14.
[4] See Gruppe, *Griechische Mythologie und Religionsgeschichte*, Bd. II, § 223, p. 618.

Troy, and the Homeric poets dwelt with unusual insistence on the brilliance of his fame bound up with the doom of his early death[1]. It might be supposed to be an accident that the thought of mortality and disaster is uppermost in the evolution of this legend, except that such is the tone of the whole *Iliad*. Battles are not always a κρατερὴ ὑσμίνη but more often θυμοβόρος, κρυερός, δήιος, δακρυόεις[2]. It is not for nothing that among the Olympians Ares is humiliated and traduced, nor can his ignominy be due solely to his alleged Thraco-Phrygian origin. Apollo was at this time worshipped in Lykia and many noble Lykians, especially Glaukos, Pandaros and Sarpedon, were fighting for Troy. Yet though Apollo is consistently an enemy of the Acheans, he is portrayed as the minister of Fate, the most brilliant and powerful of the subordinate gods, or at least as the equal of Athene. Dr Farnell has suggested that Ares may be "the divinity of some more primitive and backward tribes who were submerged leaving only as a heritage the savage god and a certain tradition of savagery."[3] But Ares must have inspired hatred for another reason. His character as depicted by Homer is very different from what it became in later literature. In one of the *Homeric Hymns*[4] he is honoured as stout of heart (ὀβριμόθυμος), the saviour of cities (πολισσόος) and strong of hand (καρτεροχείρ). He is invoked to shed a benign ray from above, so that the suppliant may drive from his thoughts all cowardly instincts, and at the same time may refrain from ruthless fury (μένος ὀξύ). These are the qualities assigned by Homer to Athene and Apollo, who seem in some way to share the honours of a god of war. Ares is always βροτολοιγός, μιαιφόνος, τειχεσιπλήτης, μαινόμενος, τυκτὸν κακόν, ἀλλοπρόσαλλος, or in a word ταλαύρινος πολεμιστής. Are we to suppose that this monster represents a third god of war, concerned only with strife and carnage? Or does he not rather represent what was later to become an idea of death? The whole problem of death is discussed with some fullness in a separate chapter[5], and we shall then see how the Greeks

---

[1] *Il.* IX, 410 ff.   [2] Cf. *ibid.* XIV, 85; XIX, 221–4.
[3] *Cults of the Greek States*, vol. V, chap. X.
[4] VIII.   [5] *Post*, chap. VII.

of the Heroic Age succeeded in reconciling themselves to the
thought of annihilation. For the present it is enough to note
that we get glimpses from time to time of a spirit, generally
quite distinct from Hades, Pluto, Tisiphone, or the Fates—
the Θάνατος who was called so often by Philoktetes and came
unbidden to Alkestis[1]—and that the warrior caste, about whom
Homer sings, had apparently formed some idea of this spirit
and associated him with a god of strife and bloodshed. It is
not unknown for Death to appear as a warrior. He is so depicted in *The Phoenix*[2], and Seneca records how Herakles, when
invading Pylos, encountered the spirit (generally reported to
be Pluto) but described as *mortis dominus*, leader of *pestiferas
manus* and armed with a three-forked spear[3]. In fact the trick
which Pherekydes[4] records to have been practised on the
actual god of death, is almost the same as the outrage which
was inflicted on Ares by Otos and Ephialtes[5]. When man
feared some spiritual enemy, he tried to imprison him in a
hole or vessel[6]. The beings who dealt with the soul after
death might be like vampires or dreams, but Ares is a danger
to the living. In him the uncertainties of life and the certain
terrors of death are depicted as clearly as in a dirge or an
elegy.

VIII. *Homeric pathos subservient to the main theme, but perhaps
    unduly emphasised in some of the (later?) accretions to the
    poem; particularly in the case of Lykaon and Hektor.*

This other aspect of the *Iliad*, its note of triumph, must not
be overlooked. Some admirers of the *Iliad* have so far appreciated the Homeric spirit of regret and its touches of pathos,
that they believe the poet to have been out of sympathy with
the victors. He may have imbibed the hatred of war so deeply
that he abhorred all violence; he may even have lost sight of
that other traditional function of the epic—the glorification
of the hero. Apart from the love of armour and of horses and
of good cheer, the whole story may be one magnificent protest
on behalf of the victims. In discussing this objection, we meet

---

[1] Soph. *Philokt.* 797–8; Eur. *Alk.* 24 ff.   [2] ll. 485–510.
[3] *Herc. Fur.* 560 ff.   [4] Pherek. *F.H.G.* 1, 91–78.   [5] *Il.* 385–91.
[6] Frazer, *The Golden Bough: The Scape Goat*, chap. 1, § 6.

for the first time indications that the *Iliad* is not the work of one generation or age, much less of one single brain. From the first word to the last a certain spirit of enthusiasm and activity seems to predominate and therefore the narrative has a certain uniformity of tone which we call epic. But at the same time the reader will easily discover certain strata or layers of sentiment which belong to different ages or to very different temperaments, and must have superimposed themselves one on the other by some process of accretion[1].

So it is with the touches of Homeric pathos. They are often counterbalanced and sometimes overwhelmed by gusts of ferocity. It must be remembered that the Acheans are the true heroes of the *Iliad*, especially Achilles, and that in its present form the setbacks and misadventures of the story are intended to bring out the importance of these warriors. In some early stage of its development the epic must have contained a song of barbaric triumph, and traces of this phase are easily discernible in the manners of the chieftains. They sometimes sell their prisoners' lives for a large ransom, but they do not recognise any virtue in withholding their strength. They are more often represented as roaring terribly and glaring fiercely with their eyes. Above all their epic greatness is meant to show itself in their taunts and yells of derision. Sometimes, indeed, we meet with a consciously dramatic or rhetorical utterance, as when old Priam, from the walls, watches Achilles working havoc, and condenses his hatred into irony[2], but generally the instinct of battle finds expression in savage glee.

When a warrior is pitchforked out of his chariot on the point of a spear, he is compared to a fish caught by an angler. When another is hit by a stone on the forehead and plunges head first over the rim, Patroklos cries out that he dives like an acrobat. The Acheans, like the Danes[3], thought that an unusually ugly wound humiliated his enemy. When the Acheans are penned within the palisade, Hektor's elation knows no bounds. He orders the Trojans to encamp on the plain and to light watch fires, lest their enemies should slink away under cover of darkness,

---

[1] See *post*, chap. III.   [2] *Il*. XXII, 41–3.
[3] Saxo Grammaticus, *Gesta Danorum*, VII, lxix[a], p. 341.

and he counsels his followers to send to the town for provisions, so that they can spend the hours in feasting, before it is light enough to make an end of their enemies.

It is when the Homeric characters thus abandon themselves that we realise how far they are removed from our modern ideal of sensibility and self-restraint. They were egoists and individualists. An epic warrior must not be cribbed and cabined by responsibility to the common welfare; he must not be one of those in authority who are thrice a slave; his greatness must arise from perfect freedom. His first duty (if they had recognised such an obligation as duty) was to himself. We have noticed that Achilles typifies the brevity of life, but he also embodies the intensity, ruthlessness and abandon of the Heroic Age. If some earlier version of the Μῆνις were ever to be discovered, we should almost certainly find the son of Peleus to be so much the protagonist, that the other characters only contributed to the spectacle of his invincibility. The Trojan warriors would probably be interesting as his victims and as nothing else; they would be mere illustrations of what his wrath could accomplish and their fate would serve only to glorify their victor. It is not surely a coincidence that when Andromache[1] recounts that all her kin have perished in war, we learn that they have every one gone down before the spear of Achilles, as her husband is fated to go down. But in the later and more expanded version which we possess, the treacherous adversaries of the Acheans are beginning to assume an additional *rôle*. As one by one they suffer the just vengeance of the more powerful and more glorious invaders, each victim nevertheless is made to typify the misery and disillusionments of war. This blending of two sentiments probably marks the next phase in the development of the epic. Again and again, as the warrior falls before the murderous impetuosity of his antagonist, we are reminded of his wife and children or of his far home and aged father; or again of the horses he had trained or of the broad lands which he hoped to enjoy. One of the best examples of this type of character is Priam's grandson Lykaon[2]. Though a mere adolescent, he has already

---

[1] *Il.* vi, 414 ff.   [2] *Ibid.* xxi, 34 ff.

suffered the bitterness of capture and slavery and now, after
regaining his home and enjoying for eleven days the prospect
of his old happy life, he finds himself helpless and half dazed
before the furious Achilles. Surely if there was one soldier in
the whole Trojan army who deserved to enjoy his share of
happiness, it was this unlucky youth. His passion for life is
rendered all the more piteous by the ruthlessness of his slayer.
He is a mere cipher, a helpless and unoffending creature who
has happened to cross the path of this destroying daemon.
As if to mock his misery, the poet makes him clasp Achilles's
knees, and with child-like simplicity implore mercy of the
avenger still maddened by the thought of Patroklos's death.

But the utmost bitterness of death is reserved for Hektor,
and here we probably reach in the complete union of the
elegiac and warlike moods a third and more developed stage
of epic poetry. To understand this hero's tragedy we must
remember his wife and child. According to Dares[1], Andromache
is warned in a dream that Hektor will be slain in battle, and
after fruitlessly trying to persuade him to withdraw, she prevails
on Priam to forbid him to leave the walls. The Homeric poet
assigns no such active *rôle* to this or any other Trojan woman,
but he causes both the wife and the child to exercise an influence all their own. He uses them as ties to bind Hektor
to life; to make him realise that his death is much more than
a loss to himself. To bring out the full poignancy of such a
situation the poet resorts to a transparent artifice to enable
the warrior, at the crisis of the battle, to snatch a few minutes
intercourse with those who are nearest and dearest to him[2].
The artistic effect more than justifies the means. Instead of a
lament or a monologue or a comment by the poet, we have
a speech from Andromache herself describing how defenceless
she and her son really are and how utterly dependent on her
husband's protection. Then comes Hektor's reply, which is one
of the most artistic achievements in literature. He has all the
passion for glory and the consciousness of his position which
you would expect from an Homeric warrior. But in addition
he has a premonition of Troy's defeat and foreknowledge of his

[1] *De Excidio*, xxiv.   [2] *Il*. vi, 369 ff.

own death. A modern man would be depressed with melancholy or would argue with destiny and perhaps brood on suicide. Hektor accepts his own fate without a trace of fear or of revolt. This readiness to yield to the inevitable, this unwillingness to stretch out futile hands to grasp an elusive ideal, are characteristic of all true epic poetry. Even Achilles shows much the same spirit when warned by the horse Xanthos of his approaching end[1]. But Hektor enjoys the melancholy distinction, among epic heroes, of feeling his losses more keenly than any other combatant. He may not be greatly troubled about the welfare of his native city provided that his own good name is preserved, but he cannot quiet or disregard the instinct of every male to defend his womenfolk and children. With the keenness of perception which this emotion arouses, he cannot help foreseeing how they will be led into captivity and put to servile tasks under the mocking eyes of their enemies, while he himself is a corpse, covered by the earth. When it is remembered that Hektor is just returning to a losing battle which could probably be descried from the low wall, the full effect of Andromache's appeal cannot escape the most prosaic reader. His wife's supplication, with the charming glimpse of his little boy, enables us to picture the thoughts which accompanied him into battle and were to haunt his moments of solitude. As far as we know, he never spoke to Andromache again. Within four days he was ignominiously slain and, as his soul speeds to Hades, he hears that his body shall be left to rot and to be devoured by dogs. We shall discuss in another place[2] what might be called the religious aspect of Hektor's fate, and it will then be shown that the Trojan warrior was not all unblessed of the gods, nor exiled from their favour. But assuredly Homer had already worked into his career all the ills of war. And yet not quite all. The same or some other poet has again taken up the theme of Hektor's sorrows and has described the grief and consternation which followed his death. Again the longest speech is from Andromache[3]. She and Hektor have already told us what fate befalls the widow of a vanquished warrior, but we have

---

[1] *Il*. XIX, 420 ff.   [2] *Post*, chap. III, § 8.   [3] *Il*. XXII, 477 ff.

not yet been reminded of what the future must have in store for Astyanax: and so, to complete the tale of misery, she now bewails in all its piteously graphic details the unhappiness and degradation which must henceforth be her son's portion. In both these passages we are dealing with a kind of composition which differs from the main body of the *Iliad*. The poet is describing calamity for its own sake; he is telling the story from the point of view of the victims or perhaps to expose the cruelty of the gods[1].

Yet it would be a mistake to conclude that pity or pathos inspires the *Iliad*. Here and there some poet, possibly in a more complex and sentimental age, may have added touches which draw tears for their own sake. Even then, the poet probably began with the intention of glorifying the stout arm of Achilles or some other victor, but went too far. In the main, these glimpses of distress and disillusionment are part of the tradi- tional atmosphere and in Homer's hands serve to heighten the splendour of life. It is nearly always the Trojans or their allies who excite the compassion of the modern reader. Neither the fate of Patroklos nor the destiny of Achilles brings with it that sense of irony and regret which we recognise, from our modern point of view, in the deaths of Lykaon, Sarpedon and Hektor. And yet the Acheans are the true heroes of the *Iliad*. Their deeds are meant to excite the highest admiration and to inspire the noblest feelings. Their characters and family histories are expected to arouse more interest and so are described with finer touches and with greater wealth of detail. Even at the height of the Trojans' short-lived success, Aias, Menelaos and Odysseus outshine them in heroism. So if pity were the pre- vailing note of the poem, we cannot believe that the minstrels would have reserved their deepest pathos for the inferior race. While telling how many perished in braving the Achean anger, the poets have realised that life was just as pleasant and death just as bitter to these presumptuous Pelasgians as to their own ancestors, and now and then, in some portions of the narrative, their sympathies have outrun their purpose.

---

[1] Cf. *Il*. xxii, 403–4.

IX. *The* Iliad *is not characterised by adolescent discontent or philosophic melancholy.*

So far we have discussed only the actual occasions for lamentation. We have seen why individual sorrows are so plentiful, and why the poet has dwelt on them with such deep sympathy and insight. We have also seen that the heroes were capable of the most intense joy and self-realisation. We have now to inquire whether this optimism is not, after all, occasional, and perhaps confined to a particular stage in the evolution of the poem. Has there not supervened a more comprehensive melancholy? Were not the Homeric warriors (at any rate in the more developed parts of the poem) sufficiently logical to deduce that in the face of so much misery, life was not worth living? The test case is, of course, Achilles's celebrated address to Priam, in which this impetuous and invincible warrior describes how Zeus keeps two jars[1], one full of evil gifts and the other of blessings, and generally draws from both in his dealings with mortals. Thus even the mightiest of the earth, like Priam himself, have to taste sorrow as well as joy.

Butcher has fully discussed this passage, and claims that Achilles "rises above the personal sorrow to the height of human pity, and draws a picture never yet surpassed of human destiny."[2] But is the tenour of Achilles's consolations really suggestive of melancholy? In any distinctive sense of the word, melancholy implies a distaste for life; a conviction that either oneself or one's fellow-creatures, or the social order, are so debased that solitude and inactivity are preferable to a career. We can arrive at the true significance of abstract words only by examining the examples which they seem to fit, and such is the meaning of melancholy as implied by St Augustine, Hamlet, Pascal, Senancour, Schopenhauer, and Thomas Hardy. Such moods may not have been unknown in Homeric times, as we learn from the perhaps interpolated note on Bellerophon's fate[3]. But such a state of mind is not characteristic of any of the warriors of the *Iliad*, and the poet speaks of the mood as a stroke of god-sent madness. Least of all does Achilles

---

[1] *Il.* XXIV, 518–51.   [2] *Some Aspects of the Greek Genius.*
[3] *Il.* VI, 200–2. *Cf.* Hother in Saxo, *Gesta Danorum*, III, xxiii[b], p. 122.

give way to apathy or monomania. In this speech he is merely
recognising things as they are. Even before his day it must
have been well known that all life is accompanied by suffering,
especially active life and more especially warfare. Consequently
all great literature, except a few comedies and a not very large
number of lyrics, is touched with sadness. We have already
noticed this quality when discussing the influence of dirges
and lamentations[1]. Besides, narrative and dramatic poetry are
bound by the very requirements of their plot construction to
make the most of this aspect of human activity. In the first
conclave, which the gods hold in the *Odyssey*, Zeus complains
of men

$$ο\dot{\iota} \ \delta\dot{\epsilon} \ \kappa\alpha\dot{\iota} \ \alpha\dot{\upsilon}\tau o\dot{\iota}$$
$$\sigma\phi\tilde{\eta}\sigma\iota\nu \ \dot{\alpha}\tau\alpha\sigma\theta\alpha\lambda\dot{\iota}\eta\sigma\iota\nu \ \dot{\upsilon}\pi\dot{\epsilon}\rho \ \mu\dot{o}\rho o\nu \ \ddot{\alpha}\lambda\gamma\epsilon' \ \ddot{\epsilon}\chi o\upsilon\sigma\iota\nu[2],$$

and it is clear from the remainder of the speech, that were it
not so, we should have missed the story of Aigisthous, Kly-
temnestra, Elektra and Orestes. In another passage, Odysseus,
after receiving some kindness from Amphinomos, declares

$$o\dot{\upsilon}\delta\dot{\epsilon}\nu \ \dot{\alpha}\kappa\iota\delta\nu\dot{o}\tau\epsilon\rho o\nu \ \gamma\alpha\tilde{\iota}\alpha \ \tau\rho\dot{\epsilon}\phi\epsilon\iota \ \dot{\alpha}\nu\theta\rho\dot{\omega}\pi o\iota o$$
$$\pi\dot{\alpha}\nu\tau\omega\nu \ \ddot{o}\sigma\alpha \ \tau\epsilon \ \gamma\alpha\tilde{\iota}\alpha\nu \ \ddot{\epsilon}\pi\iota \ \pi\nu\epsilon\dot{\iota}\epsilon\iota \ \tau\epsilon \ \kappa\alpha\dot{\iota} \ \ddot{\epsilon}\rho\pi\epsilon\iota[3].$$

He goes on to explain why: because in his hour of strength and
glory, man believes himself to be invincible, and then when
the gods send misfortune, he has to bear his afflictions with
steadfastness. The poet is thinking of Odysseus himself and of
his followers; had his words not been true, there would have
been no *Odyssey*. A poet could not have composed an epic
without bearing these conditions in mind, but he need not
therefore allow his characters to give way to them. In the
Iliad, one would, at the first glance, imagine that it was
Homer's express design to sound the depths of woe. The utmost
ingenuity and genius are expended in devising situations almost
unheard of in their poignancy. We might perhaps expect to
find depicted the agony of a warrior who faces his doom, or
even Hektor foreseeing his fate while he caresses his son. But
when we come to Andromache watching her husband's corpse
dragged in the dust round Troy, or, above all, to Priam
kissing the hand which slew his son[4]—we feel that art has

---

[1] *Ante*, § 6.   [2] *Od.* I, 33.   [3] *Ibid.* XVIII, 130–1.   [4] *Il.* XXIV, 505.

transcended our wildest guesses at human capacity for suffering. Yet there is no reason to suppose that these tremendous
situations reflect a pessimistic mood, for in one way or another
they redound to the honour of the participants. The reader
will gather some idea of what is meant, if he compares Hardy's
more gloomy novels with *The Dynasts*. In the prose we have
minute studies of human futility. The characters are like
creatures caught in a trap. Their qualities, sometimes sublime,
count for nothing, unless it be to fill the reader with disgust
for life. So, at first sight, it seems to be in *The Dynasts*. But as
we study that broader canvas more closely, we discover that
the chief characters are not really futile. They fulfil the law of
their being; they find elbow-room for their powers; they rise
to greatness even in the hour of defeat. So it is with Homer.
The protagonists accomplish all of which they are capable,
and the reader leaves the description with a sense of exhilaration and of renewed confidence in the possible greatness of
man.

But this aspect is only half the solution. In a very celebrated
passage, Zeus pities the horses of Achilles, because they have
been doomed to associate with man:

$$\text{οὐ μὲν γάρ τί πού ἐστιν ὀιζυρώτερον ἀνδρὸς}$$
$$\text{πάντων ὅσσα τε γαῖαν ἔπι πνείει τε καὶ ἔρπει}[1],$$

and this pronouncement seems to voice a more comprehensive
and fundamental sadness. The poet seems to despair of the
human race, not because of the hardships involved in the
pursuit of honour, but from the very nature of our destiny
on earth. Butcher explains this despondency as being the
melancholy of youth; the pessimistic mood which "follows
close upon other movements when the pleasure of existence
and the vision of the world's beauty have penetrated and
possessed the mind."[2] Presumably Prof. Chadwick means
much the same when he says that "the qualities exhibited
by these societies, virtues and defects alike, are clearly those
of adolescence."[3] But nothing is more deceptive than to speak

[1] *Il.* xvii, 446–7.   [2] *Some Aspects of the Greek Genius.*
[3] *The Heroic Age*, chap. xix, p. 442.

of epochs and ages in terms applicable to individuals. The
warriors who fought round Troy would undoubtedly seem
young when judged by a generation which produced *Back to
Methuselah*, and in mind they would certainly be considered
child-like. But their civilisation was far from embryonic. As
will be shown[1], it had already passed through many stages of
development, had reached its climax and was perhaps verging
towards decay. This note of philosophic sadness is not the result
of youthful disillusionment, it is the depression, almost the envy,
which comes from making comparisons. In the next chapter
it will be shown how Achean civilisation tended to invent or
remodel its deities so that these became symbols of progress.
In fact their deities were their ideals, and from time to time
lent to mortals some portion of their own excellence. Every
upward step was made by raising their gods yet one step
higher above men. Sooner or later these human beings were
bound to pay the price of such idealisation—the too acute
realisation of the gulf between the mortal and the immortal.
In order to magnify the gods, they were bound to belittle the
mortals. We shall note in a subsequent chapter how unmistakeable this melancholy becomes in Hesiod and in the
Homeric Hymns. Pindar is forced to recognise the essential
difference, while claiming that men and gods are of the same
breed[2]. But in the *Iliad* they have not yet found anything bitter
or humiliating in the contrast. They realise that the gods can
enforce homage, the greatest boon on earth or Olympos,
without incurring death or the risk of disaster. They are in
the words of a later poet:

$$\mu\alpha\kappa\acute{\alpha}\rho\omega\nu \; \gamma\acute{\epsilon}\nu o\varsigma \; \alpha\grave{\iota}\grave{\epsilon}\nu \; \acute{\epsilon}\acute{o}\nu\tau\omega\nu^3.$$

That was the essence of their superiority; it was only when
reminded of this difference that human destiny (apart from
the adventitious evils of war) seemed so depressing. For it must
be remembered that mortals do not feel discontent, till they
compare their destiny with that of the gods. As often as not,
it is a deity and not a mortal who discovers the pathos of
human life. The whole doctrine is revealed during the battle of

---

[1] *Post*, chap. III.   [2] *Nemean*, VI, I.   [3] *Theogony*, 33.

the Olympians. Poseidon challenges Apollo to fight, reminding
him of the injustice they both suffered at the hands of Laomedon.
He recalls how he was forced to build the walls of Troy, how
he was cheated of his payment and declares that his hatred
against the city has never since that time been lessened. There
speaks the old barbaric type of god. Very likely, as Dr Farnell
suggests, this connection with the walls of Troy, recalls some
distant legend that Poseidon was once a god of the city. What
is Apollo's reply?—that men are not worth quarrelling about.
The god does not add that they are sordid or inert or corrupt,
but that they are perishable as leaves and therefore best left
to war on each other[1]. In a certain limited and specialised
sense these sentiments may be termed melancholic, but they
are really the reverse side of an ideal. Had it been otherwise,
the hero who laboured most under the curse of mortality, who
is indeed the poetic embodiment of life's short span, would
not have been Achilles, the most inspiring figure in all epic
literature.

[1] *Il.* xxi, 462–7.

CHAPTER III

GODS AND MEN IN HOMER

THE theology of the Homeric poems is often belittled or
even ridiculed. Dictys and Dares ignore the gods. As
Voltaire says, "nous rions, nous levons les épaules en
voyant des dieux qui se disent des injures, qui se battent
entr'eux, qui se battent contre des hommes, qui sont blessés
& dont le sang coule."[1] Prof. Chadwick sums up religion in
the Heroic Age as "the worship of a number of universally
recognised and highly anthropomorphic deities—coupled with
the belief in a common and distant land of souls."[2] Dr Leaf
characterises the divine government of the Homeric world as
an "epiphenomenon."[3] Yet, to the present writer, it seems
incontestable that the immortals of Homer represent one of
the greatest efforts of the epic spirit[4]. Without them the mightiest
"eaters of the fruits of the earth" would lose their indescribable
touch of superhuman grandeur and we, the students of Homer,
would have missed perhaps the most valuable of all insights
into man's ways of enlarging and fortifying his self-esteem.
In the previous chapter, we studied the Homeric attitude to
life. In the present chapter we are really inquiring how that
epic spirit was formed and maintained, and what adverse
influences threatened its serenity. The truth seems to lie in a
saying of Herakleitos, which is dark because of its paradox.
"The gods are mortal and men immortal. The death of the
former is the life of the latter."[5] That is to say: imagine a god
just falling short of his godhead, and doomed to sink gradually
into the impotence which ends in death, and you have an
idea of man. His fire is divine, and though it is soon quenched

---

[1] *Du Poème Épique.*   [2] *The Heroic Age*, chap. XVIII.

[3] *Homer and History*, chap. I.

[4] It has sometimes proved impossible to refer facts quoted in this chapter
to the authorities who first used them. Still, the present author does not
wish to conceal his indebtedness to J. G. Frazer, *The Golden Bough*; Gruppe,
Griechische Mythologie und Religionsgeschichte; L. R. Farnell, *Cults of the Greek
States*; J. E. Harrison, *Prolegomena to the Study of Greek Religion*. His deductions
are his own.

[5] *Frag.* 62.

in each individual, it spreads to his successors and so is immortal as well as godlike.

1. *Traces of primitive fear and primitive magic in Homer. The
Age of Terror.*

To appreciate this point of view, it is necessary to realise
the religious phases through which the Acheans seem to have
passed. At some very early stage they or their ancestors must
have believed, like other primitive peoples, that man's happiness, prosperity and in fact life, depended on daemons or
spirits who supplied all that is good, such as the rain, the
harvest, the spring; and all that is evil, such as pestilence and
famine. Numa must have been convinced of these doctrines
when he appointed fire to be worshipped as the origin of all
things. He must have felt in some obscure and perhaps un-
reasoning way that life is dependent on motion and heat, and
that fire possesses these two qualities more conspicuously than
any other element[1]. The effort to control these powers and
influences and to win a certain measure of confidence in their
presence was surely among the first spiritual conquests achieved
by human beings. Men who were cleverer or stronger than
their fellows learnt to work spells and symbols and so were
credited with a certain influence over these spirits and daemons.
This recognition of the supernatural and the will to master it
were, no doubt, immense strides in the progress of mankind,
but they cannot have brought more than a measure of assurance and of hope. The sorcerer and the medicine man, as
Frazer observes, were liable to failure, spells and incantations
must often have proved powerless and as men became more
skilful and intelligent, they must have discovered that each
new advance was hampered by new difficulties. Contact with
the supernatural involved a more lively appreciation of the
forces of evil. Human beings must have realised that for every
daemon or spirit which could be tamed or enlisted in man's
service, there was one too powerful or too malevolent to be
cajoled.

The Acheans must have passed through some such phase

[1] Plut. *Vit. Camill.* xx.

as this, because they were applauding epic poetry, and perhaps
living it, at a time when the belief in malignant and vindictive
deities was far from dead. Sarpedon declared that the air was
thronged with dangerous and deadly spirits, waiting for an
opportunity to capture human lives[1], and it has already been
noticed how completely the character of Ares answers to the
conception of a hostile and persecuting daemon[2]. Water spirits
such as Skylla and Charybdis are believed to be dragons of
appalling ferocity, and other godheads, more highly placed
and more piously revered, can yet hardly be persuaded from
evil-doing by the odour and smoke of sacrifice. Zeus may
have acceded to Thetis's petition[3], because he deemed it wise
to lessen the dwellers of earth[4], but Hyperion threatens to
turn his light into Hades and to deprive this world of the sun,
merely because the unintentional slaughter of his oxen is un-
avenged[5]. Athene was so vindictive that her wrath could not
be turned away by human supplication and humility[6], Helen
in her heart mistrusted Aphrodite[7]. In fact the bitterness and
hatred of the gods was a commonplace of human experience,
especially in the *Odyssey*. Agamemnon was deemed a fool for
not knowing how inflexible they are[8], and Odysseus, the wisest
of all men, was ready, in the hour of danger, to suspect that
some one of the gods was weaving a deception to his discomfiture[9]. As in the days of Achan, it was believed that a
man who had once incurred the enmity of the gods, would
extend their hatred to all who befriended him[10]. Such phrases
as κακὴ Διὸς αἶσα παρέστη[11] or Ζεὺς δέ σφισι μήδετ᾽ ὄλεθρον[12]
became almost proverbial expressions for the presence of
danger. Human sacrifice was still spoken of, not so much to
put new vigour into the king-god, as the Massagetai sacrificed
horses to the sun τῶν θεῶν τῷ ταχίστῳ πάντων τῶν θνητῶν
τὸ τάχιστον δατέονται[13], or to vitalise the land, as was practised
long after the Homeric Age[14], but because some spirits were
so bloodthirsty and implacable that they required human

[1] *Il.* xii, 326 ff. [2] *Ante*, chap. ii, § 7. [3] *Il.* i, 493.
[4] *Cypria*. [5] *Od.* xii, 382. [6] *Il.* vi, 31 ff.
[7] *Ibid.* iii, 399. [8] *Od.* iii, 146. [9] *Ibid.* v, 356.
[10] *Ibid.* x, 72. [11] *Ibid.* ix, 52. [12] *Ibid.* xiv, 300.
[13] Herod. i, 216. [14] See *post*, vol. ii, chap. xi, § 2.

flesh to satisfy them. Iphigeneia and Polyxena were thus
devoted to the winds, and Achilles[1] sacrificed Trojan youths
at the pyre of Patroklos, if not as a Ποινή, because his friend
liked to kill them when alive. In contradistinction to these
aspects, critics have dwelt on what seems to us to be a very
different picture of the gods. They have urged the well-known
examples of Olympian horseplay and brutality[2], and Dr Leaf,
quoting[3] one scene, has attributed it to the scepticism of the
aristocratic Achean[4]. The reader must be left to himself to
decide how far such characterisation is really representative
and how many passages are likely to be fairly late accretions
and represent a different age when anthropomorphic deities
provoked ridicule rather than fear. But the origin of the *Iliad*
and *Odyssey* must certainly be looked for in an age of feuds
and depredations and if men's hands were raised against each
other was not that an additional reason for imagining their
deities to be just as dangerous[5]? Besides, the gods who were
ready to hurt men must be considered ready to hurt each
other, and being immortal, they could not do more than
exchange blows and insults, or put outrages upon their fellow-
gods[6]. The roaring of these giant daemons, as when Poseidon
came up to earth to aid the Acheans[7], need not be less inspiring than the appearances of Beli or Thrud Gelmir, the sea
giants of Teutonic mythology, and at some periods, mortals
stood so much in awe of them, that it was considered dangerous
to behold them with the eyes of the flesh[8]. Even when not thus
provoked, they had been known to strike men with madness[9].

These and such other imaginings, some of which have survived in popular folklore down to the age of steam, are
significant in studying Homer because they illustrate the
tendency to fear, which is characteristic of primitive man. He
feels himself menaced by many things which he cannot understand, and consequently is prone to attribute supernatural
power even to inanimate objects. Thus we hear much of the

[1] *Il.* xxi, 28.   [2] *Ibid.* viii, 10; xiv, 246; xv, 14.
[3] *Ibid.* xxi, 385.   [4] *Homer and History*, chap. vii.
[5] Cf. *Il.* xviii, 361-7.   [6] *Post*, chap. vii, § 2, on the origin of Tartaros.
[7] *Il.* xiv, 148.   [8] *E.g. Il.* xxiv, 462-4; *Od.* xvi, 175.
[9] *Il.* ii, 5; vi, 200; *Od.* xx, 345.

mysterious *aigis*[1], probably a goatskin revered as a talisman, its tassels perhaps possessing the power to enmesh and bind, and of a magic wand[2] by which Hermes controlled the dead and induced sleep and Athene metamorphosed the living[3]. Men were so used to expect hostility from a god, that any sign or revelation connected with his powers generally foreboded evil. When the thunder muttered or the lightning flashed, Zeus was devising harm[4]. There are many other traces of pre-Hellenic magic in the Homeric poems, such as accompany an age of rank and timorous superstition. The primitive rite of binding a ghost or spirit in a hole so as to control his potency finds an echo in the story how mortals imprisoned Ares in a pot[5]. Aiolos seems to have been some recollection of a medicine man controlling the winds[6]. It was still imagined that a king might be sufficiently a god to render the earth fruitful[7]. Iron frightens ghosts and spirits like Kirke, because of its hardness, so different from their nature, and also because of its newness, and this same Kirke converts men into beasts by putting parts of animals into a specially prepared broth, as do the human-leopard societies of Western Africa[8]. The Δολώνεια, though admittedly an interpolation, and therefore probably late, contains what is likely to be a survival of sympathetic magic. When Dolon[9] started out to spy on the Grecian camp, one scholiast suggests that he threw over his shoulders a wolf's skin because it was cold[10], another because that animal suited his rank[11] and Mr J. A. K. Thomson believes that he wished to appear like a were-wolf[12]. It is just as likely that he sought to acquire the subtlety of a wolf by contact with its skin.

Of course these allusions and indications present only one side of Homeric life, and suggest the recollections of some far-distant, prehistoric age. Even if the data were far more plentiful .

---

[1] *Il.* II, 446; XVIII, 203; XXIV, 20.   [2] *Il.* XXIV, 343; *Od.* V, 47.
[3] *Od.* XVI, 172, 456.   [4] *Il.* VII, 478; VIII, 75; *Od.* XIX, 457.
[5] *Il.* V, 385. *Ante*, chap. II, § 7.   [6] *Od.*   [7] *Il.* XIX, 109-14.
[8] Cf. examples from savage tribes in Frazer, *Golden Bough*, vol. III, chap. II, p. 83.
[9] *Il.* X, 334.   [10] K. 23.   [11] K. 458-9.
[12] *Studies in the Odyssey*, chap. I, p. 10.

than is the case, our own era is too hopelessly out of sympathy with these times for any investigator to form a clear idea of how human beings then thought and worshipped. But it seems to be incontestable that for many centuries primitive man passed through a phase of civilisation which ought to be called the Age of Terror, and that during this time his mind was busy discovering or inventing formidable beings, recognisable by their superhuman power to hurt. Abundant evidence has been collected of primitive peoples such as the Sofala of South-east Africa or the Futuma of the South Pacific or the Tibetans, who deify evils which afflict them, while the Futuma deify as the greatest spirit their sovereign and so submit to any tyranny from him[1]. So many and so persistent were the plagues and persecutions of spirits and ghosts that savage tribes perform periodic rites of expulsion and purification[2]. Such is the effect produced on the human mind by the struggle for life. We shall find, in the course of this inquiry[3], that a similar disposition recurs again and again, as civilisation advances, and that one of the problems of man is to recover some measure of equanimity, confidence and pride, in face of this discouragement and alarm. At each period, when men succeed in thus possessing themselves, their triumph is marked by the growth or consummation of an epic, and the real inspiration in what seems to be a poem of action, is the consciousness of victory expressed or implied over these nightmares. Dr Leaf has written some interesting pages on what he claims to be the "compromise by which Achaian religion might be recognised side by side with the 'Pelasgian.'"[4] We are going to trace that "compromise"—as far as "Pelasgian" and "primitive" are to be assumed to be synonymous—and to show that it was no sceptical or calculated rearrangement but a long and mostly unconscious effort to reckon with all the terrors attendant on existence and to replace or overpower them with other less demoralising phantasies. So it comes about that the Homeric narratives preserve different strata of beliefs. There are enough of the early

[1] Frazer, *Golden Bough*, pt I, vol. I, chap. VII.
[2] *Ibid.* pt VI, chaps. II, III; pt VII, vol. I, chap. V, § 3.
[3] See *post*, vol. II, chaps. II, VIII, IX, X.
[4] *Homer and History*, chap. VII, pp. 261 ff.

superstitions to show that the influence of the Age of Terror had not yet entirely passed away, but the most inspired and inspiring parts of the two epics illustrate how these misgivings and apprehensions were overcome, and the Homeric character was evolved.

II. *The doctrine of Fate becomes the bulwark against the fears of primitive religion.*

The first step was to imagine some consistent and dependable power, no empirical system of sorcery, but an established part of the spiritual world, which could be relied on to oppose and limit the malignity of the superhumans. So there arose the doctrine of Fate. This belief probably originated in the conception of a personal life spirit, which apparently associated itself with each mortal, as soon as born, and shadowed him throughout his career, either guarding his life, or leaving him to perish. The ancestors of the Greeks seem also to have believed in three female spirits who attended the birth of every child, and received offerings and in some way influenced the infant's powers and normal span of life. These conjectures are partly based on the primitive beliefs of other countries, or the *fylgja, Urðr, Wurt, Vyrd, Norni, Mânes, Parcae*, to be discussed in a later chapter[1]. But we know that a Κήρ was believed to accompany each child through life and that the spirit or spirits who were present at each birth were akin to the Μοῖραι. When warfare became the most engrossing pursuit of one caste within each community, and the virtues of self-assertion and individuality were prized above all others, it was natural to make a cult of these personal daemons and to regard them as apart from the other more general deities. Besides, when forcing their way into a strange land the intruders would be immensely reassured if they could think that their life's span depended on these intimate companions and not on the vengeful power of their enemies' gods[2]. So Achilles had two

[1] Vol. II, chap. II, §§ 1, 5.

[2] Cf. Gibbon: "The doctrine of predestination, so favourable to martial virtue, was carefully inculcated by the king of the Huns (*sc.* Attila), who assured his subjects that the warriors protected by Heaven were safe and invulnerable amidst the darts of the enemy"—*Decline and Fall*, chap. XXXV.

Κῆρες between which he might choose and Zeus put two in a balance to decide the death of Hektor[1]. But as Κῆρες is also the name given to the spirits whom Sarpedon dreaded[2] in war, we may conclude that the idea of this life spirit, thanks to its association with battle, was already beginning to symbolise the dread and menace of death in war, and by the time that the *Shield of Herakles* was composed, these Κῆρες have become grim, white-fanged daemons, each shadowing his mortal, ready to pounce upon him and drink his blood the moment that he fell wounded. We find that the *mara*, *Walriderske* and *Valkyrie* develop a like character in the north. But the warriors could by now afford to add these fiends to the array of their ghostly adversaries, for they had already accomplished their salvation, thanks to the Μοῖραι.

Though we do not know the dates and stages of this victory, we can still detect the mental process by which the sense of security was achieved, and the goddesses connected with birth became as it were a shield between the warrior and his spiritual enemies. The feat became possible as soon as men realised that "homoeopathic" or "contagious" magic was so much more powerful than the gods, that the gods were not above conforming to it and using it themselves. Such is the possible significance of the Διὸς ἀπάτη[3]. It has been quoted as an example of the scepticism of the Acheans, but only because we do not ourselves believe in charms. Once accept the possibility of magic and the story becomes a matter of supreme earnestness. This aspect will most easily be understood, if the reader remembers that one of the chief uses of sorcery, both negative and positive, was to influence human beings or spirits by performing in miniature and in symbolic fashion something that in real life would bring happiness or misery. The proper manipulation of these processes gave men a peculiar power. In fact a spell, whether operated intentionally, like the roasting of a wax image, or unintentionally, like passing inadvertently through a cleft tree trunk, could not be nullified except by a more powerful counter-spell. "Thus," says Frazer, "it is a rule with the Galelareese that when you have caught

Il. IX, 410 ff.; XXII, 208–13.   [2] *Ibid.* XII, 326.   [3] *Ibid.* XIV.

fish and strung them on a line, you may not cut the line through, or next time you go a-fishing your fishing-line will be sure to break."[1] So far magic is regarded as a power in the hands of men to influence the spirit world. But the generation which believed that if Hera wished to lull Zeus to sleep she could do so by applying a charm, was able to deduce that sorcery may become an independent power. For what is the function of the *Norni* and Μοῖραι in the Heroic Age? They observe almost the same ritual as the Galelareese, they weave and cut lines; only they exercise their power on a higher plane than do the spirits of earth and air and they apply it to the issues of life and death. Such was the doctrine of Αἶσα or Πότμος. Their virtue resides in this action. They are not fully individualised like Athene or Hephaistos or Aphrodite. Αἶσα is mentioned alone in the *Iliad*[2] and two Κλῶθες are associated with her in the *Odyssey*[3], but the description goes no further than to represent them as spinning. They do not act according to their own wills or foreknowledge, they are not personified more than is necessary to bring the idea into touch with the processes of sorcery.

One legend illustrates the evolution of this idea; it is the story of Meleager. Althaia, mated to Oineos, gives birth to a son. The ancient primitive Fates—they might just as well have been Norns[4]—attend his birthday feast. One gives him high birth, the second strength and courage, and Atropos[5], the third, grants as a favour that his life shall last as long as a firebrand burning on the hearth is preserved. So it looks as if the gift of immortality had been bestowed on him. The mother gathers up the brand and deposits it in a chest. The son grows up and becomes an invincible warrior. Finally he slays a boar of monstrous size and strength which Artemis had sent to ravage the land. He proposes to give the skin to Atalanta, but the sons of Thestios, his father-in-law, oppose him, claiming that they come before any woman. Yet such was his power, that he slew them all and carried out his will. This

---

[1] *G.B.* pt. I, chap. III, § 2.
[2] XX, 127.   [3] VII, 197.
[4] See *Helgakvitha Hundingsbana*, I, stanzas 2–4 for an almost exact parallel.
[5] See particularly Hyginos, *Fab.* CLXXI.

blood feud was his undoing. His mother, furious at the death of her brothers, flung the brand into the fire and the hero perished. What stronger proof of man's weakness and vulnerability? Yet not altogether so. Meleager was exposed to one fate only. Apart from the brand, no enemy need be feared, human or divine. Thanks to his identification with this perishable object he had grown up, as Apollodoros says, ἄτρωτος καὶ γενναῖος[1]. That is to say, men had discovered "the external soul," they believed that a man's life might be bound up with some object quite independent of that most perishable of all things—his body. Similarly the "city of Alkathoös" depended on the purple lock which was conspicuous amongst the grey hairs of Nisos the king[2], and Taphos on Pterelaos's golden lock[3]. Troy was believed to be impregnable as long as the tomb of Laomedon remained untouched over the Skaian gate[4], or the palladium was guarded in its original place within the walls[5]. The story of Meleager reaches us through Ovid, Apollodoros and Hyginos, that is to say, through writers who took a modern interest in archeology and folklore. Perhaps they selected a primitive, pre-Homeric version, gathered, no doubt, from among the Pelasgian legends which came to the surface after the passing of the Heroic Age. Or perhaps they amused themselves by adding a touch of contemporary sentimentalism, so that the ancient story should appeal to the taste of imperial Rome. In either case they would tend to represent the mortal as at a disadvantage—as liable to be tricked by the obscure promise of a god, or as vanishing in disaster when his position seemed secure. But such was not the necessary consequence. The conditions under which Meleager perished might easily be turned to the encouragement and strengthening of man. There was needed only the assurance that the "external soul" was in the keeping of some friendly or impartial deity and not of a capricious and impulsive mortal.

The warriors had found that assurance in the Μοῖραι. Instead of a brand, each soul was associated with something represented in later literature as a thread or the incline of a

[1] Bibl. I, viii, 2.
[2] Metam. VIII, 6.
[3] Apoll. Bibl. II, iv, 7.
[4] Servius, Aen. II, 241.
[5] Dictys, De Bello Trojano, v, 5.

balance, and either symbol was controlled if not applied by
the impartial and inflexible Fates. The scientific minds of the
twentieth century may at first wonder how a belief in predestination became an incentive to action and a cause for
pride. Yet the doctrine was a triumph of this same scientific
spirit. One of the chief anxieties of early civilisation arose from
the supposed double-dealing and deceptiveness of the gods.
We shall see later how profoundly the post-Homeric Greek
dreaded being hoodwinked by his own oracles[1], and even the
Homeric warrior had ample reason for guarding against the
trickery of the gods. One remembers how Achilles was more
than once baulked of his prey and how Hektor was lured to
his doom by illusions[2]. But the Μοῖραι worked by the laws of
impersonal magic; they were an assertion of cause and effect;
they brought a measure of certainty into the world haunted
by Ἄρης ἀλλοπρόσαλλος. This creed meant release from the
most capricious and vindictive tyranny that man has ever
invented for himself. Henceforth the spirits who presided over
the different spheres of human emotion and activity might
harass and persecute, but they were baulked of their supreme
vengeance.

Even in modern times men derived great encouragement
from the idea of destiny. Dr Sayce, himself saturated in ancient
literature, was so fortified by the belief, that he never needed
to hesitate in a really dangerous enterprise[3]. The heroes of both
the *Iliad* and *Odyssey* again and again encouraged themselves
with the assurance that neither man nor god could overwhelm
them before their time. We shall shortly have to discuss how
far this belief is changed in the poem's most modern form.
But for the moment it is enough that the doctrine of Fate must
have been supreme during one phase of Homeric development.
Nor can it be denied that the actions of men seem somehow
to be solemnised and rendered less petty or futile by the consciousness of this invisible and impersonal power, which shapes
their course. The reader will think of the prophecy of the horse
Xanthos[4], or of the Trojans, triumphantly encamped opposite

[1] *Post*, chap. VI, §§ 6, 7. [2] *Il.* XXI, 600 ff.; XXII, 226 ff.
[3] *Reminiscences*, Macmillan, 1923.
[4] *Il.* XIX, 404 ff.

the palisade, joyously expecting to annihilate the Acheans on the morrow, while the star-sown heavens brood peacefully on the fire-lit plain[1].

iii. *The heroes who believe in Fate, believe also in their own divine ancestry.*

Before leaving this aspect of the *Iliad*, it should also be noted that the confidence in destiny, though so widespread, is confined to certain classes and to certain ages. There are legends in plenty which still recognise the power of the immortals as unlimited. It is only in the case of warriors, either god-born or god-favoured, that Fate has marked out the span of life, and then only while they are engaged in some great enterprise. It seems that only men of this calibre had the courage and self-reliance to invent or accept such a creed; and they themselves certainly believed their origin to be different from that of ordinary folk. Their subjects and dependents were of the earth, earthy. The Aiakeidai believed that those over whom they ruled were sprung from ants. The Lokrians thought that their underlings originated from the stones which Deukalion and his wife threw over their shoulders or from the clay which Prometheus kneaded. But as far as can be traced, the ruling castes seem to have been the real or imagined descendants of conjurors and magicians, who began by controlling the powers of nature, and were then believed to be the channels through which these powers worked, and so were at one time themselves reverenced as deities. Dr Farnell has shown how Achilles, Diomed, Aeneas, Glaukos, Pandaros and Sarpedon were each at one time the centre of a cult and enjoyed divine honours[2]. Tribes had gradually come to regard these and other such deities as ancestors of reigning families. They are still half-divine. They speak directly to their gods without the aid of priests, and the gods speak directly to them and grant their prayers. In fact, they are the priests. Θεοῖς ἐπιείκελος or ἀντίθεος was no mere metaphorical exaggeration. The priest Dolopionos was still actually worshipped as a god[3]. Proteus

[1] *Il.* viii, 553 ff.   [2] *Cult of the Greek States*, vol. ii, esp. chap. xxi.
[3] *Il.* v, 77.

changes into the forms of innumerable animals as an Egyptian magician of the twelfth or thirteenth century might[1], but Telemachos lays violent hands on him and controls him by the charms, which the newer gods have given him.

An excellent example of the transition from god to hero is to be found in Diomed's ἀριστεία[2]. Originally he appears to have been an Argive deity and his cult was almost certainly associated with that of Athene. Traces of his divinity still linger round him, for during the battle the mist which obscures the vision of mortal eyes is withdrawn[3] so that he may discern the presence of gods among the press of fighters, and later in the day he is enabled to put to flight two alien deities. But in other respects he is a mortal, of rather doubtful status, and may really have lived and fought during the siege of Troy[4]. An example of the passing of this hero-worship is to be found in fourth-century Egypt. Herodotos[5] records that the kings and priests are now of purely human origin, back to the most distant ancestor, but he adds that a race of gods had once ruled over the country, of whom Orus the son of Osiris was the last.

In the lives of the warriors who partook of both the divine and the mortal, the power of Fate is regarded as irresistible. The ghost of Patroklos confessed that his doom had been fixed at birth[6]; Hektor used this thought to give comfort to Andromache[7] and in his hour of triumph looked to the same power to overcome Achilles[8]; Aeneas is warned by Poseidon that he is fated to fall by the hand of no warrior, unless he encounters Achilles[9]. Agamemnon[10] ascribes his folly in thwarting Achilles to Zeus and Μοῖρα, as well as to Ἐρινύς and Ἄτη. Odysseus cheers his followers on Kirke's island, by reminding them that they need fear no death, till the appointed day has come upon them[11].

---

[1] Bérard, *Introduction à l'Odyssée*, t. i, chap. iii, p. 201.   [2] *Il.* v.
[3] *Ibid.* v, 127–8.   [4] W. Leaf, *Homer and History*, chap. i.
[5] ii, 144.   [6] *Il.* xxiii, 78.   [7] *Ibid.* vi, 486.
[8] *Ibid.* xvi, 860.   [9] *Ibid.* xx, 332.   [10] *Ibid.* xix, 87.
[11] *Od.* x, 174.

IV. *They remodel ancestor worship into the cult of the qualities which they most admire. The idealisation of Zeus, who comes to preside over the dispensations of Fate.*

This ability to take refuge in the idea of Fate—to believe that some impartial and impersonal power has placed your ultimate destiny beyond the reach of spirits partial to particular races and localities—this comforting assurance was, then, the prerogative of certain warlike castes. In the men who cherished this belief we discover another characteristic which marks the second stage in the development of epic civilisation. The warriors who trusted in Destiny found themselves strong enough to command the friendship and assistance or to challenge the antagonism of the lesser auxiliary gods. On this question, like so many others, it is impossible to speak with certainty. One can only review the available data, until they group themselves into a picture which suggests fresh ideas and seems to agree with what we know of humanity. We have already seen that the greatest Achean and even Trojan warriors traced their ancestry back to some deity who was originally a priest, but we find that this belief did not stop short at the claims of ordinary ancestor worship. The majority of chieftains seem to have ignored or discarded the memory of their original progenitors. But they did not therefore discard the belief in a divine origin. In fact the more they became conscious of progress and development the more they regarded themselves as descendants of a deity. Instead of satisfying themselves with the cult of some traditional totem or medicine man, they claimed kinship with some god or goddess, either local or imported, whose qualities they most admired. Thanks to Fate they found themselves partially independent of other deities, but they did not therefore ignore the spirit world. Men seem to have grown so rapidly in power and confidence that they arrogated to themselves something of its strain.

Thus they tended to adopt as an ancestor deity the spirit who could represent some excellence at which his descendants are supposed to aim. That is why so many of the ruling caste imagined their progenitor to be Zeus, the type of majesty and kingship. It should be noticed how well the Homeric "Father

of gods and men" fulfils this ideal. Whether the Olympic ruler
was originally conceived as the god of the bright or the dark sky,
or as the "sky pillar," the *Irminsûl* of the Saxons, the Homeric
poets succeeded in creating a wonderful portrait of authority
sua vi nixa[1]. It is noticeable that however firmly Zeus may be
established, we are never allowed to forget that he is an intruder; a conqueror who holds his position by force. Here's
opposition to his authority ought, probably, to be taken quite
seriously. According to Dictys[2], Hekabe played a more in-
fluential part than did Priam in bringing Troy to defy Greece.
And in the next place Zeus is ἀγκυλομήτης: that is to say, he
sees further than his vigorous and unruly subordinates and
lays plans which reach their fulfilment by devious paths. As
such he is not a mere despot, an Agamemnon of Olympos,
who prevails by sheer weight of kingship. On the contrary he
is a statesman, more like a divine Odysseus whose will cannot
be withstood. At some stage of the *Iliad's* development, poets
or chieftains were so impressed by these attributes that they
were bound to recognise the complete autocracy of the god.
After picturing him as ταμίης πολέμοιο[3], there was nothing left
but to believe him to be also the dispensator of destiny. After
exalting Fate as a bulwark against the gods they came to
cultivate a god as the bulwark against Fate. For Zeus inter-
feres not to impose but to avert death. This impersonal power
is now to be vested in a deity who can be conciliated[4]. On
one occasion different warriors sacrifice to different gods,
praying to escape death, as if there were no Fates[5].

This new stage of fatalism may have been the creation of
epic poetry or at any rate gave it a fresh impulse, for mortals
had now some one to blame[6]. The sentiments of revolt or of
resignation were alike inspired anew by the thought of a
personal dispensator; in fact the whole idea of the *Iliad* springs
from this interference of Zeus in the normal course of events.
At the same time a reaction seems to have set in against the
tendency to acquiesce in Olympic tyranny. Perhaps it was

[1] *Il.* i, 511–604; iv, 1–67; viii, 38–40; xv, 4–77; xxii, 182–5. Cf. A. B.
Cook, *Zeus, passim.*   [2] *De Bello Trojano,* i, 10.
[3] *Il.* xix, 224.   [4] *Ibid.* viii, 5–40; xx, 242–3.
[5] *Ibid.* ii, 400–1.   [6] *E.g. ibid.* xii, 162.

found that warriors could not scorn danger unless they trusted in an impersonal Fate; perhaps the feudal independence of the chieftains made them unsympathetic towards centralised authority even in Heaven. Or again some bard in a later age, when the early Ionic philosophers were turning men's thoughts towards monotheism, may have revived the old fatalistic cult, in a spirit of antiquarianism. In any case we find many passages in which the decrees of Fate stand as originally ordained, and Zeus is regarded only as their administrator[1]. Hektor is the most striking example of this evolution. While talking to Andromache he twice confesses to his belief in Fate[2], but later he is represented as carried away by his confidence in Zeus[3]. Yet never was a warrior more cruelly deceived by the destiny which dogged his steps so relentlessly[4].

v *The cult of the Olympic gods accompanied by freedom from superstition. The condescension of the immortal causes the ascension of the mortal. The gods free men from fear in battle.*

On the whole we may conclude that the worship of Zeus does not fully satisfy Homeric idealism. That deity inspired too much awe, and was too far-reaching in his designs. He suggested the post-Homeric helplessness of man, on which Hesiod dwells[5], and reminded them of feudal, as well as patriarchal authority. It is through the conception and present-ment of the lesser gods that the heroic spirit appeared in its full glory. We have already noticed how many traces of animism and of primitive magic are to be found in the poem, but in order to understand how much they achieved by their polytheism, we must first realise how many other superstitions had been overcome. Besides converting sympathetic magic into a saving confidence in Fate, they had ceased to believe in the connection between the weapon and the wound, in telepathy in battle, in taboos. They did not try to annul unfavourable omens by magic, nor did they imagine that Hephaistos needed

---

[1] *Il*. XVI, 431–61; XX, 300–5; XXI, 82–4, 516–17.
[2] *Ibid*. VI, 447–9, 487–9.   [3] *Ibid*. XII, 237 ff.; XVIII, 309.
[4] *Ibid*. XV, 59–77, 610–14.   [5] *Post*, chap. VI, §§ 2–4.

keeping alive by perpetual fires. They did not suppose fire to
be a god, as the Persians thought, or a wild animal as the
Egyptians believed[1]. The soul was no longer considered to be
a manikin, which could escape during sleep or sickness or
be captured by evil spirits. Herodotos records that when a
Skythian had killed his first man, he drank of his blood and
in all his subsequent career he kept the scalps of his enemies
strung on the bridle of his horse[2]; and we learn in *Fafnismol*[3]
that Regin cuts out the heart of Fafnir, the treasure-guarding
dragon, and drinks his blood, and that Sigurth cooks the
monster's heart. The Acheans felt no desire to acquire the
qualities of their friends or foes by such practices. Many
savage peoples preserve the bones of animals or even of men,
believing that the spirit is thereby enabled to return to these
remnants and the flesh to grow on them again, as in the
"Valley of Dry Bones," and it is likely that the Egyptians
embalmed their dead because the spirit would remain powerful
while the body existed. But the Homeric warriors do not seem
to have believed seriously in any immortality except the in-
destructibility of emotions and personality. They had no fear
of ghosts. Achilles welcomed the soul of Patroklos and Odysseus
sought out the spirit of his wife[4].

While releasing themselves from the burden of these superstitions they looked elsewhere for worthier gods to take their
place and often found them, as we have said, in the local or
agricultural spirits of the land they had conquered. Here was
an aboriginal goddess of the earth, worshipped at Argos.
Artemis was first of all associated with waters, wild vegetation
and with trees in Arcadia and was later believed to be the
patroness of wild beasts. Hermes was also worshipped in
Arcadia from the earliest times as one of the earth divinities
of vegetation. Athene was worshipped in so many parts of the
Greek world, that she must almost certainly be a primitive
Hellenic deity, and must have held sway, at least in Athens
and Ithaka, before the time of the Homeric poems. Sometimes
the Acheans went further afield. Aphrodite, originally a

---

[1] Herod. III, 16.   [2] *Ibid.* IV, 64.   [3] Stanzas 30–41.
[4] *Il.* XXIII, 93 ff.; *Od.* XI.

vegetation deity and perhaps the patroness of birth and generation, belonged to the east, and she is probably connected with
the sea because her cult was brought westward by seafaring
folk.

The conversion of these ancient spirits into gods and goddesses brought with it a remarkable revolution of thought. In
totemistic religions a tribe was supposed to draw nearer to its
deity by assuming the form or the skin of the beast which they
considered to be mysteriously related to themselves and to be
an embodiment of the god or goddess. The Homeric Age
reversed the process. They imagined that their deities approached them, by human means if not in human guise. For
this reason we hear so little about Ἅιδης. In the earliest times
this silence is natural, since a ritualistic name such as "The
Unseen" would have no fructifying, magic force. But by the
Heroic Age, his influence and dignity had grown immensely.
He was the counterpart of the great sky-god, a kind of Zeus
καταχθόνιος, as Dr Farnell styles him, and if human beings
neglected so formidable a deity it could only be because he was
unlike man and partook of shadows and darkness and depths.
Compare the obscurity of this subterranean spirit with the
honour and reputation which accrued to Apollo. Apollo was
not, apparently, a local deity. He was of Aryan origin and was
almost certainly brought to Hellas by the invaders. Like other
deities, he was worshipped as a god of vegetation, but as the
title Λύκειος was soon bestowed on him, and as from quite
early times he is thought of as plying a bow, he must have
become a patron deity of people who lived by the chase, and
though once worshipped as a wolf, he may for that reason
have become one of the first superhuman allies against these
enemies of man. At any rate as a hunter he was eminently a
deity who would *meet men half-way*, and so his worship spread
over all Greece and extended as far as Lykia. He is certainly
one of the most honoured and admired of the Homeric gods,
though an ally of the Trojans; and he is called Φοῖβος,"bright"
or "radiant," though not yet connected with the sun.

These ancient gods of vegetation and streams are of course
profoundly changed. To begin with they become dwellers of

mountains, for Olympos in the *Iliad* seems to have stood for any suitable hill, and so it is supposed that the Acheans came from the northern mountains. Then, again, these deities are grouped as members and dependents of a great household, suggestive of the beer hall or the *comitatus*. But the essential difference between gods and men—the condescension of the immortal causing the ascension of the mortal—is not so universally understood. At every crisis which calls for a hero's supreme courage or strength or judgment, a deity seems to take possession of his mind and for better or for worse to direct his actions. In those crowded moments man becomes, in a certain sense, a part of the deity. Though never expecting to become immortal, he enjoys for a brief space the attributes of immortality. It is not that Homer misunderstood the origin of thought[1]. In one place Here's flight from Ida to Olympos is compared to the rapidity with which memories rise of their own accord in the mind of a much-travelled man[2]. Besides, such phrases as θυμὸς ἐποτρύνει or θυμὸς ἐνὶ στήθεσσι κελεύει seem to have been familiar. But as soon as a warrior is called upon to suppress some cowardly or vicious impulse, or to steel his resolution for some heroic effort, this raising and ennobling of his spirit was represented as an alliance with one of the immortals.

In some instances the poet may have been influenced by the tendency among primitive peoples to personify the abstract. This explanation is particularly acceptable when discussing Athene. According to the oldest legends, she was the goddess of war, averse to love, while other stories, probably as ancient, represent her as the daughter of Μῆτις, and yet others record that her birth was assisted by Prometheus and by Hephaistos. Thus all available evidence points to the belief that she was one of the earliest deities, who presided over the arts of life, instead of the activities of nature, and we should expect her, even in those early times, to stand out as the patroness of self-restraint, reason, cunning and the warlike but well-directed aggressiveness which in those days accompanied the growth of civic communities. On the other hand we should expect to

---

[1] Cf. Plut. in *Vit. Coriol.* 32.   [2] *Il.* xv, 80–2.

meet at least a suggestion of the kind of symbolism which is so frequent in more sophisticated literature and is supposed to characterise primitive religions. We are prepared to find that Γῆ and Νέμεσις remain abstract in Homer though personified in the *Theognis*[1] or that Δεῖμος, Φόβος and Ἔρις help Ares to marshal the Trojans[2] and when the other gods leave the battle at Zeus's command, only Ἔρις remains[3]. Athene and Ares may also be symbols. Their appearance may also be influenced by the old belief that the victorious nation is the one with the strongest and most zealous gods[4]. Even the invincible Achilles recognised that Hektor's god might well ensure the Trojan's escape unless his own proved the stronger[5].

Yet we must admit that the epic genius made far better use of their religion. One of the most suggestive lines in the *Iliad* is the utterance

$$συμφερτὴ \ δ' \ ἀρετὴ \ πέλει \ ἀνδρῶν \ καὶ \ μάλα \ λυγρῶν^6.$$

The words are spoken to Idomeneus, who had withdrawn to the huts to help a wounded comrade and is now preparing to return to the battle. The day has definitely turned against the Acheans; one warrior after another is falling or retiring wounded; and the chieftain is now preparing to go into danger of his own accord after a respite. Of all the trials imposed by warfare, this is the hardest and requires the greatest effort from a soldier, but the full significance of the utterance arises from the fact that the help which he needs comes from a god. It is Poseidon, disguised as Thoas, who offers the encouragement of his company and friendship. Undoubtedly the chief moral problem before the Homeric Age was the mastery of fear. We have already noticed what progress men had made in overcoming the terrors of their primitive religion. Now in these poems they were learning how to get the better of the more human and earthly agonies of battle and adventure. In describing dread or distress, Homer is more pathetic and

[1] l. 223.   [2] *Il.* IV, 439–45.
[3] *Ibid.* XI, 73–7.
[4] *Ibid.* III, 439; IV, 44–67 and 6–11; VIII, 30–7; XIII, 15–31; XV, 12–235.
[5] *Ibid.* XX, 449–54.   [6] *Ibid.* XIII, 237.

forceful than any other poet, even than Shakespeare. Such lines as

"Έκτορα δειδιότες κρατερὸν μνήστωρα φόβοιο[1]

or

ἡμεῖς δὲ κλαίοντες ἀνεσχέθομεν Διὶ χεῖρας
σχέτλια ἔργ᾽ ὁρόωντες· ἀμηχανίη δ᾽ ἔχε θυμόν[2]

can have been created only in an age which felt and appreciated fear to the core. But in Homer we do not only learn how deeply men suffered from this emotion, we also see one of the most spirited attempts at overcoming it. We see a race who did not so much make fear a cause of shame or reproach as one which was capable of imagining that the spirits of earth, sky and water could become their allies and protectors and above all lend them that spiritual companionship which is the most enduring incentive to heroism.

VI. *The Age of Homer was largely aniconic, so their religion was not wholly anthropomorphic nor yet wholly animistic. They seem to have evolved a kind of spiritualism, which gave the widest and highest scope to their idealism.*

To understand the relationship between Homeric gods and men, it must be remembered that the age was partly if not wholly aniconic. Professor Chadwick has raised doubts. "A number of statuettes, apparently representing deities, have come to light in deposits belonging both to the Mycenean and Geometrical periods, while primitive female figures, often in a sitting position, are quite common. The finding of a large image would now scarcely call forth much surprise."[3] All depends on the purport or symbolism of that same hypothetical statue. Except for the mysterious image of Athene[4], worshipped so fruitlessly in Troy, and the palladium, we learn nothing of the external presentiment of their gods. We are told in the *Iliou Persis* that Aias in dragging Kassandra tore away with her the image of Athene, and was nearly stoned for it by the Greeks. But the original must surely be as late as Arktinos

---

[1] *Il.* XII, 39.
[2] *Od.* IX, 294.
[3] *The Heroic Age*, chap. x, p. 205.
[4] *Il.* VI, 301–10.

of Miletos[1], and the word is ξόανον. In another passage, Penelope is compared to Artemis or to Aphrodite[2], and, of course, the celebrated allusion to Zeus's eyebrows may, as Pheidias thought, be indications of his powerful gaze[3]. But for the most part, the Homeric gods were not known to their worshippers by the beauty or majesty of their outward form. In fact, as in the folklore of other countries, it was not permitted to a mortal to behold a deity as he really is. The *Iliad* does not suggest that the Olympians were different in form from human beings, yet what student of Homer can form a definite picture, except of Zeus or Hephaistos, and of these two the fire-god's limp may be merely a reminiscence of the halting, bickering character of a flame, while Zeus's eyebrows and locks may mean anything? When Athene[4] arms for battle, the poet is obviously thinking not so much of the personality of the goddess, as of the dread which these preparations should inspire, and the passage in which Agamemnon's[5] face and eyes are compared to Zeus, his breast to Poseidon, and his waist to Ares, is obviously a later addition. The poets decline every opportunity of describing their deities as they really were. At most the menace of their presence might be appreciated by dazzling light, such as the fire which blazed over the crest of Diomed, brilliant as the autumn star[6], or the flame which shot out of a cloud over the head of Achilles, like a beacon fire in a beleaguered city[7], even as Telemachos suspected the presence of a god because the walls and roof beams seemed to glow with light[8]. Sometimes the deity, when mingling with men, is merely alluded to as a vulture, a sea eagle, a swallow or a hawk. Once Apollo is described as visiting the Achean nost like night[9], and Ares as rising from the battlefield like a mist[10]. On neither occasion did the human beings know by their own senses that a god was present.

If a god wished to come into contact with some chosen

---

[1] *Fl.* 776 B.C. (?)   [2] *Od.* XVII, 37.
[3] Macr. *Saturn*, v, xiii, 23; Farnell, *Religious Cults of the Greek States*, vol. I, chap. VI.
[4] *Il.* v, 733–52.   [5] *Ibid.* II, 477.   [6] *Ibid.* v, 4–8.
[7] *Ibid.* XVIII, 205–14.   [8] *Od.* XIX, 36–40.   [9] *Il.* I, 47.
[10] *Ibid.* v, 864–7.

mortal, he generally assumed the guise of some human being, often that of one of the lesser warriors and sometimes that of a stranger. Apparently the disguise was selected without any reference to the spirit's attributes; Athene appears only twice as a beautiful woman[1]; and when thus transformed their god-head was sometimes completely unrecognisable. Diomed at the height of his ἀριστεία is confronted by Glaukos, he pauses and asks for his antagonist's name. That was the only safe way of avoiding a god in human form[2]. On one occasion Athene, who came to restore Odysseus to his true shape, remains invisible to Telemachos, but is discovered by the dogs[3]. On another occasion Poseidon, the deity famous for his rapid journeys, was just detected, under the guise of Kalchas, by his feet and knees[4]. Paris came nearest to seeing a deity in its true form when he recognised Aphrodite by her neck, breast and eyes[5].

One is tempted at first to suppose that the Acheans and Trojans were still under the influence of some kind of primitive animism, and for that reason had never developed a definitely anthropomorphic idea of their deities. Yet the winds do not appear to have been worshipped, though many similes show how deeply their power and picturesqueness had impressed the Homeric world. There was no cult of the sun, for Apollo was still only a god of warfare and archery and in some way the minister of Zeus and of Fate. If any traces of animism lingered, they are to be found in the cult of the old rivers. But though sacrifices were made according to the ancient animistic fashion in the stream of the river and not on the bank[6], and though Skamandros[7] fights Achilles with the volume of his waters and not as an armed warrior, yet that river harangues like a human being, and all of them are summoned to Zeus's council[8], no less than the Olympians. The poets had forgotten more of animistic worship than they had learnt of anthropomorphism.

Yet Homeric religion was not rudimentary. But it had only

---

[1] *Od.* xvi, 15–18; xx, 31. [2] *Il.* vi, 123. [3] *Od.* xvi.
[4] *Il.* xiii, 13. [5] *Ibid.* iii, 396. [6] *Ibid.* xxi, 130.
[7] *Ibid.* xxi, 211 ff. [8] *Ibid.* xx, 1–12.

just begun to develop along the lines familiar to us. Prof. Lévy-
Bruhl has pointed out that savages believe the ordinary business
of life, such as hunting and fishing, to be more dependent on
mystic and invisible powers, than upon physical processes[1].
The Acheans seem to have followed out this idea and to have
evolved a worship apparently anthropomorphic, but really
touched with a sublime spiritualism. It is to be noticed that
when a deity came close to a human being, though invisible
or indistinguishable to others, he was immediately made known
to the mortal to whom he specially addressed himself. Thanks
to the lack of plastic or pictorial forms, the Achean mind came
into direct immediate contact with the god. Art did not stand
between them as a barrier. When Apollo succoured Hektor,
prostrate because of the boulder with which Aias felled him, the
god entered straight into his thoughts without using any inter-
mediary at all[2]. This idea of spiritual contact, of exchanging
words and emotions, and sometimes of transferring divine
energy, is apparently peculiar to the Greek Heroic Age. In
many passages there are traces of earlier and cruder beliefs;
but now and then the poet seems to have had insight into a
complete communion without the mechanism of magic or even
of visual recognition. This intercourse led to a blending of the
worshippers with the worshipped, till the human bid fair to
equal the divine. Thus a stage was reached of immense importance in the progress of man. The gods are recognised to be
nobler and more powerful as the allies than as the tyrants and
persecutors of man. The discovery is marked by an ancient
story recorded by Apollodoros[3]. When the new struggling
dynasty on Olympos was confronted by the old evil deities,
the earth-born monsters, the younger gods received the oracle
ὑπὸ θεῶν μὲν μηδένα τῶν Γιγάντων ἀπολέσθαι δύνασθαι,
συμμαχοῦντος δὲ θνητοῦ τινος τελευτήσειν. The superiority
of the new order was marked by an alliance with men. Yet
the Homeric gods do not become immensely exaggerated types
of human prowess with the added virtue of immortality. They
are not honoured for their ancient and impossible feats of

---

[1] *Primitive Mentality*, authorised transl. by L. A. Clark, 1923.
[2] *Il.* xv, 239.   [3] *Bibl.* I, vi, I.

strength, cunning and endurance, as were some of the deities of Norse mythology. So far, again, they are not anthropomorphic. But each divinity is honoured so far as he ministers to human prowess and raises it to his own level.

VII. *The influence of the gods on the warriors is seen in their prayers, their remonstrances, their moments of disappointment or despondency, and in times of danger.*

What passed between daemons and mortals, during their temporary alliances? We have already seen that the human being was thereby strengthened to overcome fear. Even when shut up in the Kyklops's cave, where he watched two of his comrades devoured every day, Odysseus retained the spirit to plot revenge, because he felt that Athene might yet give him victory[1]. We have now to see that at every crisis of his career, a warrior had learnt to rely on some deity. It is part of the fascination of Homer, that we cannot help brooding over this remarkable phase of human development. Men believed that the divine purposes were almost identical with their own; that gods and goddesses mingled with humans either as allies or adversaries, but employed mortal arms and manhood to accomplish immortal ends. Assuredly such imaginings must have enabled actual warriors to face the hazards of war with more steadiness and confidence and must have led them to feel that human excellence, thus elevated and supported, was hardly distinct from godhead. So we conjecture, for we have no direct evidence. What we possess are the highly poetic and artistic uses which Homer employs to create the most wonderful picture in literature of the warrior's soul.

Of such quality are the prayers which Homer gives to his warriors. In these supplications he shows the highest thoughts of which a hero was capable; witness the orisons offered by Odysseus and Diomed[2], when they set out by night, like two lions, to raid the Trojan camp and to loot the horses of Rhesos. Friendship and paternal love moved others to the purest generosity of thought, as when Hektor prayed that his son might grow up to eclipse his father's fame[3], or the arrogant,

---

[1] *Od.* IX, 316–17. [2] *Il.* X, 277–95. [3] *Ibid.* VI, 476–81.

self-centred Achilles yet prayed that Zeus might grant honour to Patroklos instead of himself, and bring back his friend safe to him after the victory[1]. In the heat and stress of battle the prayers of the warriors are sometimes intensely dramatic. Take, for instance, the outburst of Aias when fighting desperately to rescue the corpse of Patroklos. He realises that his own side are losing courage and strength and he cannot find a messenger to send for help because the struggle is shrouded in a thick mist. His thoughts have none of the romanticism of a pseudo-epic. As would befall in real life, he feels only too keenly the helplessness that seems to have fallen on himself and his comrades, and he gives expression to the horror, inborn in all men, of perishing in the darkness. But where a less heroic warrior would surrender to despair, he is saved because he can address a god and give vent to his bitterness in a prayer to be allowed at least to die in the daylight[2]. An example of yet intenser feeling will be found in the struggle between Achilles and Skamandros. The Trojan forces found their retreat barred by the river and had to jump into the stream. Achilles plunged in after them, impatient of any obstacle between himself and the slaughter of his enemies. Then the old river god, in the scene we have already discussed, beat against the intruder with huge waves, loosened the gravel under his feet, and Achilles, at the height of his triumph, found himself faced with an ignoble death, "for gods are stronger than men."[3] His prayer to the gods is a masterpiece of realism and of self-revelation. The thought of drowning fills him with loathing, but he feels no fear, much less despair. His indomitable spirit is filled with the keenest disappointment and this bitterness finds outlet in reproaching his mother, the goddess Thetis, who had promised him a glorious death under the walls of Troy[4].

So the attitude of the Homeric warrior is different from that of the post-epic worshipper. Why is it that the staunchest admirer of Milton yet feels that Adam is devoid of all epic grandeur? It is not that "our grand father" achieves no victories on the battlefield. We shall see later that it is possible

[1] *Il.* XVI, 233–48.

[2] *Ibid.* XVII, 629–47.

[3] Θεοὶ δέ τε φέρτεροι ἀνδρῶν. *Ibid.* XXI, 264.

[4] *Ibid.* XXI, 200–83.

to retain the very essence of epic idealism, without even suggesting the prowess of the warrior. But Adam, like the great Miltonic archangels, suffers from one fundamental defect; his virtues are given to him. He depends on a supernatural power for all that is most admirable in his nature. But it will be noticed that the Homeric warrior looks to his god only for encouragement and help[1]. His virtues are his own, independent of all Olympos. The greatest are so confident of their moral sufficiency, that they even turn upon the god in resentment as often as the immortal fails them. These gestures of defiance had undoubtedly come down to Homeric civilisation from a primitive age. It is quite a usual practice among warlike savages to be revenged on their gods. Herodotos tells us that the Thrakians used to shoot arrows at the thunder and lightning by way of insult[2]. Such a tradition easily becomes a trap for the boastfulness and blasphemy of later and more civilised generations, especially after many poets have successively handled the theme. Thus when Biarke realises that his overlord is dead and his castle is burnt, he not only curses Othin, he actually asserts that he will slay him in mortal combat[3]. When Charlemagne feared that God would withhold his support, he threatened to overthrow his altars and to abolish his churches[4]. The Acheans are not betrayed into such atheistic folly. In each case the human being undoubtedly believed that a deity had played the chief part in his discomfiture; he acknowledges a superior power with whom he knows that he cannot cope. But at the same time he is too conscious of his innate worth to submit. His superb impatience at opposition actually finds expression in reviling the gods in whom he believes and without whom he cannot triumph[5].

In these instances the man first appeals to the god, but just as often the god comes first to the man. In such cases, the poet employs the situation to develop an even nobler aspect of the

---

[1] *E.g. Il.* III, 380–2; XII, 290–301; XVI, 715–30; XVII, 322–41 (perhaps the best example in the *Il.*), 544–96.

[2] IV, 94.

[3] Saxo Grammaticus; see Olrik's brilliant reconstruction of the duologue; see also *post*, vol. II, chap. II, § 6.

[4] *Ferabr.* 1211, 1428.

[5] See esp. the expression in *Il.* III, 365–8, 399–420; XXII, 15–20.

Homeric warrior. It is noticeable that in Homer men rarely
cultivate between themselves that expansiveness which makes
up the modern idea of friendship. The intimacy between
Achilles and Patroklos is impaired by the latter's dependence,
while Odysseus and Eumaios enjoy only the fellowship of
destitution. But the heroes open their hearts to their gods.
Bacon has said "that whosoever hath his mind fraught with
many thoughts, his wits and understanding do clarify and
break up in the communicating and discoursing with another.
...Finally he waxeth wiser than himself."[1] So it is in Homer.
The poet uses the dialogue between mortals and immortals
almost like a catechism to reveal in the privacy and sug-
gestiveness of conversation the more complex and intimate
thoughts of a warrior. Two of the most significant examples
of such intercourse will be found in the scenes between Thetis
and Achilles; one after his humiliation by Agamemnon and
the other when the death of Patroklos had been added to these
grievances against Fate[2]. On both occasions the goddess
hastens to his side, though still invisible, and though she well
knows the cause of his sorrow, she asks him to tell her his
troubles. Thus Achilles has the opportunity of revealing the
very recesses of his mind and we learn why the warrior is so
passionately desirous of immediate fame and why this almost
morbid yearning obscures the natural generosity of his character.
The poet goes yet further. Thetis, thanks to this interchange
of confidences, betrays an almost fierce concentration of love,
which is unmatched in the whole range of Homeric poetry.
Penelope is hardly capable of more than a profound attachment
to her home and to the memory of her famous husband, and
Andromache is lost in her distress for her son's future. It is
probably not accident that the full intensity of maternal egoism,
the readiness to sacrifice the whole world for a son, finds full
expression in the character of a goddess[3]. Another interesting
revelation of character will be found in the episode in which
Athene accompanies Here to the scene of battle and finds
Diomed "cooling the wound which Pandaros had dealt him

[1] "Of Friendship."   [2] *Il.* I, 357 ff.; xviii, 70 ff.
[3] *Ibid.* I, 348–427; xviii, 35–144.

with an arrow." Her questionings and upbraidings, together
with his answers, give vivid shape to the warrior's eagerness
to equal or surpass his father's reputation, and the weariness
or dread of battle which prompts the suspicion that a god is
fighting for the enemy[1]. These hesitations and moments of
discouragement are intensely human and the greatness of a
warrior was then, as now, largely shown in the ability to regain
self-confidence and enthusiasm. So human beings, however
great, are rarely left to overcome their own weakness unaided
by divine power. It is the god who supplies the encouraging
thoughts which the hero needs. Perhaps the best example will
be found in the *Odyssey*. Odysseus lies awake tormenting his
brain over his plans and realising only too clearly the almost
insuperable difficulties which beset his path. Athene appears
to him and asks the cause of his sleeplessness. Shortly and con-
cisely he explains how overwhelming the odds are which he
must encounter. In reply, she reminds him that a goddess can
bring more comforting and effective help than the stoutest
comrade in whom a brave man trusts, and counsels him to seek
tranquillity in sleep[2]. The man supplies his own courage and
energy, and regains his own calm, but his mood has all the
grandeur and inspiration of being a gift from the gods.

The warriors who imagined that their noblest thoughts were
the words of deities, could hardly trust to their own unaided
might in the actual business of fighting. Here again it will be
seen that the interposition of the gods was in most cases hardly
more than an unconscious idealisation of man's own efforts.
Athene did not exterminate the suitors as Jehovah exterminated
the hosts of Sennacherib. She merely stood by her hero's side
and by guiding his missiles and by rendering vain those of his
enemies she helped him, step by step, after many hazards and
efforts, to win the day[3]. Such beliefs did not only elevate their
hopes of victory; they lessened the disgrace of defeat. It has
already been noticed that the Acheans and Trojans were surprisingly ready to acknowledge a fault, though by no means
the kind of men who cultivated humility, and we have seen

---

[1] *Il.* v, 792–834.   [2] *Od.* xx, 45–53.
[3] *Ibid.* xxii, 224–56.

that this disposition was partly due to self-confidence[1]. But this freedom from self-reproach was not reasoned; it took the form of a religious belief. Nearly all questions of merit or demerit related to the battlefield and there, it was held, no warrior had the monopoly of divine aid. Zeus, who so zealously aided and heartened the Trojans and at one time stirred up a great dust storm "which made weak the mind of the Acheans and gave fame to the Trojans and to Hektor,"[2] yet another time filled Hektor with a "coward's spirit."[3] When later he was taunted with cowardice, that hard-bitten and well-tried hero declared as his philosophy of warfare that however stout of heart a man might be Zeus was even stouter and could take away courage as easily as he could give it[4]. Menelaos felt that none of the Danaans could reproach him if he abandoned the corpse of Patroklos to Hektor, ἐπεὶ ἐκ θεόφιν πολεμίζει[5]. In fact the gods were supposed sometimes to counsel cowardice. Hektor was warned by Iris to avoid conflict with Agamemnon[6] and Apollo urged Aeneas to keep out of the way of Achilles[7].

VIII. *Above all, the gods reconciled the warriors to the humiliation of death. The killing of Hektor.*

To the Homeric warrior, the greatest terror of battle was not dishonour or even captivity, but death, and we have seen that this abhorrence arose not so much from dread of the next world, as from reluctance to leave this one. No amount of imagination could mitigate the bitterness of severance, but we have seen how its uncertainty was sometimes lessened by the belief in fate. Death could not be dealt at random by either gods or men[8]. It was sacred and part of the higher scheme of things. We have now to see how far the humiliation of mortal defeat could be softened by a belief in the gods. When Onesilos heard of Artybios's wonderful horse, trained to rear and to fight a hoplite, his shield-bearer remarked that a king or a commander should engage only with his like because ὑπὸ ἀξιοχρέου καὶ ἀποθανεῖν ἡμίσεα συμφορή[9]. It halves the

---

[1] *Ante*, II, § 5. [2] *Il.* XII, 252–5. [3] ἀνάλκιδα θυμόν. *Ibid.* XVI, 656.
[4] *Ibid.* XVII, 175–8. [5] *Ibid.* XVII, 101. [6] *Ibid.* XI, 186–94.
[7] *Ibid.* XX, 375–8. [8] *Ante*, § 2. [9] Herod. V, 111.

calamity to perish by the hands of a worthy foe. The poets
have given to this grandiose idea a peculiar touch of epic
heroism. They do not allow some of their greatest heroes to
meet their doom, except at the hand of an ominous and awe-
inspiring deity. A mortal is not allowed to rob them of this
life, even if the golden scales have turned against them. It is
surprising that Sarpedon, though the undoubted son of Zeus,
and marked down by Fate against the Olympian ruler's will,
should be suffered to perish by the hands of a mere mortal[1]
and this inconsistency supplies one of the many reasons for
thinking that the *Iliad* is not the work of one brain. But his
slayer, Patroklos, is later confronted by the terrible figure of
Apollo wrapt in mist and the deity smites him on the back
with his magic hand and thus enfeebled and bewitched, he
is at last spitted on Hektor's spear[2]. In the case of Achilles, the
horse Xanthos makes clear that his real conquerors are θεός
τε μέγας καὶ Μοῖρα κραταιή[3]. But, of course, the best example
of all is the death of Hektor. His overthrow is in some respects
the consummation of the poem, and the poets lead us slowly
and inevitably to the close, through a series of reversals and
surprises, till the hero is finally betrayed by Athene and falls
without striking an effective blow. "Why should Athene," asks
Dr Leaf, "be invoked to turn against Hektor at the last, and
worst of all to delude him by treachery at the moment when
all help was gone? The aesthetic answer to these questions is
not easy to find—at least I have never been able to satisfy
myself." Nor perhaps could Dares. According to his sources
Hektor returns to the battle after an enforced absence, draws
on himself the onslaught of Achilles, by the havoc which he
works on the Acheans, and perishes only after a heroic fight[4].
Almost any modern would prefer this version, yet to an Achean,
both the rise and the fall of Hektor probably seemed to be
a masterpiece. It must be remembered that Hektor is not one
of the greatest. He is not διογενής except through his most
distant ancestors. Here makes it quite clear that he has no
right to more than an ordinary warrior's due[5]. He has already

---

[1] *Il.* xvi, 431 ff. [2] *Ibid.* xvi, 788–854; cf. xix, 413–14.
[3] *Ibid.* xix, 410. [4] *De Excidio*, xxiv. [5] *Il.* xxiv, 58.

been granted far more than his proper share of success. The Trojan who could slay Patroklos, drive Aias to despair, and even threaten Achilles, had indeed good reason to consider himself fortunate. The Father of gods and men had used Hektor as the poor instrument of his sovereign will, and could even find it in his heart to pity the mortal who forgot his own subordination[1]. Yet the mortal had no reason to complain. Although life was sweet to the epic warrior, in all probability there still lingered the tradition that death on the battlefield was an obligation. The northern races held to this requirement; most of the warriors who left Troy alive had little reason to consider themselves lucky; Ovid (at any rate a respectable antiquarian) describes the chief grief of Meleager to be his ignoble death[2]. Zeus had granted Hektor the means of winning honour beyond his wildest dreams—partly out of gratitude for his piety[3]—so now his downfall is saved from dishonour. He is slain by the greatest hero of the war and even then only because Apollo withdraws his aid and Athene directs the fatal blow. Dictys preserves some traces of the same spirit when he represents Pyrrhos as glad that his father was slain *non in certamine, neque in luce belli* so no one could say that he was fairly vanquished[4].

IX. *The interpretation of omens in the Homeric world. The Acheans assert the dignity and independence of human nature without sacrificing the supremacy of the gods. The superstition of the "dying man's curse" transformed.*

It will readily be appreciated how many of the Homeric heroes would have agreed with the utterance of Peisistratos, πάντες δὲ θεῶν χατέουσ' ἄνθρωποι[5]. Pride of life, possessions, power and enjoyment were theirs as human beings, but every special triumph of skill or fortitude was associated with a deity. Even in material things no true excellence was unmixed with divine influence, but the true province of the gods was the mind and the spirit of men. They dealt with the horror of omens in much the same way. Hektor does indeed betray an

---

[1] *Il.* XVII, 198–208.   [2] *Metam.* VIII, 518.
[3] *Il.* XXII, 169–72.   [4] *De Bello Trojano*, IV 15.   [5] *Od.* III, 48.

attitude very like modern scepticism and so does Eurymachos[1]. But the Trojan was carried away by his short-lived success and his over-confidence in Zeus, and the other was one of the suitors, already doomed for his arrogance and blindness. For the most part the Acheans, or at any rate their poets, discovered in this superstition another resource against the possible wilfulness and double-dealing of the immortals. There are two ways of obtaining knowledge of the future, described in the *Phaidros*[2]. In one form a god enters into a man and through the mortal's ecstatic utterance proclaims his divine will; in the other form certain indications are given and the human being, whose intelligence is sufficiently keen, may discover the hidden meaning behind the symbol. The first kind of augury—the μαντικὴ ἔνθεος—was hardly practised in Homer. There are perhaps signs of it in the *Odyssey* when some divine manifestation is followed by the utterances of a simple and unwitting mortal, such as thunder in a clear sky and the prayer of the old woman at the mill in Odysseus's house[3], or the belief that minstrels really were possessed by a god[4]. The second form—ζήτησις τοῦ μέλλοντος or *divinatio*—is found in two guises. Sometimes it is the cry of an eagle, hawk, heron or raven which seems to be a promise of help from a god. We are told that Melampos learnt to understand the voices of birds because serpents cleansed his ears while he slept[5] and Helenos and Kassandra, according to a scholiast[6], learnt soothsaying in the same way. But this belief is a later development of the Homeric idea. In the *Iliad* men deduced an omen merely from the sound or the quarter whence it came. It has been well argued[7] that such conjectures are not augury but a relic of totemism. The bird or animal refers to the deity; it is, in fact, the god himself who speaks. The true and characteristic augury of the *Iliad* was either the direct inquiry of heaven's will by noting the order in which pebbles leapt out of a shaken vessel, or another of those intelligent and courageous adaptations of sympathetic magic, which must now be discussed.

[1] *Il.* xii, 237–42; *Od.* ii, 178 ff.   [2] p. 244.   [3] *Od.* xx, 102–19.
[4] *Od.* viii, 44; xvii, 518–20.   [5] Apoll. *Bibl.* i, ix, 11.
On *Il.* vii, 44.   [7] J. A. K. Thomson, *Studies in the Odyssey*.

We have already alluded to the prehistoric belief that like produces like; that because something is happening, it probably causes or foretells the happening of something else analogous. Consequently every important design of the gods was prefigured in some similar though less portentous occurrence in the world around us, and there grew up in many different countries and ages the science of tracing connections between earthly events and heavenly purposes. The Homeric warriors cultivated these arts with more than ordinary zest, because they found thereby an outlet for their imaginative sympathies, as well as an insight into the future. The true Homeric omen is an inverted simile. It is a miniature drama in the animal world; some tragedy between an eagle or snake and its victim; he who had an eye for the allegories of natural life could detect the designs of the Olympians figured in this vision of victory and defeat[1]. So even in these poems of warfare and adventure, we have glimpses of yet another human ideal: a man such as Polydamas[2], or Halitherses[3], or Kalchas[4], who became a leader of men thanks to their insight and powers of imaginative interpretation. Or the greatest of all, Teiresias, who was permitted to retain his mental powers after death, when all other spirits were shadows[5]. Sometimes without the aid of an interpreter, the warriors themselves are represented as quick-witted enough to recognise the symbolism of the omens and to make the right application, either so as to gather fresh courage, or to foresee and guard against some unfavourable turn of destiny[6]. These faculties were to become so valuable that men ended by prizing them at least as highly as warlike qualities, and we shall then be able to trace the rise of the intellectual hero[7]. But in the *Iliad*, the warrior is still supreme, and μαντοσύνη subserves his desire not to disprove magic, but to understand and to control it[8]. Compare the cult of oracles in Herodotos[9]. Men have perhaps an even more consuming desire to know the future, but they

---

[1] Chief examples: *Il.* II, 299–330; Apoll. *Epit.* III, 15.

[2] *Il.* XII, 210–19.   [3] *Od.* II, 157.   [4] *Il.* I, 70–2.

[5] *Od.* X, 494. See J. A. K. Thomson, *Studies in the Odyssey*.

[6] *Il.* VIII, 245–50; X, 274–7; XXIV, 314–21; *Od.* XV, 160–78, 525–34; XXI, 413–15.

[7] *Post*, chap. VI, §§ 4–7.   [8] *Il.* XII, 20–207; *Od.* II, 146–76.

[9] *Post*, chap. VI, § 7.

are no longer so sure of themselves. They find that the responses of the gods have become hopelessly ambiguous and that their own passions or prejudices blind them to the right interpretation of the riddle. But in Homer the wisdom of the gods is not a quality to contrast with the folly of men. Even when Zeus did not vouchsafe some special sign of his intentions, his "crooked counsels" could be read by the intelligence and intuition of human beings.

Another ancient menace which the Acheans outreasoned and transfigured was that of the dying man's curse. There was a primitive belief that an enemy's last words, issuing from his lips with his spirit, became somehow a part of his ghost, a kind of Ἐρινύς, and stirred up other malignant spirits, and the greater the soul of the dying man, the more formidable his curse. Traces of this superstition are found in the reluctance of Siegfried to tell Fafnir his real name, lest the wounded dragon, when at the point of death, should know whom to curse[1], and Odysseus, in the original story, probably had a similar reason for misleading Polyphemos[2]. But by the time the *Iliad* reached its present form, this superstition has been completely transformed. An heroic age would be almost impossible if one's enemies had such deadly power, so this malignant faculty was changed into second sight. Confidence in Fate again saved the hero from magic. The dying warrior was enabled to foresee, though not to precipitate, the doom of his slayer, and perhaps two of the most impressive touches in the *Iliad* occur when first Patroklos and then Hektor reveal with their last breath how far each is permitted to θεῶν μήνιμα γενέσθαι, to draw on his vanquisher the wrath of the gods[3].

x. *The story of Hektor's corpse illustrates the progressive stages of Homeric civilisation. The characteristics of the Homeric warrior summed up.*

In conclusion, we may explain Homeric religion as a cult of spiritual conquest; the means of winning a larger and nobler idea of one's own powers. The picture of the Kyklops dwelling

[1] *Fafnismol*, 1. [2] *Od.* ix, 364–7.
[3] For Patroklos, xvi, 851–4. For Hektor, xxii, 358–62.

in uncouth isolation, ignorant even of the arts of cooking, lighting a fire, as did Grendel's dam, to illuminate the shadows of his cave, and independent of Zeus and the θεοὶ μάκαρες, by itself suggests that the gods of Olympos were the product of a newer and higher civilisation. In fact, it will be shown in subsequent chapters that epics cannot arise except in some such atmosphere of progress and spiritual freedom. In the *Iliad* and *Odyssey* this tendency is so powerful and consistent, that just as we catch glimpses of a quite primitive and terror-stricken age, so we also have a foretaste of a later and more humanistic epoch than any yet described, a time when deities are worshipped for their freedom from all taint of humanity. Some such indication is found in Phoinix's famous tirade on the clemency of the gods and the mediation of the Λιταί[1] or in Odysseus's allusion to Ζεὺς ξείνιος when trapped in the Kyklops's cave[2]. But the profoundest and most striking example is the story of Hektor's corpse.

This celebrated episode has often[3] been discussed, but it is too significant to be omitted for that reason, since in no other instance can we trace so clearly the progress of Homeric civilisation. We are told that in Travancore[4], after a murderer is hanged, his heels are cut off so that, in the words of the scholiast on Sophokles[5], ἀσθενὴς γένοιτο πρὸς τὸ ἀντιτίσασθαι τὸν φονέα. In the original story, Achilles must have been prompted by some such motive, and so, presumably, was Menelaos when he outraged the corpse of Alexandros, whom Philoktetes had slain[6]. Similar precautions were taken in post-Homeric times. When Kambyses entered Saïs, he dragged out the corpse of Amasis from its coffin, and burnt it after inflicting unspeakable outrages[7]. Xerxes beheaded and crucified the corpse of Leonidas[8]. Apparently both Asiatics had good reasons. The corpse of Amasis was embalmed, and the dead man's

---

Il. ix, 496 ff.   [2] *Od.* ix, 270 ff.
[3] See esp. G. Murray, *Rise of the Greek Epic*, chap. v. The points raised in the present work are not fully discussed in the *Rise*.
A. Oldfield, "The Aborigines of Australia." *Transactions of the Ethnological Soc. of London*, iii (1865), p. 287.
[5] *Elektra*, 445.   [6] *The Little Iliad.*
[7] Herod. iii, 16.   [8] *Ibid.* viii, 238.

spirit might well be strong to pursue, while the flesh remained intact. Xerxes probably expected that the Spartans preserved their dead. But by the time that the *Iliad* assumed its present form the Acheans or their poets had freed themselves from the fear of the dead. Their corpses were burnt, and as we shall see later[1], this ritual destroyed all effectual access to the world of the living. In so enlightened an atmosphere, the actions of Achilles would appear unreasoningly inhuman, and consequently Homer has given them another aspect, a little more worthy the dignity of an epic hero. Hektor's ankles are mutilated to serve the triumph which Achilles celebrates immediately after his victory[2]. This episode probably marks the second stage of the story; the poet still dwells on the remorselessness of Achilles, as if it were an honour to be vindictive[3], and up to the last, Here, Athene, and Poseidon are as implacable as he[4]. Another and newer phase of civilisation is introduced when Apollo upbraids the gods for their cruelty and compares Achilles to a lion who is too tyrannical and impetuous to refrain from slaying sheep and pronounces the famous

$$\tau\lambda\eta\tau\grave{o}\nu \ \gamma\grave{a}\rho \ \mathrm{Mo\hat{\iota}\rho\alpha\iota} \ \theta\upsilon\mu\grave{o}\nu \ \theta\acute{\epsilon}\sigma\alpha\nu \ \grave{a}\nu\theta\rho\acute{\omega}\pi\omicron\iota\sigma\iota\nu^5.$$

Zeus more than the others is wroth at the hero's barbarity[6], and feels a purely human pity for old Priam as he sets forth to beg his son's body[7]. Finally Achilles himself, who throughout the poem has been glorified as the incarnation of sternness and pride, now recognises what the will of Zeus really is and only fears that his headstrong passions may outrun his will[8]. This opposition between two stages of civilisation is brilliantly illustrated by a story[9] outside Homer. In the battle against Thebes, Tydeus slew Melanippos, after first receiving a wound from his victim. Athene begged a healing charm ($\phi\acute{a}\rho\mu\alpha\kappa\omicron\nu$) from Zeus and then in Homeric fashion flew to the succour of her favourite. But Amphiaraos, to satisfy his revenge, cut

---

[1] *Post*, chap. VII, §§ 2, 3.
[2] *Il.* XXII, 376–84, 396–404.
[3] *E.g.* XXIII, 17–34.
[4] *Il.* XXIV, 25 ff.
[5] *Ibid.* 49.
[6] *Ibid.* 113–16.
[7] *Ibid.* 332–3.
[8] *Ibid.* 560–70.
[9] Apoll. *Bibl.* III, vi, 8 and viii, 1.

off Melanippos's head and gave it to Tydeus, thus tempting him to revert to an act of barbarous superstition. Tydeus yielded, split open the skull and swallowed the brains. Athene, filled with loathing at the sight (μυσαχθεῖσα), turned her back on her beloved warrior and withheld the boon which would have conferred immortality.

So at length our conception of the hero of the *Iliad* is complete. We picture him as a chieftain who realises his full self in everything that he does; who has acquired so intense an admiration for the possessions and appurtenances of this life that he can dream of nothing more desirable; who enjoys so keenly the sense of mastery and power, that his spirit has not learnt to look for felicity from without; a warrior so convinced of his own merit that he recognises no other duty than the task of establishing his fame. Men who can imagine for themselves so magnificent a pattern of human self-sufficiency are highly civilised, and Homeric tastes and manners are characterised by ἀστειότης—the dignity, refinement and luxury which Longinus associated with city-life. Are we then to suppose that their philosophy of life led them no further than the worship of man? Could the intelligence which enabled them to enjoy and admire so keenly, fail altogether to discern something behind or above this world? We find, on the contrary, that the Achean had achieved this serenity and self-confidence by gradually winning a victory over the hereditary and traditional terrors of the spirit world, and by inventing a theocracy of tutelary deities a little nobler than himself, who are continually stretching out hands to raise him higher. He is continually climbing up on to their level. This is not the portraiture of an historical type; it is an impression gathered from the records of poets and stands for an ideal or a tendency, not for a fact. The poet does not even pretend to be describing a type; he is telling a story. These characteristics reveal themselves amid actions which seem to be the warrior's one absorbing occupation. While struggling for victory and reputation they develop and evolve these spiritual qualities, which mark a tremendous advance in the progress of the race. While aiming at the consciousness of success, they display a higher consciousness of themselves. It is characteristic of this attitude to regard one's ancestors as greater than oneself, or at least as no less, but in reality each generation surpasses the ideal of its fathers. Whatever the individual acquires of the divine, dies with him, his successors look higher still and in this sense the Herakleitean saying is proved true. The immortal god continues to die and the mortal continues to live.

CHAPTER IV

THE *ODYSSEY* AND ITS HEROIC TYPE

THE foregoing chapters have been written with the object of showing how, even after the lapse of many centuries, the reader can borrow from the *Iliad* a sense of power and of self-possession, a vicarious pride, not only in the achievements of these long-haired bronze-plated impulsive warriors, but in the spirit which Homer gave them. In fact the two aspects go together. Their idealism, their superiority to superstition, their idea of divinity, their desire for glory and hatred of death, are known to us through their strenuous activity, through the deeds and emotions arising from warfare. By this artistic combination, Homer enables us to share, in sympathy and imagination, their intensity, their enthusiasm and the plenitude of their fame. Such is the art of the first complete epic. How does the *Odyssey* conform to this standard? The question is worth asking because this other Homeric poem is often regarded as a romance, a domestic idyll, a theme for moralisation, and is sometimes ignored when heroic poetry is discussed. Let us then see what this second poem contains.

1. *In what respects the* Odyssey *resembles the* Iliad.

The student of Homer will easily recognise many touches which remind him of the *Iliad*. There is a similar love of magnificence and ostentation and an even greater enjoyment in the beauty or craftsmanship of one's possessions. The palace of Alkinoos has a towering roof, with walls of bronze, while the golden doors, fitted into silver frames[1], were wrought by Hephaistos and will last for ever. Golden statues held up torches to illuminate these halls by night, and the seats, ranged round the walls, were covered with the best robes. The building glittered like the sun or moon[2]. When Penelope demands gifts from her suitors, she receives a magnificently coloured robe with twelve brooches, a golden chain strung with amber beads,

---

[1] σταθμοί (?). *Od.* VII, 89.   [2] *Od.* VII, 84–102. See also *ibid.* 172–4, 335–8.

ear-rings with three drops and a necklet[1] (περικαλλὲς ἄγαλμα). Mechanical devices, which seem so commonplace to our modern ideas, were then full of interest, and are described with admiration. The threshold of Penelope's chamber was of polished oak and built in a straight line. When she unbound the door-handle and shot back the bolts with the key, the beautiful doors rang, as a bull roars in the pastures, and flew open[2]. When Odysseus built his bed onto the stump of the olive tree, he adorned it with gold, silver and ivory[3].

Just as in the *Iliad* the poet seems to be keenly sensitive to the beauty of the human form. Though the story requires that his heroes should sometimes be transformed or degraded, he never misses an opportunity of restoring their manhood with added grace and charm. When Hermes comes to the help of Odysseus before Kirke's house, he is endowed with all the charm of adolescence[4]. It is remembered that though Hermione was Helen's only child, she was as beautiful as golden Aphrodite[5]. When the crew, at Kirke's island, are transformed again into human shape, they appear younger, taller, more beautiful than they were before their bewitchment[6]. When Penelope has resolved to appear before the suitors, Athene lulls her to sleep and then steeps in ambrosial beauty her fair face, and makes her skin as pure as ivory, so that she seems as wonderful as Kythereia and all the suitors are smitten with desire[7]. Though the *Odyssey* recounts achievements very different from those which took place on the plains of Troy, yet the poet recalls as often as possible the thrill which the *Iliad* gives. The Phaiakians are just as eager as the Acheans or Trojans for an athletic contest, and Odysseus's feat with the discus is hailed with admiration[8]. When Odysseus has at last caught all his enemies unarmed in the hall and begins to slay them, the poet has managed here and there to bring into the scene that grimness and disdain and intensity which make the heroes of the *Iliad* appear so great. The death of Leiodes is a striking example. The soothsayer begs to be spared, because he has

---

[1] *Od*. xviii, 290–300.
[2] *Ibid*. xxi, 43–50.
[3] *Ibid*. xxiii, 195–200.
[4] *Ibid*. x, 279.
[5] *Ibid*. iv, 14.
[6] *Ibid*. x, 395–6.
[7] *Ibid*. xviii, 187–205.
[8] *Ibid*. viii, 97 ff.

merely practised his art among the suitors, without sharing
in their wantonness. Odysseus will not listen to his plea, but
picks up the sword which the slain Agelaos had let fall and
stabs him in the neck. But it is the swiftness of the avenger's
reply, the sureness of his accusation and an indefinable air
of mastery and confidence which recall the best epic manner[1].

There is also much suggestive of the *Iliad* in the part played
by the gods. It has been noted how often the heroes of the
Iliad seem to compel a larger tribute of wonder and admiration,
when they are aided by supernatural powers[2]. Assuredly no
modern reader, however sceptical, can help being moved by
one passage in the interminable record of conflicts following
on the breaking of the truce. The two tutelary deities of the
Acheans, Here and Athene, rise in their might to vanquish
an inferior hostile god, and through the might of Diomed they
drive him from the field[3]. There are no such scenes as this
in the *Odyssey*, but the most prominent characters, Penelope,
Telemachos and above all Odysseus, enjoy to the full that
added prestige and importance conferred by the services of
an immortal. For the audiences of the ancient world, a chieftain
was raised to a higher plane by divine assistance. When Hermes
had given Odysseus "moly" that would baffle Kirke's spells,
the human being became something of a demi-god himself,
the equal and in this case the conqueror of any immortal[4].
Nearly every crisis in his career is graced and solemnised by
the presence of Athene and her intervention is nowhere more
impressive than during the last battle with the suitors. This
dangerous business is planned by Odysseus and by his three
confederates without counsel from Olympos. Every contingency
is foreseen and provided for by the cunning and experienced
adventurer. But just as the narrator of the *Iliad* loved to
prolong a struggle and hold the victory in the balance,
allowing it to incline now this way and now that, so the climax
of the *Odyssey* is suspended and for a moment it looks as if the
suitors will overwhelm the men who have trapped them. It is
at this supreme moment that the battle becomes worthy of

[1] *Od.* XXII, 320–29.
[2] *Ante*, chap. III, §§ 5, 8.
[3] *Il.* v, 722–867.
[4] *Od.* x, 274–306.

the gods. Athene raises aloft the destroying *aigis*; then at last a panic seizes the intruders and they flee like a herd of oxen; Odysseus and his confederates fall mercilessly upon them as vultures pounce on a cowering flock of birds[1].

II. *Yet the tone and spirit of the* Odyssey *are those of an age which has suffered some humiliation. Its chief characters labour under afflictions, the dominant class is vilified, some of the best speeches are protests against poverty and ill-treatment. Warfare is abhorred. Mortals stand more in awe of the gods.*

Thus many features of the *Odyssey* recall the spirit and artistry of the *Iliad* and at the first glance the poems might appear to be the work of one man or group of men. And yet the careful reader who passes from the one to the other will find that he is no longer in the same world. Many of the people and the places may seem familiar, but their social order has undergone a transformation; their energies have found a new and wider scope; they prize other forms of excellence—in a word, their outlook on life is not that of the warriors who fought round Troy. It may be urged that this disparity is due to the particular conditions amid which either poem is unrolled. The *Iliad* is an epic of war time and the Achean chieftains, under the stress of camp life, would naturally display a spirit impossible in men of more settled lives such as the *Odyssey* represents. This explanation may account for a great deal. On the one hand it may account for that almost universal magnanimity and singleness of heart peculiar to the *Iliad*. It may also explain the sense of natural scenery in which the *Odyssey* excels: visions of a coastline of smooth rock rising up sheer from the fringe of foam[2], or Kalypso's vine-clad cave, near four bubbling streams, which fretted a meadow of violets and parsley[3]. For though the poets of the *Iliad* were keenly alive to the world of sight and sound, their eyes could not escape for long from the sandy plains of

---

[1] *Od.* XXII, 297-309. Note how δὴ τότ' at the beginning of the passage suggests the long expected climax. Bérard believes that the number of suitors was raised to an overwhelming figure, in order that Athene might be introduced to help in their slaughter. The goddess is the λύσις to an ἀπορία such as Porphyrios loved to propound. *Introduction à l'Odyssée*, t. I, chap. VI.

[2] *Od.* v, 400-16.

[3] *Ibid.* v, 63-74. For other examples, see XII, 70-9; XVII, 208-11.

Troy. But the *Odyssey* is something more than a poem of travel
and of peace time. It is the epic of a race or of a generation
which has undergone some great humiliation and which has
learnt wisdom in sadness.

As this assertion cannot, in the ordinary sense of the word,
be proved, the reader may well ask why it is advanced. He
may go further and demand that he be left to enjoy the poem
in peace until the commentator can produce some measure of
certainty wherewith to justify this intrusion. It should be urged
in reply that no poem can be enjoyed till it be understood. No
doubt the student can read his own meanings and spirit into
the text, and can thus learn to discover himself. But he cannot
get that further view which sees through the story to the collective spirit behind and thus learn to discover what is beyond
himself. Besides, though it can never be established what
particular misfortune had been undergone, there are unmistakeable signs that, for whatever reason, the spirit of
defeat was abroad; and unless this tone is appreciated, the
epic qualities of the *Odyssey* will not be properly understood.
To begin with, the chief characters in the second half of the
poem are not representatives of an established and victorious
caste. All seem to be labouring under some disability. They are
not merely confronted by dangers and difficulties; they are
cramped, ill-treated, oppressed and defrauded. One of the
most interesting and pregnant characters is an old swineherd,
once the son of a king, but stolen in early childhood by the
Phoinikians and sold as a slave to Laertes[1]. Under the old order
he had been his lord's favourite but now he has fallen upon evil
days, and goes about his menial duties still courteous and
trustworthy, his head bowed under oppression in patient disdain. Andromache, in the *Iliad*, though already stricken with
the foreknowledge of Hektor's death, is still, after Hecuba, the
most honoured lady in Troy. Her only affliction is the menace
of what may happen to the foremost warrior of her city. But
Penelope is a queen only in semblance. In the height of peace
time and wooed by three hundred suitors, she is a victim of
treachery and indifference, ignored by her own handmaids.

[1] *Od.* xv, 403–84.

One servant is faithful to her, the only other minor character described with sympathy; Eurykleia, an aged slave, verging on dotage, who still treasures her recollections of the old order. How does the poet consider that he ought to portray the men of the rising generation? In the *Iliad* they are conspicuous for their courage and impetuosity. In the *Odyssey* the one youth with whom we are expected to sympathise is Telemachos, the son of one of the greatest men on earth, but as consistently flouted and insulted as is his mother, who writhes under the insolence of the intruders and is threatened with foul play as soon as he is old enough to resist their outrages. The others, the so-called "Acheans," dominating the Kephallenes or country folk, are caitiffs and poltroons, chieftains from the neighbouring isles, but tainted with the greed of traders[1], neither διογενεῖς nor σκηπτοῦχοι, haunted by such sycophants as Iros and Melanthios who salve their own humiliations by bullying those more defenceless than themselves. Even the peerless and far-famed Odysseus, though the hero of the story, is intentionally portrayed as a man of sorrows[2]. He interests us first as a shipwrecked wanderer and then as a poverty-stricken beggar. The kingdom which he ruled in the *Iliad* has dwindled to a large fortified house and some farming estates[3]. His genius is to conquer misfortune and to bide his time— ἀκέων κίνησε κάρη, κακὰ βυσσοδομεύων[4]. In his final hour of triumph he reappears as the terrible and remorseless conqueror, a veritable hero from the Trojan war. But the poet does not for long retain the old epic spirit. His hero seems to have suffered too much while planning his stratagem; his nearest and dearest are too slow to recognise him; his mind is too full of suspicions and the issue of the whole ignoble business is too doubtful. How can he remind us of Aias making his last stand at the ships or of Patroklos pushing his counter-attack up to the walls of Troy?

All these characters must have been conceived and portrayed to please very different audiences from those who first listened to the *Iliad*. The contrast is even more significant when the

[1] *E.g.* Noemon, IV, 630–7.   *Od.* VII, 208; XII, 258; XIII, 90.
[3] *Il.* II, 631 ff.; *Od.* VII, 225.   *Od.* XVII, 465.

student comes to compare the speeches of the two poems. No critic, of course, has the right to select any one passage and to claim that it is more representative than all the others. But most lovers of Homer will agree that one of the finest and the most characteristic passages in the *Iliad* is Sarpedon's exhortation to Glaukos, which enforces the aristocratic obligation to sacrifice ease and even life to honour[1]. Which are the finest speeches in the *Odyssey*? Here again there is bound to be the widest divergence of opinion, but many students of the *Odyssey* will feel that one of the most typical speeches is either the indignant outburst of Odysseus when he is struck on the shoulder by Antinoos's footstool and gives voice to the resentment of the whole immemorial race of beggars[2]; or his warning to Amphinomos that human beings are tempted into insolence the moment they are granted a fleeting hour of prosperity, and forget their own feebleness and the certainty of approaching death[3]; or again the words with which Eumaios explains that Argos is neglected since slaves have not the heart to care for so splendid a hunting dog, and need to be driven by their masters[4]. In fact, while the *Iliad* harps on the qualities of leadership, the *Odyssey* is attuned to the spirit of the defeated and the hatred of oppression. When the wraith of Achilles in Hades searches for an example of the most wretched kind of existence in the world above, he speaks of being bound a serf to one who has not even inherited land[5], and Herakles remembers how he suffered misery beyond measure because he was bound in servitude to an inferior master[6]. Eurymachos is told that he uses his power and position with such arrogance and harshness because there are no strong men to oppose him[7]. It has often been noticed that in the *Iliad* all except the chieftains are ignored as if beneath contempt. In the *Odyssey* they are still beneath contempt, but they are no longer ignored.

[1] *Il.* XII, 310 ff.
[2] *Od.* XVII, 468–76. W. Moellendorf (*Hom. Untersuch.* pp. 28 ff.) and V. Bérard (*Introduction*, t. I, chap. V; t. II, chap. XI) suspect an interpolation, the former because the episode is repeated, the latter because the speech is beneath epic dignity. Yes, unsuited to the *Iliad*, yet perhaps repeated because not beneath the dignity peculiar to the *Odyssey*.
[3] *Od.* XVIII, 125–50.   [4] *Ibid.* XVII, 312–23.   [5] *Ibid.* XI, 487–91.
[6] *Ibid.* XI, 620–2.   [7] *Ibid.* XVIII, 381–3.

Their vices often play a leading part in the story. When Odysseus, after the manner of the privileged, god-descended chieftains, has been presented by Aiolos with the sack containing all the dangerous winds, so that he can complete his journey in calm weather, it was thanks to the greed and mean-spirited distrust of his companions that his greatest disaster befell him[1]. Again, fighting seems to have lost its glamour. The besiegers of Troy spoke of war as δήιος or δα-κρυόεις[2], but the men of the *Odyssey* speak of weapons as something to be abhorred. When Odysseus disguised as a beggar describes himself as the son of a wealthy Cretan, he admits that he was always attracted by warfare and adventure, but adds that javelins and arrows are things at which others generally shudder[3]; and later he tells Eumaios that it is a hungry belly which drives men to man ships and carry war to their neighbours[4]. Besides, weapons are twice regarded as dangerous to peace and good fellowship, αὐτὸς γὰρ ἐφέλκεται ἄνδρα σίδηρος[5]. No essential difference exists between the theology of the *Iliad* and the theology of the *Odyssey*. But a contrast of tone can be detected in the two poems. Thus it is not forgotten, even in the *Iliad*, that the Immortals are unquestionably more powerful than men, yet some of the Achean warriors, in their great moments, revile and even defy their deities[6]. In the *Odyssey* the gods and goddesses still resemble human beings in form and thought, but human beings stand in awe of them. Mortals are humbled when they think of the dwellers of Olympos. They no longer dare to blaspheme them, but like people who have themselves suffered oppression, they look to their deities as the avengers of impiety. When the gods meet at the beginning of the poem to decide the fate of Odysseus, Zeus himself exclaims at the blindness of men who blame the capriciousness of the immortals, when they themselves, like Aigisthos, provoke the condign punishment[7]. When Nestor, in the presence of Telemachos, recalls the events of the Trojan war, he is full of regret at the lawlessness of the Acheans, and at the impiety

---

[1] *Od.* x, 1–75.
[2] *Ante*, chap. ii, § 7.
[3] καταριγηλά, *Od.* xiv, 226.
[4] *Od.* xvii, 286–9.
[5] *Ibid.* xvi, 294.
[6] *Ante*, chap. iii, § 7.
[7] *Od.* i, 32–8.

which brought disaster to their journey home[1]. We have already noticed how far in both the *Iliad* and the *Odyssey* a god's assistance was necessary to the full glory of a human deed. In the former poem the heroes are now and then portrayed as over-slow to recognise divine help and as over-inclined to claim the full honour for themselves. But in the later epic the greatest of them is willing to give the entire credit to his tutelary deity. When Odysseus speaks to Eurykleia of the vengeance that he is plotting, he says

$$εἴ χ' ὑπ' ἐμοί γε θεὸς δαμάσῃ μνηστῆρας ἀγανούς[2],$$

and later, when the victory is won and the old woman is ready to shout for joy at the sight of the corpses, he bids her be silent, because it is unholy to triumph over the slain[3]. When Penelope is told of her husband's return and for proof is assured of the slaughter of the suitors, she yet thinks it to be far more likely that some god has achieved the deed, in punishment for their impiety[4]. In fact men had, for some reason, grown out of one phase of their self-confidence, and were at any rate beginning to realise that life was fuller of insidious and irresistible dangers than had appeared at the siege of Troy. The original audiences of the *Odyssey* must have experienced a rather grim and almost morbid interest in the monsters and magicians whom Odysseus encountered, because they are so mysterious and unexpected and cannot be met and vanquished like the Trojans in open battle. Men were realising that martial prowess is no longer the only guarantee of success and for this reason Kalypso's advice to the great warrior is so significant. She is explaining to him the tortuous and hazardous course which he must steer after leaving her island, and when Odysseus suggests that while eluding Charybdis he can resist Skylla, she is astonished at his simplicity[5]. Weapons of war are useless, only cunning and flight will avail against this deadly πῆμα βροτοῖσιν. It is significant, too, that the audiences seem to have been so interested in storms. Poseidon enjoys in the *Odyssey* the same kind of importance as Apollo does in the *Iliad*, but he is far more impersonal and inhuman, and his

---

[1] *Od.* III, 102–47.   [2] *Ibid.* XIX, 488.   [3] *Ibid.* XXII, 412.
[4] *Ibid.* XXIII, 62–8.   [5] *Ibid.* XII, 111–25.

visitations nearly always end in disaster. We cannot attribute this feature solely to the nautical tastes of the early Greeks. A seafaring folk does not generally dwell unduly on the perils which they have to face, but in the *Odyssey* we are not spared a single terror of the ocean. One of the descriptions must be the most thrilling shipwreck in all literature[1].

III. *The* Odyssey *probably represents the trials and afflictions of some generation subsequent to the Trojan war. Perhaps the age immediately following the Dorian invasion.*

Thus the *Odyssey* differs from the *Iliad* in the activities, pursuits and sentiments of its characters, the conception of life's dangers and difficulties, and, to some extent, in its theology and its idea of the supernatural. Men's spirits are broken and their ideals are tinged with disillusionment. There seems to be no reason for not assuming the cause of this degeneracy to be the one given in the poem: κακοΐλιον[2]. The *Odyssey* may really have taken its rise from the period of the Trojan war, portraying the stress and antagonism at home, while the ruling caste were away in Asia. Such a situation must often have arisen in the history of a dynasty founded on invasion and conquest. When the Skythians left their homes to over-throw the Medes, the sons of the conquered race actually forced their way into their places and married their wives[3]. We look forward many hundreds of years and we find Cœur de Lion's kingdom just as ready to fall a prey to treachery and violence, while the king and his nobles seek honour in the Holy Land. Such crises must have inspired enough heroism and involved enough misery to live in the memory of the people and to become a theme for popular poetry. So there arose the ballads of Robin Hood. If such be the origin of the *Odyssey*, the poem represents the sentiments, beliefs and aspira-tions, not so much of the warrior class, but of those more or less dependent on them and loyal to them.

It seems likely that the poem, in its present form, bears also the impress of the "Dorian invasion." According to ancient tradition that disaster followed closely on the siege of Troy.

[1] *Od.* XII, 403–25.   [2] *Ibid.* XIX, 260.   [3] Herod. IV, 1.

Thoukydides calculated the interval to be only eighty years. Dictys describes how dissensions began before the chiefs had left the ruins of Troy[1] and records how much they suffered during and after their return[2]. We are left in no doubt as to whether the apparent victory over Troy facilitated, or even caused, the defeat which followed it. Every story connected with the return of the heroes shows how the Peloponnese was impoverished, afflicted and disunited. There is a significant legend, preserved by Plato[3], that the Acheans returning from Troy were expelled by the new generation, but united with one Dorieus and so captured their rightful dominion. If so, they only acted like the warrior class of Egypt who, for less reason, deserted Psammetichos and joined his enemies in Aithiopia[4]. Whether the conquerors were the so-called Dorians or the mixed races from Illyria, it is probable that their victory was soon won. The Acheans themselves were intruders, the appropriators, not the creators of Pelasgian civilisation, and now they in their turn were ousted. Probably some battles were fought and then the remnants of the old ruling castes perished amid the flames of their strongholds. Probably a dynasty, defeated in war, was expected to vanish and leave no trace behind. When Kimmeria was threatened by invasion from Skythia, we are told[5] that the δῆμος prepared to evacuate the land, but the βασιλεῖς preferred to die and be buried in their own country and faced extermination in trying to coerce their subjects to their will. According to one legend Priam threatened to set fire to Troy and perish in the flames with his warriors and their treasure[6]. When Charlemagne warred on the Huns Einhard records "tota in hoc bello Hunorum nobilitas periit, tota gloria decidit."[7] When Saguntum could no longer hold out against Hannibal, the chieftains made one huge pyre in the market place and burnt first their treasures and then themselves. Attila was prepared to do the same after the battle of Châlons[8]. Those of the Acheans who remained true to their

---

[1] *De Bello Trojano*, v, 14.   [2] *Ibid*. vi, 1–4.   [3] *Legg*. iii, 6–7, pp. 682–6.
[4] Herod. ii, 30.   [5] Herod. iv, 11.   [6] *De Bello Trojano*, v, 6.
[7] *Vita Caroli Magni*, 13.   [8] *Decline and Fall*, chap. xxxv.

ancestry must have perished in some such way, and left behind only a memory. This memory became sweeter and more acceptable as the people groaned under the injustices and hardships which accompany the most peaceful establishment of a new regime. The Dorians cannot have won goodwill where William the Conqueror failed[1]. They would naturally hate the present and idealise the past. If the *Odyssey* is influenced by this period of transition and resettlement, it represents a reaction against the new order of things.

In either case the investigator will look in vain for anything Tyrtaean; any call to arms or re-awakening of a martial spirit, because the poets are not starting a crusade, but are merely giving voice to moods and feelings of the time. Nor need we expect direct allusions to the Return of the Herakleidai. *Beowulf* contains no reference to the conquest of England; the *Chanson de Roland* does not contribute any direct evidence of the collapse of Charlemagne's dynasty; the medieval romances suggest that Arthur's reign failed only through internal dissensions. So the *Odyssey* does not allude to contemporary or recent history. Its poets merely introduce their own emotions into a familiar story. Instead of breathing a revolutionary spirit, they turn in thought to "the good old times." So it comes about that on the one hand we have traces of post-Achean modernity, as in the almost universal use of iron, and familiarity with the art of riding[2], and on the other hand the σκηπτοῦχος βασιλεύς is described like a revived memory. We shall notice later how the experiences of Telemachos illustrate this attitude, and for the present it is worth remembering that the youth is not born to the manner. He needs a visitation from Athene before he feels himself inspired to emulate his father's dignity[3]. The poets are very careful to indicate when they are talking about the warlike patriarchs of the old order. Warriors are more than once compared to the immortals[4], and the disguised

[1] *Vide* character of William in Old English Chronicle under year A.D. 1087 and note how legends arose to glorify the memory of Hereward.

[2] *E.g. Od.* v, 37; IX, 50. Both describe riding as a usual practice. Of the two allusions in *Il.* x, 513, and xv, 679, the first is a makeshift because Diomed has not time to bring out the chariot and reins. The second is the simile of an acrobat.

[3] *Od.* I, 322.   [4] *Ibid.* VI, 309; VII, 5; XIV, 203.

beggar is allowed to compete with the bow because πατρὸς
δ᾽ ἐξ ἀγαθοῦ γένος εὔχεται ἔμμεναι υἱός[1]. On the other hand,
the degeneracy of the age is emphasised[2]. The race of intruders
is carefully distinguished from the true epic type. The poet
finds it necessary to define the position and influence of the
suitors[3] and to explain why they are able to afflict the great
house for so long. Besides, they are represented as traders, men
given up to the petty stratagems and calculations of gain, and
we shall see later how well these qualities would suit a caricature
of the Dorians[4]. When the civilisation of the Phaiakians is being
praised, no mention is made of the commerce by which they
must have acquired so much wealth and luxury[5]. One of them,
Euryalos, speaks contemptuously of traders[6]. But when Athene
impersonates the son of a patriarch chief, the poet pauses to
describe the charm and beauty of the breed[7]. It may be for
the same reason that the songs of minstrels are so often praised
and their influence represented as so great[8].

IV. *The education of Telemachos as an epic theme.*

Yet the *Odyssey* is as much an epic as the *Iliad.* It has altered
its scope to harmonise with an altered civilisation, but its
purpose is still the same: to portray a perfect character glorified
by action. Telemachos reminds his mother that poetry has
changed with the age and that the minstrels cannot be blamed
for adapting their songs to the sentiments of the time[9]. Let us
now see what the new ideals were.

In the first place it must be remembered that there are three
distinct stories in the *Odyssey*. The first is the epic of this same
Telemachos. The beginner is sometimes tempted to wonder
why four books are devoted almost completely to the history
of Telemachos's feelings and to his singularly enjoyable but
pointless visit to Pylos and Mykenai. It is because the audiences
of the poem were interested in the moral and social upbringing
of a σκηπτοῦχος βασιλεύς. The *Odyssey* begins, as Fénelon

[1] *Od.* XXI, 335.   [2] *Ibid.* II, 276.   [3] *Ibid.* II, 130; XXII, 48.
[4] *Post*, chap. VI, §§ 2, 4.   [5] *Od.* VIII, 246–9.
[6] *Ibid.* VIII, 159–64.   [7] *Ibid.* XIII, 221–5.
[8] *Ibid.* I, 325–8; VIII, 44, 256 ff., 471 ff.; XII, 189–90; XVII, 518–20.
[9] *Ibid.* I, 351–2.

saw, like an earthly tale of social education, a kind of prehistoric
Il Cortegiano or *Euphues* or *Wilhelm Meister*. At the beginning of
the epic Telemachos is already πεπνυμένος[1]. In one of his
first speeches, he shows that his mind has grown to understanding, that he can judge what is right and fitting and can
surprise his mother by his clearness and discrimination. When
he arrives at Pylos, he is conscious of his inexperience and asks
his supposed Mentor what are the proper forms of address and
the correct demeanour with which to approach the celebrated
and venerable Nestor[2]. When Eteoneos announces the strangers'
arrival and Menelaos gives directions for their entertainment,
the mutual respect and freemasonry among the γένος διοτρεφέων
βασιλήων are emphasised[3]. It is true that the *Iliad* gives an
impressive picture of the ceremonial observed among warriors,
but this occurs at a crisis of the war and leads up to a still more
effective scene; it is a necessary piece of setting. The entertain-
ments in the *Odyssey* have no ulterior purpose; they are there
for their own sake. If there is a climax to the episode, it is
reached when Telemachos, with admirable courtesy, takes
leave of his host and in the words which Horace so much
admired[4] declines the gift of horses[5], and Menelaos, who himself
gives an unmistakeable lesson on the duty of speeding the
parting guest, exclaims with a smile

αἵματός εἰς ἀγαθοῖο, φίλον τέκος, οἷ' ἀγορεύεις[6].

This ἀστειότης and ἀστεϊσμός, which have already been noticed
in discussing the *Iliad*, are conspicuous features all through
the *Odyssey*. Kalypso and Hermes compliment each other as
if they were mortals and are just as courteous and considerate[7].
The long talks between the old swineherd Eumaios and the
supposed beggar are not to be admired solely as studies in
dramatic irony. Both interlocutors are men of noble birth and
the original audiences must have intensely enjoyed their dignity
and refinement, and must have appreciated the contrast with
their oppressors, the upstart intruders in Odysseus's palace.
But throughout the poem, Telemachos remains the type of

[1] *Od.* i, 345–59.   [2] *Ibid.* iii, 21–4.   [3] *Ibid.* iv, 20–36, 60–4.
[4] *Epp.* i, 7–40 ff.   [5] *Od.* iv, 593–608.   [6] *Ibid.* iv, 611.
[7] *Ibid.* v, 87–104.

aristocratic culture because we watch the steps by which he
reaches perfection. His good breeding is only one aspect of his
growing self-confidence and maturity. He is also learning to
hold his own and to abash the suitors by his self-possession.
Odysseus soon recognises his reliability and trusts him with
the dangerous secret of his identity. All his qualities come to
fruition when he plays a part second only to his father in overthrowing the intruders' period of oppression and misrule,
especially by his self-restraint and secrecy as Eurykleia admits[1].
Thus the first portion of the *Odyssey* describes how the mind
and spirit of a young aristocrat grew to manhood. The poem
gratifies an interest in the courtly manners of old times, but
it also reflects the feelings of a more modern epoch. Cunning
is valued as much as courage; Telemachos himself realises that
intelligence and forethought are indispensable in this difficult
age. The scenes combine to form a poem in the true epic
spirit, because Telemachos is free from the moral weaknesses
and hesitations which characterise the personalities of later
literature. He does not suffer from the disheartening self-
criticism of Euphues, nor from the paralysing self-examination
of Wilhelm Meister. His character is lightly sketched, but we
see enough of it to catch something of his serenity and to feel
almost a certain pride in the leisurely completeness of his
development. He can even afford to confess to a mistake[2]. And
again this part of the poem is epic because the scenes, even the
mere descriptions of receptions and banquets, are narrated
with that air of admiration and enjoyment which are features
of the Heroic Age. Thus even though the old order may have
passed away or was tottering to its fall, it was natural, almost
necessary, to introduce one or more of the mighty princes in
full possession of his wealth and palaces. Menelaos seems, in
later times, to have enjoyed a reputation for riches and
splendour. Hesiod describes him as κτήνει Ἀχαιῶν φέρτατος[3],
and at the courtship for Helen as πλεῖστα παρών[4]. So it was
not inappropriate that he should supply the principal scene.

---

[1] *Od.* XXIII, 29–31.   [2] *Ibid.* XXII, 153–9. Cf. *ante*, chap. II, § 5.
[3] *Catal. of Women*, Berlin Papyri, 9739, l. 25.
[4] Berlin Papyri, 10560, ll. 43–4.

Penelope is like her son. We have already noticed the helplessness and defencelessness of her position, but it must not be
forgotten that she has the qualities that develop in suffering.
Her chief passions are love for her home, which she will never
forget, even in her dreams, and the treasured memory of her
husband, who belonged to a former, nobler generation.
Inspired by these sentiments, she defends herself by her wits
and keeps at a distance the hated necessity of re-marriage[1];
nor are we surprised to learn that her resourcefulness is famous[2].
Like Telemachos, she is versed in the duties and ceremonial of
hospitality.

v. *The character of Odysseus. Its probable origins. Its development in the poem as the man of supreme resource and self-
control.*

The two other stories deal with Odysseus himself. Every
reader will recall the widespread belief that now and then a
hero of the old order, finding the new world an impossible
dwelling-place, retires to some cavern or mountain, to await
the occasion for return. This idea is attached even to historical
characters. According to the *Kyffhäusersaga*, recorded in 1426 in
the chronicle by Engelhusius von Einbeck, Frederic II was
believed to be only asleep. Wedekind was supposed to be still
alive in a hill of Westphalia, Siegfried in his mountain castle
Goldseck, and Charlemagne in Unterberg. There was a like
expectation of Arthur's return, and as early as the ninth century
it was believed that Trajan's soul returned to his body and
was baptised[3]. The return of Odysseus is not unlike a reincarnation of this type. It is not for a moment suggested that any
Homeric poet consciously revived the legendary hero and used
him as a sort of Achean messiah to crush the Dorian antichrist.
The poet's conscious purpose was to tell a great and moving
story. In fact the ultimate source of his narrative must have
been some floating legends of the "Return of the Wandering
Husband" such as we still find in ballads of Lorraine, Brittany

[1] *Od.* XIX, 137.
[2] *Ibid.* XIX, 325–6. On the character of Penelope, *vide* J. W. Mackail,
Classical Studies, IV, "Penelope in the *Odyssey*."
[3] Giovanni Diacono, *Vita Sancti Gregorii Magni*, II, 44.

and China[1]. These recollections may have been superimposed on some other very vague Minyan-Ionic tradition of an "Eni-autos daimon," once the rival of the horse-god Poseidon, as Mr Thomson suggests[2]. Whatever the first suggestion, the feelings of the poets and of their audiences must have led them to clothe their hero in the garb of a long-expected deliverer; to group the remnants of the old order round this figure; to shroud his advent in secrecy; to describe his final victory more as an act of justice than as a deed of vengeance.

So much for the theme; but we have not yet accounted for the indescribable touch of poesy. The Odyssean minstrels were no mere annalists or versifiers. They were under the further obligation of giving expression to that which seemed best in the world around them. So we pass to the next aspect of the epic; the portrayal of its hero as the perfect man of action.

Odysseus has often fascinated latter-day sentimentalists as the embodiment of intellectual questioning, even as the ardent searcher after truth. Yet, except for his ill-timed curiosity in the Kyklops's cave and his very natural willingness to hear the Seirens, he does not display any marked eagerness to acquire knowledge or experience for its own sake. But he does in the highest degree typify the man who overcomes brute force by sheer brain power, $\grave{a}\epsilon\grave{\iota}\ \acute{\epsilon}\nu\grave{\iota}\ \sigma\tau\acute{\eta}\theta\epsilon\sigma\sigma\iota\ \nu\acute{o}o\nu\ \pi o\lambda\upsilon\kappa\epsilon\rho\delta\acute{\epsilon}a\ \nu\omega\mu\hat{\omega}\nu$[3]. In the *Iliad* he had enjoyed a reputation for resourcefulness and for persuasive oratory, so any poet who wished to retain familiar names was likely to find in Odysseus a link between the two ages and ideals. As if to introduce the character, Nestor is portrayed recalling the disputes and dissensions in the Achean councils[4], and particularly insisting that Odysseus was conspicuous for his wisdom and his cleverness in managing men. In the *Odyssey* far more is required of him. The difference between the two ages will be recognised if we compare their attitudes to old age. In the *Iliad* there are only two men who have lived long and neither has reason to be grateful for his grey hairs; but in the later poem old age

[1] A. Lang, *Homer and the Epic*; Puymaigre et Villemarqué, *Barzaz Breiz*, and *Chants Populaires du Pays Messin*; Gerland, *Altgriechische Märchen in der Odyssee*; Dennys, *China and the Chinese*.
[2] *Studies in the Odyssey*, chap. v.   [3] *Od.* XIII, 255.   [4] *Ibid.* III, 120 ff.

is praised for the wisdom which it brings[1] and for the calmness of its ending[2]. It is this appreciation of something more than strength or good fortune which characterises the *Odyssey*. Its hero is the kind of man who can save himself and others when the sword or spear alone is worse than useless. In fact martial prowess is more than once condemned. Nestor describes the warriors of the *Iliad* as μένος ἄσχετοι[3]. The Kyklopes are ὑπερηνορέοντες[4], and we hear of an expedition ruined because the men were too much at the mercy of their own warlike passions: ὕβρει εἴξαντες ἐπισπόμενοι μένεϊ σφῷ[5]. Odysseus is the hero who can triumph over these vices. One has only to remember how well he perceived the wisdom of controlling his anger when Eurylochos mutinied because his comrades were bewitched by Kirke[6]. He has the instinct and intuition which come to those who have formed the habit of calculating events. When passing by Skylla and Charybdis he himself confesses to one mistake which cost him dear[7]. Yet even in this crisis the escape of the ship is due to his self-control and his knowledge of men. The more one reads the poem the more one wonders at the hero's tenacity and resourcefulness. Yet he is of the same type as Telemachos, only infinitely developed and hardened. The poet has described his qualities as the Phaiakian ship sped towards Ithaka[8]. Perhaps Eurylochos comes even nearer to the truth:

σχέτλιός εἰς, Ὀδυσεῦ, περί τοι μένος οὐδέ τι γυῖα
κάμνεις· ἦ ῥά νυ σοί γε σιδήρεα πάντα τέτυκται[9].

VI *Many features are very ancient, especially the adventures of Odysseus, and may have existed in Pelasgian folklore both before and during the Achean domination. Their recrudescence a sign that the warlike epic was beginning to pall. These primitive themes excellent material for displaying the more modern qualities of the hero. Also the interest in travel and in domestic life. His stratagems in Ithaka; the rôle of Athene.*

Such is one side of Odysseus's character: he is the man who could travel over the known world and by his resourcefulness

---

[1] *Od.* II, 16.
[2] *Ibid.* XI, 136.
[3] *Ibid.* III, 104.
[4] *Ibid.* VI, 5.
[5] *Ibid.* XVII, 431.
[6] *Ibid.* X, 438–42.
[7] *Ibid.* XII, 234–59.
[8] *Ibid.* XIII, 88–92.
[9] *Ibid.* XII, 279–80.

and his pertinacity could triumph where others, including some of the greatest Achean warriors, would be expected to fail. Would Achilles have got the better of Polyphemos, or Aias have escaped Skylla and Charybdis or Hektor have rescued his comrades from Kirke? As we have seen, he belongs to the siege of Troy only by reputation. He becomes the protagonist after its fall, he displays his peculiar genius among a younger generation. But when we look at the background on which his character develops, we find it to be infinitely older than anything in the *Iliad*[1]. Bérard suggests that the idea of a hero wandering among the dangers of the West may have been derived from Chaldean legends current one or two thousand years before the *Odyssey* took its present form[2]. The Kyklopes according to the more historical sources were the descendants of Ouranos and Gaia, imprisoned and maltreated by their parents and by Kronos, till Zeus released them, enlisted their aid in the conquest of Olympia[3], employed them as willing craftsmen[4] and secluded them from the spheres of human activity on Lipare[5]. In the *Odyssey* these demi-gods are the descendants of Poseidon and the sea nymph Thoösa, daughter of Phorkys, and as such may once have been associated with the progress of Minoan civilisation on the mainland of Greece. But they are very different from the mighty labourers who were famed to have built the walls of Mykenai. Polyphemos and his brethren are so primitive that they know nothing of the sacred laws of hospitality, nor agriculture nor cooking. They have to light a fire to illuminate the cavernous gloom of their caves. But though portrayed from the point of view of the age of Zeus, they still retain their primeval character. They are not subjected to the god of the Acheans as Here was; they do not even recognise his rule, and they must have existed at a time when the Olympian Ruler was in very truth no more than a part owner of the universe, and less established than we find him to be in the *Iliad*, which recognises his priority over Poseidon[6] and does not mention these rebels to his authority.

---

[1] This question has already been raised and discussed by J. E. Harrison, *Myths of the Odyssey*, 1882; J. A. K. Thomson, *Studies in the Odyssey*, 1914.
[2] *Introduction à l'Odyssée*, t. I, p. 80.   [3] Apoll. *Bibl.* I, 1.
[4] *Theog.* 139.   [5] *Aen.* VIII, 416.   [6] *Od.* XIII, 335.

Many nations at many times seem to have pictured to themselves how one of their kind found himself in the clutches of
some such man-eating ogre, and devices such as Odysseus
extemporised had to be thought of again and again[1]. The
"moly" which Hermes gives him is like the "herb of virtue"
found in the folklore of many lands[2]. Though the Iliadic
heroes have discarded blood-drinking yet the ghosts in Kimmeria need such draughts to revive them. The custom of
suitors contesting for a bride is an ancient and almost universal
theme and is retained, though the inheritance is no longer
matrilinear and the successful competitor would not expect
to remain as husband and king. Even the drawing of the bow
was a well-recognised sign and test of prowess in ancient
times. The king of the Aithiopians once sent Kambyses such
a weapon and defied him to use it efficiently[3]. At times its
mastery ensured kingship. When Herakles lay with the
Skythian serpent-woman and she prophesied that she would
have three sons, her lover left behind a girdle and a bow,
and appointed that the descendant, who could draw it, was
to remain and possess the land. Skythos the youngest achieved
the feat, and hence sprang the Skythians[4].

At first it might seem unlikely that the hero who embodies
the virtues of one age should excel in feats suggestive of
periods inconceivably more primitive. As if to support this
objection we easily detect traces of a very ancient element in
his character, what A. Lang terms "the shifty lad," whose
astuteness, in popular tales, proves more than a match for
giants and magicians[5]. Surely the hero of the *Odyssey* marks
the survival and revival of some aboriginal ideal, a romanticism
which had perhaps lain hidden in the Pelasgian underworld,
and had now again risen to the surface. Such may well have
been the case, for not only are the character and the legends
ancient, both elements are much too good ever to be forgotten. Nor need we wonder if Acheans as well as Pelasgians

---

[1] Frazer, *Ulysses and Polyphemus*. See *Transl. of Apoll.* Loeb Classics,
Appendix XIII.
[2] J. E. Harrison, *Myths of the Odyssey*, pp. 70–1.
[3] Herod. III, 21.   [4] *Ibid.* IV, 9 and 10.
[5] W. Grimm, *Die Saga von Polyphem*, 1857; Merry, *Odyssey*, Excursus II.

treasured them and handed them on from generation to generation. But neither race was therefore more likely to look to this folklore for their inspiration and idealism, and to glorify it with their best poetry, unless their established litera- ture had ceased to satisfy. In fact the recrudescence of older themes is almost always a strong piece of evidence that the more recent ideals are passing away. So we find that the Olympic gods as a body play a more restricted part. Zeus is still mentioned as one of the originators of human mis- fortunes[1], Poseidon is the requisite *ressort d'action* in all the ill-luck which dogs Odysseus, and Athene is necessary to the epic portrayal of his virtues. But apart from these and a few other such manifestations, there seems a tendency to return to animism. Yet though the older spirit gods are amply recog- nised, as for instance Atlas[2] and the spirit of the storm[3], yet the worship is no longer primitive. At times there are touches of exquisite romanticism as when Leukothoe, inspired by pity, rises from the stormy deep like a bird on the wing, and after giving the shipwrecked mariner the magic veil, the only talis- man of any power in that terrific tempest, buries herself in the waves again[4]. At times the poet, like Herodotos, describes the supernatural powers merely as $\delta\alpha\acute{\iota}\mu\omega\nu$[5].

The modernisation of the poem is even more plainly shown in the more human adventures. It is especially these tales of hairbreadth escapes which have fascinated all readers since the Renaissance, because they make us admire what we know to be impossible. Nor need we doubt that the earliest audiences keenly enjoyed this atmosphere. But the primitive Greeks can- not have revelled in them as if they were nothing but fairy stories. Whether or no they believed that those encounters had taken place, they believed that they might take place. Half the charm consisted in the problems which they created for the adventurer; in the superhuman resolution which they evoked, in the glory which they reflected on their conqueror. Even in the supreme test, the conference with the bodiless ghosts, it is the strangeness and awfulness of the experience

---

[1] *Od.* VIII, 82; XX, 201.   [2] *Ibid.* I, 52.   [3] *Ibid.* I, 241.
[4] *Ibid.* V, 333 ff.   [5] *E.g. ibid.* XII, 295.

that attracted the listeners. No doubt their curiosity was excited to hear again the words of famous heroes long dead,
and they must have wept at the meeting of mother and son.
But what they really admired was the novelty and magnitude
of Odysseus's achievement. Even Achilles pays homage to his
audacity and intelligence[1]. Even Kirke wonders at the privilege
and salutes him as $\delta\iota\sigma\theta\alpha\nu\acute{\epsilon}\epsilon\varsigma$[2]. The other half of their charm
arose out of the comparison of civilisations. Here again it is
difficult for us to feel like the ancient Greeks[3] when we read
of cave-dwellers who have not yet reached the stage of agriculture or even of communal existence, but live like the ogres
of northern legends or like our own reconstructions of paleo-
lithic man[4], or of the oriental and Phoinikian-like luxury of
the Phaiakians[5]. Such revelations interest us as curiosities, not
as contrasts with our own expanding institutions. But Odysseus
represents an age of travellers who are bringing different
civilisations into touch; when thrown on an unknown coast, he
still needs to ask himself whether the inhabitants are likely to be
$\dot{\upsilon}\beta\rho\iota\sigma\tau\alpha\grave{\iota}$ and $\ddot{\alpha}\gamma\rho\iota\sigma\iota$ or $\phi\iota\lambda\acute{o}\xi\epsilon\iota\nu\sigma\iota, \kappa\alpha\acute{\iota} \sigma\phi\iota\nu \nu\acute{o}\sigma\varsigma \dot{\epsilon}\sigma\tau\grave{\iota} \theta\epsilon\sigma\upsilon\delta\acute{\eta}\varsigma$[6].
It is another characteristic of the *Odyssey* that it gratifies the
curiosity of people who are studying and cultivating the arts
of life. We have seen that the men of the *Iliad* had special
reasons for being interested in armoury and horse breeding;
the contemporaries of Odysseus do not care more for these
things than for anything else, but they are much concerned
about other observances and devices which improve man's
way of life. It is noticeable that tables are cleansed before meals[7];
that craftsmen, prophets, leeches, shipwrights and bards are
always welcome as the ambassadors of civilisation[8]; there is
an expert's description of a lumber road[9]; and after the
slaughter of the suitors the most rigorous disinfection is enforced[10]. Clearly this generation was conscious of progress. So
the hero of this age is $\pi\sigma\lambda\acute{\upsilon}\tau\rho\sigma\pi\sigma\varsigma$ and his mission in life,

[1] *Od.* xi, 473–6.   [2] *Ibid.* xii, 21–2.
[3] Cf. Herodotos's description of the Androphagoi, iv, 106.
[4] *Od.* x, 1–13.   [5] *Ibid.* viii, 246 ff.
[6] *Ibid.* vi, 119–21; xiii, 200–2.   [7] *Ibid.* i, 110.
[8] *Ibid.* xvii, 382–6.   [9] *Ibid.* x, 103 ff.
[10] *Ibid.* xxii, 481 ff.

despite his travels, is domestic and intellectual; at least such were partly the inclinations of the age which he represents. His ambitions and destiny are quite different from those of the warriors at Troy. He refuses immortality with Kalypso[1], and we are told that after one more pilgrimage, which introduces the quaint story, still current, of the man mistaking an oar for a winnowing-fan[2], he will die by the gentlest of deaths in extreme old age, in peace and prosperity[3]. He is quite free from that insatiable restlessness and impious curiosity which, according to Dante[4], drove him to explore the world till his ship foundered in the uncharted seas surrounding the mountain of Purgatory.

The Odysseus who landed in Ithaka and coped with an army of invaders, almost single-handed, seems to us less sympathetic than does the indomitable and cunning adventurer on the high seas. Yet to the people of the later Heroic Age he must have seemed to be an even more perfect embodiment of the epic hero. He is just as resolute, as far-seeing, as resourceful, and, when the time comes, as doughty as before, and if his own country does not threaten him with weird and unearthly terrors, it exacts another even more highly prized quality, the art of dissembling. It has already been suggested that the *Odyssey* represents an age which has been humiliated. At any rate its poets have a profound admiration for one characteristic of a subject people, the ability to deceive. It is not necessary to follow Odysseus in all the ingenious impostures that he practises, nor linger to share the ominous secrecy with which his plot is hatched. But it is worth noting that Athene, in these latter stages, graces him even more devotedly with her divine help and approval, and that she is now very different from the war goddess of the *Iliad*. All that to the ancient mind was inspiring and admirable in trickery finds full expression when the man and the goddess, both disguised, meet on the Ithakan shore and the deity bursts into involuntary praise of the mortal's subtlety and glibness[5]. Nor

---

[1] *Od.* v, 215-20.
[2] Dr Rouse, "A Greek Skipper," in *The Cambridge Review*.
[3] *Od.* XI, 119-37.   [4] *Inf.* XXVI, 91 ff.   [5] *Od.* XIII, 291.

does Odysseus lose anything of his virtue or nobility because
he can outwit other men. He recognises his son, but he can
restrain even the most natural and softening emotion, till the
right moment comes[1]. Nor does he lay aside his dignity and
royal bearing because he is disguised as a penniless beggar.
Even in this disguise he is not false to the Odyssean idea of a
hero. Perhaps his attitude of mind can best be illustrated by
the two Homeric presentments of Hermes. Originally this god
was probably conceived to be a spirit of ways and paths and
is therefore represented in the *Iliad* as the god of the way to
death or as the god of the crossways, haunted by ghosts. His
influence was then extended to those who travel by the ways,
that is to say heralds, and so he was soon himself invested with
a herald's attributes. Such associations still cling to him in the
Odyssey, but he is also connected with another and very different
class of those who use the ways. Thieves and tricksters are now
a class sufficiently large or important to be added to his province, and without surrendering his function as conductor of
souls, he has become the patron[2] of such rogues as Autolykos.

[1] *Od.* XVI, 191.   [2] *Ibid.* XIX, 396 ff.

CHAPTER V

THE HOMERIC QUESTION IN RELATION TO THE PRESENT WORK

WHILE studying epic poetry as a revelation of human energy and idealism, and while making Homer the starting point of such investigations, it is requisite to discover as much as possible about the conditions under which the poems were produced. In the first place we cannot form a satisfactory idea unless we know, at least conjecturally, at what stage Homer appears in the history of thought and of poetic expression. In the next place, analogies and comparisons with the Homeric Age will frequently have to be established in studying later epics and consequently references will have to be made to the established theories on prehistoric Greece[1]. Thirdly, this same word "Homer" calls up so many different impressions and theories that a statement of faith must be made before the reader and writer can be in accord.

1. *Minoan, Mykenaian and Achean civilisations. Pelasgians and Acheans.*

Let the reader, then, carry his imagination backward, over three thousand years, to the southern parts of Greece. At that time there lived a mysterious race, remarkable for industry and inventiveness, which built magnificent palaces, protected by cyclopean fortresses, and filled with objects of art and luxury, and with the true artistic spirit they rendered even their weapons of war beautiful. This civilisation probably began towards the close of the Stone Age, but the people soon became acquainted with the use of copper and with the alloy of copper and tin which we now call bronze. By about 1400 B.C. their culture had spread over the south of Greece and the

[1] In this chapter the views are discussed in too general a way to need special reference. Invaluable hints and suggestions have been gathered from the following (often conflicting) works: Ridgeway, *The Early Age in Greece*, vol. I; Chadwick, H. M., *The Heroic Age*; Murray, G., *The Rise of the Greek Epic*; Scott, J. A., *The Unity of Homer*; Allen, T. W., *Homer: the Origins and the Transmission. The Cambridge Ancient History*, vol. II.

islands of the Aegean. It had penetrated as far east as the Troad and as far west as Etruria and Latium, and is thought to have first reached its height in Crete under Minos and is therefore called Minoan.

When the relics of this vanished civilisation began to be revealed, archeologists thought that we had at last discovered the Homeric Age. But it has since been proved that this race was not the Acheans, but some earlier people, to be termed the Ionians or Pelasgians, themselves conquerors, who had probably come from Knossos, the great thalassocrat, and had become a land power in their new home. While they were building luxurious palaces, and delighting themselves with glazed pottery, inlaid daggers, embossed cups and carved gems, another race of tall, long-haired warriors, perhaps foreign invaders, perhaps Thessalians from the regions about the Spercheios and the Peneos, had made their dread presence felt. Like so many conquerors, in the periods of migrations, they had learnt the language of the conquered in whose country they had settled. These northerners, perhaps from the great fair-haired communities of central Europe, appeared in northern Greece about the fourteenth century B.C. There, perhaps because they were themselves threatened with invasion, or through love of adventure and the prospect of wealth, some bands pushed their way southward and invaded the Peloponnese, and others followed till most of the peninsula was overrun. Perhaps the huge fortifications at Argos, Tiryns and Mykenai were built to repel these invaders as well as to keep the aborigines in subjection. For these northerners had one great advantage over the Pelasgians; they were better armed. Their civilisation at that time seems to have been concentrated on the arts and crafts of war. They went into battle equipped with bronze helmets, breastplates and greaves, and some of their swords and spears were of iron, whereas the Pelasgians appear to have worn leather caps and had no other defence than oblong shields, which must have hindered their movements the more effectually they covered their bodies. We know nothing for certain of the conquest of the Peloponnese, but it is likely to have been rapid and less embittered than one would otherwise suppose.

These warlike settlers were the immortal Acheans of Homer. As they did not (like the Goths, Huns or Vandals) destroy this civilisation, but (like the Normans) took possession of it and acquired the language and some of the customs of their subjects, a new and wonderful era opened for them. They were settled, each in a newly conquered kingdom, in one of the most wonderful climates of the world, and they found themselves lords of a refinement and a culture which would have surpassed the wildest dreams of their forefathers. In fact the race must have passed through a period comparable only to the Renaissance at its height, when life lay before them full of boundless possibilities.

II.   *Theories concerning the era of Homeric composition. Difficulties in the way of accepting any of them.*

So far we can go with reasonable certainty. But as soon as we try to connect Homer with these events, as descried in the distance, we find ourselves involved in confusions and contradictions. We look first at the civilisation described in the poems —the palaces, the embroidery, the gold work, the carving and the artistic spirit of the people—and we find ourselves forced to admit that the *Iliad* and the *Odyssey* are the product of the Mykenaian Age. They belong to the culture of this earlier conquering race, dark haired and red skinned, who came from Crete, bringing Minoan civilisation, and apparently dominated Greece, till the Acheans gradually dispossessed them. So we return to the poems. But when we begin to read them in this light, we find nothing but a few fleeting references to Ionians or Pelasgians. Instead, we find that this other race, the Acheans, is always celebrated as the only heroes of the war and as the ruling caste, and that they are light haired and pale skinned. Besides we are reminded that they employed iron for implements and perhaps even for weapons of war, whereas the metal was so scarce in Mykenaian times that hardly a ring is found in the graves. Moreover the combatants are nearly always described as equipped with breastplates and short circular shields, whereas Minoan warriors are depicted naked, generally with figure-of-eight shields reaching from their shoulders to their feet. And if Troy really was once captured by the Acheans, as Prof. Chadwick, Dr Leaf and Sir James Frazer maintain, it is difficult to believe that the account of its fall should originate among an earlier folk.

So we close the *Iliad* convinced that we have read through the national epic of the Acheans, the pre-Dorian rulers of the Peloponnese; the second if not the third conquerors of Greece. Yet when we return to our commentaries and archeological studies, we are reminded that the great age of the Minoan civilisation had passed away when the Acheans appeared in Greece, that these invaders had no creative or artistic gifts, that the best which they could produce were "geometric" patterns and juvenile scrawls like the fragments of the "warrior vase," and we are invited to conclude that their civilisation could not have produced the magnificent poetry of Homer. So we are tempted to compromise. It has been noticed that though the mother city Knossos, trusting in her sea-power, remained in part unwalled, the Minoans of Argos, Tiryns and Mykenai fortified their towns, presumably to keep in check the subject races, and so it is suggested that among the con-quered aborigines there was already a portion of newly arrived and ever-increasing Acheans. This bilingual population learnt and cherished the epics of the Minoans, and when new hordes of Acheans joined their brethren who had already settled in Greece and overthrew the Minoan rule, the poetry of the defeated dynasty was handed on, translated, and adapted to the circumstances of the conqueror. It has even been suggested that the *Odyssey* came through like channels from the Minyans of central Greece. Thus the disconcerting inconsistencies of the two poems—the differences of equipment and of mythology—are accounted for. We have two poems of a superb civilisation thinly disguised, perhaps by the same hereditary caste of minstrels, to suit a later and ruder age. But unhappily the poems do not suit a ruder age, whether late or early. How did these northern warriors, said to be illiterate and inartistic, come to appreciate and assimilate the subtle and penetrating emotion of a southern race, expressed in highly wrought poetry? They must have been surprisingly docile and patient.

Nor will the modern student find all the passages indisputably reminiscent of the earlier civilisation to be the most inspired, nor those which are unmistakeably Achean to be mere interpolations, added by a less cultured age, bastards of the true Homeric Muse.

Then perhaps the two poems, as we now have them, are the product of a cult? Perhaps they never existed in the Heroic Age, except as lays and ballads; short effusions, fit for the leisure and relaxation of fighting men. Perhaps during the downfall of the Atreidai, and the "Return of the Herakleidai," and the migrations eastward which followed these disasters, the lays were preserved by a sect or caste (possibly not untouched by religious fervour), which mitigated the humiliations of the present by magnifying the glories of the past. So there may have come into existence, very likely in Asia Minor, the school of the Homeridai, professional poets and rhapsodists who rewove and "stitched together" the collected fragments, passionately intent, like their select audiences, on recapturing the vanished greatness of an early time, till the two incomparable poems reached the stage of completeness which we now know. Yet if such be the history of their evolution, we cannot help wondering why two compositions of such length, covering immense fields of legend and mythology, and apparently touching on every known sphere of human activity, contain no allusion to the invasion, whether Dorian or Thessalian—Aetolian—Doric, no allusion to the art of writing, though the linear script has been discovered on late Minoan vases. It is also surprising that Homeric thought, for all its enthusiasm and poetic insight, yet remains untinged by the reflectiveness and intellectual curiosity which begin to be noticeable in the Hesiodic Age.

III. *Uncertainty of authorship.*

The authorship of these poems is as uncertain as their era. The theory is still widely held that both poems originated in primitive lays and ballads which were gradually worked into longer connected narratives, and that the finished product was the result of the recension instituted by Peisistratos. But scholars have already begun to argue that Peisistratos never undertook any such recension and that furthermore the *Iliad* and the *Odyssey* have each an artistic unity such as no multiple author- ship could produce. The raw material may well have come from many sources, but the descriptive power, the characterisa- tion, the movement of the narrative and the sense of force and beauty are the creation of one supreme genius. Some go so far as to attribute both the *Iliad* and the *Odyssey* to a single poet.

This theory has much to recommend itself. After all, argu- ments based on inconsistencies can easily be pushed too far. What should we make of Froissart's battle of Crécy, if we knew as much and no more of bows and cannons than we do of the long and the circular shields? *Paradise Lost* is a cross-puzzle of civilisations. Deities, bearing evident traces of Olympian origin, argue against Calvinistic doctrines in a manner sug- gestive of scholasticism. Figures derived from early Hebrew mythology allude to doctrines held at the Restoration. The action takes place soon after the creation of the world, and in the cardinal portions of the narrative the leading characters are either spirits or human beings of primitive simplicity. Yet some contributor has incorporated a multitude of scenes from the New Testament, another has made countless allusions to classical mythology, yet another displays a knowledge of medieval romances, especially the Arthurian cycle, and English folklore. The inconsistencies of material equipment are just as perplexing. They range from Homeric shields, spears and chariots to Asiatic insignia of royalty, then to Dorian and Ionic architecture, whence we pass to mystic dances such as those described by Dante, to tournaments suggested by Boiado, Ariosto and Tasso, and end with a description of cannon and the telescope. Such are but a few of the difficulties which would present themselves if we tried to fix the date and authorship of *Paradise Lost*, knowing as little of Milton as we know of Homer.

Ought not such an object lesson to render us very cautious in arguing from Homeric discrepancies? Assuredly it should. But caution will lead us to notice one essential difference between the inconsistencies of Homer and those of modern poems, however long and complex. If we take, for instance, the *Divina Commedia*, we shall find almost as great a diversity of themes as in *Paradise Lost*. Characters illustrative of utterly divergent civilisations are brought together. But yet the *Divina Commedia*, like *Paradise Lost*, has what might be called the unity of moral and religious conviction. The poet, in both cases, is perfectly consistent in his sympathies, his admiration, his hatred and his fears. If any more modern poet tried to continue either poem, he would find it easy to keep to the subject and the avowed purpose of his author; he might even echo quite convincingly the professed doctrines and ideals of the original; let us even suppose that he could rival his models in sheer poetic excellence; yet he would betray himself in his judgments both human and divine. A poet cannot escape from his age in what he expects of God and man. No one could be persuaded for a moment to believe that *The Dream of Gerontius* belonged to the school of Dante, or *Phèdre* and *Iphigenie auf Tauris* to the school of Euripides, or the *Idylls of the King* to the school of Malory. Now this is just the kind of inconsistency with which we meet in Homer. Considering the length of the *Iliad* and the number of characters engaged, and the disintegrating effect of piecemeal recitation, the unity of action, atmosphere and characterisation is amazing. And yet, throughout the preceding chapters[1] we have had to notice, again and again, that other more fundamental stratification of religious and moral views. The same deities appear in different lights; they act differently to human beings, and the same warriors are, on different occasions, possessed by thoughts and motives which belong to different ages. Even the similes belong to different ages.

We have noticed the unity of style and poetic enthusiasm. This feature, despite unmistakeable lapses, is most remarkable. Yet its significance can easily be over-rated. Critics do not always realise that poetry is an art profoundly adapted to transmission. It is surprising how successfully the manner and even the vision of a master can be cultivated by his disciples. Some of the greatest poets, though themselves ardent students of Homer, have forgotten this peculiarity of their craft. For

[1] Esp. chap. III.

instance, Schiller writes to Goethe declaring that the idea of divided authorship is "nothwendig barbarisch" in view of the "herrliche Continuität und Reciprocität des Ganzen und seiner Theile."[1] Yet this same Schiller, hardly seven months earlier, confesses that his celebrated description of a whirlpool in *Der Taufer* is a study not from nature but from Homer. "Ich habe diese Natur nirgends als etwa bei einer Mühle studiren können, aber weil ich Homers Beschreibung von der Charybde genau studirte, so hat mich dieses vielleicht bei der Natur erhalten."[2] If Schiller could copy Homer to such effect while developing a theme alien to the *Iliad* and *Odyssey*, what should we expect from a rhapsodist, speaking the same language, one of a long line of imitators, and bound by honour and interest to continue and prolong the inspiration of the master? So we are tempted to suppose that there was once one poet who devoted his genius to the subject of the Trojan war (probably dealing with the part played by Achilles) and who developed this powerful, simple style, which somehow suggests and conserves the joy in human greatness. His enthusiasm was so great and his gift of expression so irresistible, that other poets have caught his spirit and manner. Thus the Δολώνεια retains the grimness and naïve enthusiasm of the earlier poetry and the ὁπλοποιία has all the Homeric art of starting with a simple theme and of then multiplying it and filling it so completely with enthusiasm that the description may pass the widest bounds of possibility, and yet satisfy the reader's mood and hold him captive.

Yet the student who can acquiesce in these opinions without searchings of heart must indeed be girt with triple bronze. The weight of authority is too heavily against him. Even if he ignores the men of his own generation or nationality as being for either of those reasons subject to error, he will hesitate when he finds how many of the great foreigners of the past insisted on the unity of Homer. Goethe, who closely studied both the *Iliad* and the *Odyssey* with a view to composing an epic on the events which lie between, replied to one of Schiller's letters already quoted, "Ich bin mehr als jemals von der Einheit und Untheilbarkeit des Gedichts überzeugt, und es lebt über-

---

[1] 27th April, 1798.　　　　　[2] An Goethe, 6 Oct. 1797.

haupt kein Mensch mehr und wird nicht wieder geboren
werden, der es zu beurtheilen in Stande wäre."[1] Welcker admitted that the original source of the two poems was to be
found in prehistoric lays and he could not deny that the inter-
polator had been at work on the finished text, but he insisted
that the real formative influence was the man of genius who
gave them their shape and impressed them with his personality[2].
Terret, in the preface to his immense work[3], concludes that
"l'opinion traditionnelle de l'antiquité qui attribue à son seul
Homère l'Iliade et l'Odyssée se concilie parfaitement avec les
découvertes les plus récentes de l'archéologie et de la philo-
logie." Andrew Lang, who gave up most of his industrious life
to the study of early poetry, wrote two able books to establish
the unity of each poem[4]. Raffaele Onorato, without attempting
to discuss the textual and archeological difficulties of the
problem, has taken in hand to prove the artistic coherence of
the *Iliad*: "nella sua orditura fondamentale di contenenza
e di forma,"[5] and even claims that what Aristotle calls τὸ
ἄλογον, the "irrazionale" of Fraccaroli[6], is really the result
of poetic insight and not of multiple authorship.

IV. *These technical questions are important because they involve
something bigger: the relationship of "Homer" to the progress
of thought and emotion. So it is proposed to see how the idea
of the hero developed in post-Homeric times; thus leading us
to the next stage of this inquiry.*

So the problem of Homeric authorship is as far removed
from certainty as the problem of date. Any of the theories
stated may be the right one; all may contain some element of
truth, but the student will be swayed in his final choice as much
by temperament and inclination as by reason. None of the
current opinions can be established by irrefutable evidence.
It is hoped that frank and frequent discussion, while sharpening

---

[1] 16th May, 1798.
[2] *Der epische Cyclus oder die homerischen Dichter*, 1st ed. 1835–49.
[3] *Homère: étude historique et critique*, 1899.
[4] *Homer and the Epic*, 1893; *Homer and his Age*, 1906.
[5] *L'Iliade di Omero: Saggio di Analisi Critica*, 1919.
[6] *L'Irrazionale nella Letteratura*, 1903.

the intellect, will stimulate thought on these subjects and encourage ingenious speculation till the truth at last appears—
confessa dea. No one would wish to see these efforts relaxed, but
it is difficult to believe that the key to Homer can be found,
till we have amassed far more positive information about the
Heroic Age and the evolution of its poetry. While awaiting these
discoveries, if indeed the material still remains to be found,
is there not some other line of investigation which will lead us
towards a closer intimacy with the greatest and most complete
epic in the world? After all, why do we investigate the historicity
of Homer? It is not only from motives of literary curiosity.
We also want to understand the mental effort. There is a kind
of chronology quite distinct from dates. It consists in tracing
the successive steps by which different civilisations reach the
same stages of moral and intellectual freedom. Each race seems
to ascend by similarly ordered gradations and each progress
can be compared and in a sense synchronised, however widely
the processions are separated in place and time. We want to
see what milestones, on such a course, are marked by the
Homeric poems. Archeology and linguistic study supply the
surest data in these speculations. But failing certainty in such
fields, is there no other means of nearing our goal?

Fortunately mankind in his ceaseless journey from generation to generation does not leave traces of his march only in
rusted weapons, broken pottery, relics of brooches, rings,
images. After digging in the stratified deposits of buried fortresses or palaces, among charred fragments of masonry and
the outlines of foundations, there are still other ways of un-
covering the past. Vanished civilisations also leave relics of
their beliefs, obsessions and ideals, often embedded in later
thoughts, like fossilised remains, which can be extracted from
their strata and pieced together into an outline of some forgotten age. They are the shapes and substances into which
human sentiment has formed itself. We have already endeavoured by these means to trace the moral and religious
effort which lies hidden in the *Iliad*, and we have seen how far
the Achean's attitude to himself depended on his attitude to
God. We have also seen that the *Odyssey*, apart from its story,

contains traces of a different effort. The hero has other virtues and accomplishments; he is no longer possessed by the same mood; he seems to respond to a different idealism. Does the *Odyssey*, then, mark a fresh stage in man's pilgrimage through the world? To answer that question we must look further into the history of man's emotions and religious thought. A solution is worth finding. For, in effect, we are asking whether epic inspiration, one of the most wonderful manifestations of human greatness, is the product of one age only in each national civilisation—dependent on a certain type of warlike society— or, rather, is a spirit running through succeeding ages of culture, adapting its energy to their varying needs, and finding expression as often as the forces of progress make themselves felt. Besides, in asking whether the *Odyssey* is a separate link in this chain, we shall be led on to the next stage of our inquiry. We shall see how the Homeric warrior gradually developed into the intellectual hero and how epic inspiration sometimes continued in an altered form, and sometimes failed.

CHAPTER VI

THE RISE OF THE INTELLECTUAL HERO

WE begin this chapter with the question "Is Odysseus really one of the old glorious race of Acheans, facing a situation different from anything at Troy, but quite congenial to the ideals of that strenuous ambitious time? Or has he been transferred to some later less confident age, where life presents more difficulties because men have developed finer faculties and subtler perceptions?" To solve this problem we must apply some test, and we shall find the touchstone which we require in the study of comparative religions. But it will not be enough to examine different systems in a theological or ethnological spirit and so trace the transference, survival and metamorphosis of deities from one civilisation to another. The problem before the student of literature is not only nor chiefly to investigate the ways in which men worship God. Indeed few things are more difficult to estimate than the symbolism under which any race has prefigured the powers above it. What we have to examine is the elbow-room which man has left for his own energy after satisfying his apprehensions of the supernatural. How much of himself do the gods leave to man, after exacting their own due? How does his consciousness of himself develop under the weight of theocracy? Such an inquiry may at first seem nebulous, unsatisfying and alarmingly attractive to figures of rhetoric. But in reality it will be found eminently adaptable to scientific treatment, and from the not unplentiful data there will emerge a test which can be applied consistently and which penetrates to the core of the most varied civilisations.

I. *The standard of humanism which men reached under the religion of the* Iliad; *another aspect of Homeric civilisation (cf. ante, chap.* III).

Let us begin by recalling the features of the *Iliad*. We have noticed that the warriors still hold fast to their belief in Fate. They are persuaded that the span of their lives is controlled by an independent power and cannot be shortened or lengthened

9-2

by the caprice of any other hostile or friendly deity. Even when Hektor discovered that Athene had tricked him into a duel with Achilles, he recognised that this deity was after all only an instrument of destiny[1]. At the same time the poet, and so his audiences, have advanced a stage beyond this conception. Their beliefs are becoming monotheistic. They cannot yet satisfy their imagination with the thought of a single god; in fact Olympos is crowded with "proud limitary" deities. But they are convinced that one stately and imposing power controls the affairs of the sky and the earth and might be expected to dominate the designs of the Three Spinning Maidens also. Zeus as we have seen is no animistic spirit but the last of a series of Olympian rulers, perhaps the representative of the northern invasion. By force and by judicious alliances he has deposed Kronos, and has arrived at a kind of stable triumvirate between himself and the rulers of the sea and the nether world. Though the poet of the *Iliad* seems to have been familiar with tales of early struggles and discords among the immortal powers, those old turbulent times are hardly remembered. Zeus has established his rule in his own element beyond serious question, by his superior skill, strength and wisdom. We have even a glimpse[2] of that Tartaros which Hesiod describes as the prison house of the monsters of the old uncivilised world. Probably Zeus's authority would have stood unquestioned in the province governed by Fate as elsewhere, had not the confidence in Destiny proved to be one of the chief comforts and mainstays of men in times of war. So, on the whole, the Olympian Thunderer proves ready to relinquish or unable to retain the control over mortals' length of life, while he enjoys the absolute disposal of their fortunes and destinies. He is the bestower of victory or defeat, prosperity or adversity, and is continually plotting and contriving events to produce the results which he has preordained.

In what mood and with what thoughts is man expected to face this attitude of the Great Immortal? The answer, as we have seen, is twofold. The warriors themselves have no anxious fears about his designs. They do not recognise any perplexing

[1] *Il.* xxii, 297–305.   [2] *Ibid.* xx, 61–5.

and disheartening mystery in the workings of the divine purpose. They expect the Olympian monarch to make his will
clear to the dwellers of earth, and in the main their expectation
is justified. Apollo descends from Heaven to warn Patroklos; a
horse is endowed with speech to settle the doubts of Achilles;
Zeus is known to declare his purposes by dreams or by auguries
which, for the most part, need only imagination and experience to interpret. Thus the warriors themselves labour
under few or no doubts. But the poets are not so satisfied that
the Olympians are all straightforward friends or enemies of
man. The chief events in the *Iliad* arise through the gods
misleading men. Driven by their passion for fame, mortals
blindly hasten to accomplish a divine purpose, quite different
from what they themselves desire. Even the lesser deities are
to a certain extent deceived. In fact the irony of the situation
is so apparent to the modern world, that people have sometimes been tempted to interpret the *Iliad* as a satire on human
destiny. Homer certainly never intended to go to that length,
for the deceptions practised on man are not represented as
complete. Except in that one glorious evening of triumph,
Hektor is not tricked into forgetting that his own and his
city's doom are sealed. Even when the Achean fortunes are
at their lowest, a portent intimates that victory will yet incline
to their side. In fact the poem represents some state in Achean
culture when the poets have still half gained or retained an
epic confidence in the will of the gods. They realise in how
portentous a sense Zeus is ἀγκυλομήτης; and while they feel
the urgent necessity for reading the will of heaven, they begin
to lose confidence in the accustomed methods.

So as regards the mortals, they are very far from considering
themselves the masters of creation. But they are equally far
from regarding the warrior caste as mere playthings of the
gods. In fact their greatness seems to arise out of the uncertainty of their position. Even deities can still be persuaded,
cajoled, influenced, won as friends. Nothing is beyond hope
and effort, except the certainty of death. We have already
seen what self-respect and pride of life developed under these
beliefs. It should also be noticed that the warriors had reached

no mean level of civilisation. They admired and appreciated eloquence hardly less than Hesiod himself[1], and with good reason, since the fate of an expedition, perhaps of a dynasty, might depend on some speaker's power of conducting an embassy or swaying the Assembly[2]. Again, though valour is of such supreme importance in an age of warfare, the heroes are sufficiently civilised to use their reason when facing danger. They have reached the stage at which men calculate the strength of their opponent, before engaging him, and weigh the risk with the chance of success. They not only shrink from a warrior when aided by a god or daemon, as much as did Sigvaldi[3] some twenty centuries later; they give way before superior forces and even admit the folly of engaging a warrior who is recognised to be their superior.

Such characteristics seem to denote a complex development. But it should be remembered that they arise only in connection with war. Apart from strategy and tactics, the Homeric mentality betrays a child-like simplicity. Their poets seem quite content with a disappointingly naïve explanation of the supernatural and they represent their warriors as even less speculative. Apparently we have before us one of those short-lived epochs (to be noticed several times in the course of this work) in which civilisation has reached an equilibrium. Theory corresponds to practice, ideals are satisfied in conduct and there results a kind of sensitised materialism, soon to disappear as life fills itself with fresh dangers and disillusionments.

II. *The Age of Hesiod compared with the Age of the* Iliad. *Men appreciate the gods more and themselves less. They tend more and more to admire craft and astuteness.*

Let us now pass over the *Odyssey* for the time being and look forward to the so-called Age of Hesiod; yet perhaps not so very far forward as the poet of *The Works and Days* cannot be more recent than the end of the eighth century, and may be far older. Of course we shall at once notice many conspicuous

---

[1] *Il.* III, 204–24.   [2] Cf. *ibid.* II and IX.
[3] *Jomsvikinga Saga*, Cap. 44 (tenth century A.D.).

differences. Hesiod represents the attitude of the settled land-owner. His father left Aiolia and settled in Boiotia, not as a dispossessed tyrant or fugitive involved in a blood-feud, but simply as an agriculturist[1]. At the same time the necessary differences which arise from occupation and interest can easily be over-rated. Even if the heroes in the Troad are not repre-sented as engaged in agriculture or cattle rearing, some of them owned broad acres and were rich in flocks and herds. The fiercest warriors depended to a large extent on the labours of the farmer and shepherd and many of the similes prove that the poets and their audiences were familiar with rural pursuits.

In one respect Hesiod, or any other farmer poet, was bound to differ from a warrior, whatever their respective circumstances or temperament. Whereas a soldier need fear disaster only to himself and even then only if his armour failed him and the Fates or Zeus were hostile to himself or his comrades, the lands-man could suffer in a hundred ways in every field that he had sown or head of cattle that he had reared. From the earliest time to the present day, the tiller of the soil or the breeder of livestock depends on innumerable influences outside his control or calculation, and thus rural districts harbour such diversity of superstitions, just as soldiers up to the present time believe in Fate and Chance. In fact some communities were so conscious of the multiplicity of gods and of the difficulty of knowing which one to appease, that they set up altars to the "Unknown God," at Phaleron, Olympia and Athens, in order to cover every eventuality, and sometimes victims for sacrifice were let loose to roam, till they indicated the deity who demanded worship, by stopping near the haunt of some god or spirit[2]. If the reader prefers some concrete example, he has only to turn to the description of the winds in the *Theognis*[3] and ask himself how many of these considerations would trouble any soldier of Agamemnon's army, and even then only when crossing the sea. So we are not surprised to find that Hesiod recognises far more influences to propitiate than does Homer,

[1] *Works and Days*, 637.
[2] Frazer has collected similar examples from savage races. See note on Paus. i, i, 4; *Transl.* vol. ii, pp. 33–4.
[3] ll. 870–85.

that he is far more careful of ritual and of taboo, and more distrustful of human confidence.

But there is another fundamental difference between Hesiod and Homer. The former is possessed by the sense of degeneracy. This sentiment is due to the lapse of time and is passed down the ages in ever increasing volume[1]. It is sometimes argued that the material with which Hesiod deals belongs to the most ancient Boiotian culture, and represents the thoughts of Minyans, Ionians or Mykenaians. Such may well be the case and we shall discover throughout the post-Achean or Dorian Age a tendency to revive the most ancient beliefs and traditions. But we shall also find that the spirit in which they are received is apparently not so old. Hesiod himself, in his celebrated description of the Five Generations[2], admits that he does not belong to the Heroic Age, the ἀνδρῶν ἡρώων θεῖον γένος, but to the γένος σιδήρεον, the common folk who employ the metal of husbandry and endure the settled peaceful life in which the evils of civilisation appear. The contrast must have been like that between Odd, the adventurous and lordly colonist and Ufeig, his crafty and underhanded but utterly indispensable father in *Bandamanna Saga*. The feeling is summed up in the *Contest of Homer and Hesiod*, which belongs to a still later age. When Hesiod asks

πιστεῦσαι δὲ βροτοῖς ποῖον χρέος ἄξιόν ἐστιν;

Homer answers

οἷς αὐτὸς κίνδυνος ἐπὶ πραχθεῖσιν ἕπεται[3].

Yes, danger brings out the steadfastness of man in action, but now that bracing influence has vanished, and as a result the age has lost the virtues as well as the vices of the warrior caste-spirit. So we hear much of the meaner and more plebeian faults of human nature[4], and especially of the lack of mutual confidence. On the other hand it is an established article of faith that the heroes and demi-gods have for ever passed away, either slain at Troy and Thebes or summoned by Zeus to dwell apart from mortals at the uttermost bounds of the earth[5].

[1] *Post*, vol. II, chap. IX, § 1.   [2] *Works and Days*, 109 ff.   [3] P. 321.
[4] *Works and Days*, 156–60, 171–201.   [5] *Ibid.* 160–70.

In the *Catalogue of Women*[1] we are told that Zeus resolved to slay all the demi-gods, so that the descendants of deities should no longer mate with mortals.

The next feature of the Hesiodic era is the advance which has been made towards monotheism. In the invocation to the *Works and Days*, Zeus is recognised as the deity who really controls the race of men, belittling the proud and exalting the humble. Powers, no less extensive, are suggested in the *Iliad*, but by now they are insisted upon and given prominence. As his position grows more assured, the deity himself becomes more mysterious. Clement of Alexandria has preserved a fragment in which the poet declares that no one now knows the mind of Zeus[2]. By the time that the *Theognis* was composed the Fates are no longer described as powers outside his sway[3]. They are his daughters by Themis and support him in the war against the earlier elemental forces.

Here, as we should expect, we find that men have not changed their ideas of their gods without changing their idea of themselves. We have already discussed the strain of melancholy[4] which is supposed to have run through Greek epic poetry and we have found that the sadness arose chiefly out of contrast with the fortune of the immortal gods. But in the age of Hesiod self-pity has sunk much deeper into human sentiment. Since the mid-nineteenth century we have become so used to regard the race as a succession of generations steadily ascending from humble and tentative beginnings, that we find it difficult to realise the attitude of people possessed by the contrary opinion. Nor can we easily realise how the circumstances of their lives contributed towards these mournful reflections. The few thinkers and humanists at the beginning of the Dark Ages were strengthened in their conviction of Original Sin, when, amid their surrounding desolation, they became aware of the ruined monuments of Roman splendour and greatness, like relics of some giant race which had passed from the earth[5]. In much the same way, the contemporaries

---

[1] II, frags. numbered 4–10.   [2] *Stromateis*, v, p. 259.
[3] *Theog.* 901 ff.   [4] *Ante*, chap. II, § 6.
[5] *E.g. The Wanderer*, 87; *Andreas*, 1492.

of Hesiod and of the so-called *Homeric Hymns* must have been
further convinced of their decadence when they not only saw
or heard tell of the cyclopean structures of the Mykenaian
Age, but seem also frequently to have discovered the bones
of huge extinct animals whom they could not help believing
to be the remains of heroes and giants. So strong was this
belief that even in quite late times the bones of heroes used to
be exhumed and identified[1]. In addition to these reminders of
the greatness which they had lost, there was the ever present
necessity for unremitting labour, because of the many failures,
miscalculations, improvidences and supernatural interferences
attendant on agricultural life. And so there grew up the belief
that the gifts of the gods are baneful things, if possible to be
avoided, as Prometheus warned his brother[2], but generally to
be borne with resignation[3]. So we are not surprised to find
that the more men felt their own littleness, the more they
reverenced the gods. Perhaps a period of earthquakes and
eruptions may have increased their dread and helped to burn
into their consciousness the belief in giants and monsters. For
as Hesiod says in the fragment quoted by Plato, ἵνα γὰρ δέος
ἔνθα καὶ αἰδώς[4].

What virtues did these generations most admire? In answering
this question, we should consider the probability that the
Dorians may have conquered the Acheans, partly as the
Normans conquered the Saxons, by superior ingenuity. We
know that the two ideals of the Spartan training were bodily
endurance, amounting to self-mutilation, and deceitfulness.
Neither quality is conspicuous in the *Iliad*, but both are
noticeable in the legends of a later age, especially cunning.
No doubt there were still enthusiasts who affirmed that the
race of Herakles should not make war by stratagems, but the
greater number seem already to have learnt, as Lysander
phrased it later, "to sew the fox's skin on to the lion's skin."[5]
It will be remembered how scrupulously just the Homeric

---

[1] *E.g.* Orestes, Herod. I, 68; Pelops, Paus. v, xiii, 4; the Indian god
Orontes, *ibid.* viii, xix, 4; the giant Hopladamos, *ibid.* viii, xxxii, 5; Hyllos,
ibid. I, xxxv, 6.

[2] *Works and Days*, 85–8.   [3] *Hymn to Demeter*, 147–8, 217.
[4] *Euthyphron*, 12 A.   [5] Plut. *Lys.* vii.

warriors were about drawing lots. But when the three Dorian conquerors were dividing the Peloponnese, Kresphontes threw in a clod of earth, instead of a stone, so that the other two pebbles must perforce arise and he have the first choice[1]. We shall shortly have occasion to notice that in the *Theognis*, Zeus is endowed with all the wiles of a statesman, but the most famous example of this propensity is the *Ode to Hermes*, which reads at first like a *fabliau* and in its picturesque and rather humorous story allegorises the qualities indispensable to an age of chaffering and internal development, as well as the arts of a subject race.

III. *This transition marks the beginning of what we might call the age of intelligence. Under the pressure of altered requirements, very ancient stories assume a new importance and are endowed with a fresh significance.*

A change of spirit was coming over the prehistoric Hellenic world, producing an attitude of mind not unlike that which prepared the way for Christianity in Northern Europe. It will be shown in a later chapter[2] how the Teutonic races, which accepted the new faith, were yielding, at any rate in some avowed cases, to the desire for a more penetrating and comprehensive explanation of life and destiny. Now that their position was more settled, they were beginning to be involved in the difficulties of civilised existence. Their culture was becoming more artistic and magnificent, but at the same time more complex. For both reasons, they had grown too intelligent to be satisfied with the old mythological explanation of things. The generations which followed the Dorian Conquest seem also to have become more thoughtful and introspective. As such, we should expect their taste for epics and stories to change. But how comes it that these post-Homeric Ages seem to have reverted to the earlier and more primitive kind of legends? A similar phenomenon appears in the Middle Ages. Such epics as *Beowulf*, *Waltharius*, *Chanson de Roland* are practically untouched by most of the primeval and superstitious traditions which are collected and discussed in *The Younger Edda*, or

[1] Apoll. *Bibl.* II, viii, 4.   [2] Vol. II, chap. II, § 6; chap. III, §§ 2, 3.

Saxo's *Historia*, which form the basis of such romances as *Gawayne and the Green Knight*, and are surprisingly familiar to Malory and the courtly narratives from which he compiled his book. So in ancient Greece we find the newer generations embracing legends and tales which must have existed long before the Age of Homer, and which the poets of the *Iliad* and the *Odyssey* almost certainly knew but ignored. For instance we are told nothing of the origin of Areion, the immortal steed of Adrastos[1], or of the battle of the cranes and pigmies[2]; or of the more barbaric and inhuman proceedings connected with the concealment and upbringing of Zeus, and of the conquest of Kronos[3]. These ancient tales were apparently known but passed over in silence, as being unworthy of audiences who first listened to the fame of Achilles. Yet these, and such-like stories, must have proved wholly acceptable to the ages following the Dorian Conquest. Although so unmistakeably primitive they must have appealed to the generations which were becoming more sophisticated. Otherwise they could not have survived in such abundance till Pindar, Apollodoros, Hyginos, Pausanias, Vergil and Ovid collected them and gave them permanence, nor would so many of them have served the Athenian tragedians.

One is tempted to explain this revival as being simply the third or the last of the four stages of epic evolution so well set forth by Professor Chadwick[4]. But when we attempt to classify this material according to any of these four stages of evolution, we find that an immense body of lore and legend seems hardly to fit exactly into any one compartment. We are apt to forget that several stages must occasionally have been in operation at the same time. In the *Odyssey* we find that the Achean tradition is still strong, but that another mass of legend and folklore, immeasurably older, has risen to the surface, while all the time the demand for novelty is so insistent that the suitors have already grown tired of the stories which Telemachos could remember.

[1] *Il.* xxiii, 346.   [2] *Ibid.* iii, 3.

[3] *Ibid.* Many other cases of expurgation are discussed by Murray in *Rise of the Greek Epic*, chap. v.

[4] *The Heroic Age*, chap. v.

So it is with the type of legend which has been preserved
for us by the poets and folklorists both of ancient Greece and
of medieval Europe. At some time and in some form they may
have been recited by popular minstrels or handed down from
father to son among peasants and traders. And yet they are
a great deal more than fables which circulated among serfs
and helots; old wives' tales or monstrous imaginings, which
have survived from the dawn of time, because they could stir
crass and narrow intelligences. The legends preserved by
Apollodoros and the epitomisers of the Homeric Cycle (to
mention no others) have ceased to be primitive. They have
changed their character and they have undergone a vigorous
process of selection. But the influences to which they have
been subjected do not qualify them for any special audience
to be classified as warriors, or farmers or townsfolk. On the
one hand the tales are profoundly pessimistic; they emphasise
the wickedness and demoralisation of man, his helplessness
before the terrific powers of nature, his dependence on mocking
and ironical deities, who take pleasure in mystifying mortals.
On the other hand they glorify the only powers that will save
human beings in this desperate plight: intelligence, resourcefulness and the ability to discern the hidden purposes of
Providence. Such a purport cannot very well have been given
to the tales by the fabulists who collected them in a later age.
As we have seen, the poetry of Hesiod describes the awakening
of this spirit, and it was probably for this reason that emphasis
was laid on the truthfulness of the Boiotian as compared with
the falsity of Homer[1]. Besides, we shall be able to trace the
continuous development of the mood down to the time of
Herodotos. We have before us, undoubtedly, the ideal of the
post-Homeric hero. Dr Leaf[2] has very aptly characterised this
phenomenon as the fusion of the new and old; the blending
of the "folklore of the autochthons with the epic spirit of
Homer." No doubt some such interchange of sentiments took
place. But this transformation must also have been accompanied by the fusion and recasting of classes. In the obscure

---

[1] *Theognis*, 27 ff. *Contest of Homer and Hesiod, passim.*
[2] *Homer and History*, chap. VIII.

welter of races and ambitions which has clouded this unexplored age, some new type must have risen to the surface,
perhaps by virtue of race, but more likely through innate
ability. We hope to show that the surviving fragments of literature, even if their earliest germ is in the Stone Age, are the
record of what this aristocracy thought and felt.

IV. *These stories insist on the wickedness and weakness of man,
on the disillusionments which accompany experience, on the
dangers which encompass existence, and on the supreme need
of insight, ingenuity and foreknowledge. The legends of Prometheus and Teiresias in these connections.*

Let us examine a little more closely the kind of mythology
and folklore which seem to have been appreciated at this
period. We notice at once a surprising insistence on vice and
crime. Many of these originated in some ancient tradition of
cannibalism, and might have been expected to pass into forgetfulness with the practices which they illustrated. For instance,
we learn how the sons of Lykaon entertained Zeus in human
form and, in order to test his divinity, gave him human flesh
mixed with other meat, and thus drew down on themselves
the vengeance of his thunderbolts[1]. Or how Prokne, aided by
her sister Philomela, killed her son Itys and served him up to
her husband Tereus[2]. Perhaps the most striking example of all
is the story of the "Thyestian banquet" from which the sun
averted his gaze, and which occasioned the ill-omened flight
to the court of Thesprotos, and all the dismal sequence of
incest, assassination and deception, extending to the second
generation[3]. A tale of such horror could not have been attached
to the ruling house of Mykenai, till after the fall of the strong-
hold, and whether first applied out of hatred and disgust, must
have persisted for other reasons. It will be noticed that in every
story the crime appears in its most horrible and pathetic form—
a parent eats his child, and does so unwittingly; and secondly
the criminal is really the victim of a plot—he is rendered

---

[1] Hyg. CLXXVI.
[2] Apoll. *Bibl.* III, xiv, 8; Ovid, *Metam.* VI, 580 ff.
[3] Apoll. *Epit.* II, 13 ff.; Paus. II, xviii, 1; Hyg. *Fab.* 87, 88.

guilty by the machinations of others. Apparently the stories gratified a horror of sin and at the same time emphasised how unexpectedly the most heinous acts might be committed.

This tendency to arrive at an ulterior meaning will be seen in tales arising out of some recollection of human sacrifice. Medeia restored Aison to youth by draining off his old blood and by infusing into his veins her magic potions[1]; and induced the daughters of Pelias to murder their father with the assurance that they could bring him back to life and even to immortality by a ritual of boiling water[2]. When Pelops had been murdered and served up to the gods as food by Tantalos, his father, they restored him in the same way[3]. In these few examples, chosen out of many, it is noticeable that the element of depravity and crime is retained and that the aboriginal and now discredited basis of the story is ignored. In its place, our attention is turned to the possibility of immortality. This feature is extremely suggestive. The heroes of the *Iliad* did not expect to live for ever. Even Thetis, for all her mother's care, had no thought of rendering her darling son immune from death. But as we explore the remains of post-Homeric literature, we find that the idea has grown familiar. There is frequent mention of drugs and other antidotes which suddenly heal wounds or restore life; and heroes such as Herakles are raised to the status of gods after their career on earth is ended. Again, as the idea of Hades becomes clearer, and is more fully developed, other very ancient stories, connected with the revival of vegetation in springtime, grow into accounts of how persons were actually fetched back alive from the abode of the dead. Hyginos has collected a considerable list[4]. Probably these and such-like stories were remembered and repeated in this form because men were growing more and more dissatisfied, restless and inventive. They could not help changing their lot, at any rate in imagination.

It is characteristic of the age, that as men came to recognise the possibility of immortality, they began to suspect it. Sarpedon, it will be remembered, wished without hoping to

---

[1] Ovid, *Metam.* VII, 251.   [2] *Ibid.* 297 ff.   [3] Pindar, *Olymp.* I, 26.
[4] CCLI. For full discussion of this subject see *post*, chap. VII, § 4.

live for ever. Odysseus declined the honour because it would
involve certain loss of home and kingdom. Apollo offered the
Sybil immortality if she would surrender to him her virginity,
and then offered to grant any other request as proof of his
sincerity. She asked to live as many years as there were grains
in a certain heap of sand, and had already endured seven
hundred winters of ever increasing age when she told Aeneas
the tale[1]. Tithonos suffered to the full the bitterness of immortality, and so did Cheiron till Prometheus consented to
assume the onerous privilege[2]. These stories must, in some
cases, have survived as an answer to the aspirations of an earlier
time—the comment of experience on the dreams of youth.
Whatever the horrors of death, they seem to have dreaded
yet more a continuation of the complexities and disillusionments of life.

And with good reason. In addition to a sense of degeneracy,
the people of this time seem to have been acutely conscious
of physical dangers, and therefore to have taken so deep an
interest in the Nemean lion, the Parnassian lion, the serpents
swarming in Greece, the boars at Kalydon, Erymanthos and
Krommyon. It is likely that these monsters first appeared in
pre-Homeric epics of Minoan origin, and represent how
Southern Greece was cleared and settled by the explorers from
Crete. There is certainly an atmosphere of heroism about the
feats, and we find that similar themes figure conspicuously in
early northern poetry[3]. So we might be content to conclude
that these survivals were reconstructed into the epic of the
Dorian Age, as we shall find that the Anglo-Saxons did with
Beowulf[4], except that no finished poetry of this type and period
has survived, and what literature we do possess is so different
in tone. So it seems that the persistence of these legends should
be interpreted as one more indication of man's sense of insecurity. Such was the impression which they made on
Pausanias. Though a sceptic, inclined to believe that the old
story-tellers veiled their true meaning in allegory[5], he has no

[1] Ovid, *Metam.* xiv, 130.   [2] Apoll. *Bibl.* ii, v, 4.
[3] *Post*, vol. ii, chap. ii, § 2.   [4] *Post*, vol. ii, chap. i, § 3.
[5] i. viii. 3. Plut. records the theory that Phaia, the wild sow of Krommyon,
was an obscene and murderous woman who lived by brigandage, *Vit. Thes.* ix.

difficulty in believing that these formidable creatures once existed and were cherished by some deity as an affliction to mankind[1]. Besides, unlike the slayer of Grendel, Perseus, Herakles, Theseus and Laomedon do not overcome the wild beasts without divine aid. In this connection one cannot help recalling the stories of how jealously the gods guarded the barrier placed between themselves and mortals, and how swift they were to punish human self-sufficiency. Alkyone and Keyx perished δι᾽ ὑπερηφάνειαν; for Alkyone claimed Zeus for her husband and Keyx claimed Here for his wife[2]. Perhaps the most memorable example is the fate of Niobe who dared to challenge comparison with Latona.

But if the myths and legends which we are discussing made nothing of human strength and self-sufficiency, they placed enormous value on human brain power. It is worth noting that such feats as the cleansing of Augeias's cattleyard, the slaying of the Hydra and the Stymphalian birds, or the bringing back of the apples of the Hesperides, in which Atlas was induced to help, could not have been accomplished without cunning and resourcefulness. Among the most primitive savages we find stories current of how some god started the human race by moulding figures out of earth or clay. We have seen[3] why such a legend continued throughout the Heroic Age, but how was it that so unambitious a theory captivated the imagination of men till the age of Perikles? Partly no doubt in reaction from the dogma of divine descent, but also because the miracle was associated with Prometheus[4]. This mysterious figure was once merely the son of Iapetos and Klymene and brother to Atlas, but his memory lives as the prototype and god of a new order. He does not wield power, nor seek dominion; on the contrary he is the enemy of force and the breaker of privilege. His influence lies with the humbler, more industrious folk of a later age who rely on the knowledge of arts and inventions and are resigned to suffering while working out a dream of progress. It should also be remembered that Prometheus had a knowledge of the future. In tracing

[1] I, xxvii, 9.
[3] *Ante*, chap. III, § 3.
[2] Apoll. *Bibl.* I, vii, 4.
[4] Apoll. *Bibl.* I, vii, 1.

the development of ideas we shall see how this power was more
and more highly prized and eagerly sought for. It becomes the
most valued and the most uncertain of human possessions. So
it is significant that Prometheus knows the secret on which
the Jovian dynasty depends[1], and according to one version
obtained his release after thirty years, thanks to this prescience.
The legend of Daidalos is also worth noting. The story as told
by Ovid[2] is the least satisfying part of the fable. The real
charm of the adventure comes in the sequel. Minos was deter-
mined to recover the escaped artificer so he followed him,
proclaiming everywhere a rich reward to anyone who could
thread a certain spiral shell. Kokalos the tyrant of Kamikos
in Sicily undertook the task, and after a hole had been bored
in the shell an ant was introduced with a fine thread
attached. Minos recognised the hand of the master in this
device and demanded the surrender of Daidalos[3].

We have noticed that the only man of intellect in the *Iliad*
was Machaon, famous for his skill in surgery. Eustathios,
in his commentary on that very passage[4], quotes Arktinos in
the *Iliou Persis* repeating this praise of the Homeric leech,
but (in the light of the requirements of more modern culture)
adds that the other physician Podaleirios, whose name is twice
coupled with that of Machaon[5], had a profounder knowledge
and was able to diagnose secret diseases and cure maladies
which seemed past help. It was he who first detected the seeds
of madness in Aias's past rage. This Podaleirios, because of
his science and skill, became a myth, almost a cult. Pausanias
saw his portrait painted on the temple of Messene, side by
side with that of Machaon because both had been at the
Trojan war[6]. Stephanus Byzantius says that he healed the
princess of Karia who had fallen from a roof and after receiving
her in marriage founded two cities. According to Lykophron
he died and was buried in Apulia and those who slept on sheep-
skins on his tomb were visited in dreams by his ghost and so
learnt the future[7]. It has already been suggested that this

---

[1] Hyg. *Fab.* 54.   [2] *Metam.* 183–235.   [3] Apoll. *Epit.* I, 14, 15.
[4] *Il.* XIII, 515.   [5] *Ibid.* II, 732; XI, 833.   [6] IV, XXX, 12.
[7] *Cassandra*, 1047 ff. See Frazer, *Transl. of Pausanias*, note on III, XXVI, 10,
vol. III, p. 403.

period resembled the Middle Ages, and we shall find that Vergil, like Podaleirios, was first admired as a man of profound learning and wisdom, and then venerated as a superman, a magician and a source of prophetic knowledge. In neither case was this worship confined to the superstitions of the common folk, as Dr Leaf suggests with reference to Vergil[1]. In the case of the Greek it was an established cult.

From the earliest times there seems to have existed the peculiar obsessions known as lycanthropy and cynanthropy, under which the patient imagines himself to be a wolf, a dog, a fox or a cow. These delusions must have been connected in some way with the totemistic worship of animals[2], and they might have been expected to cease with that superstition. Yet we find that such fables, generally based on the metamorphosis of men into beasts, retained their hold on the imagination for centuries, because they gratified curiosity and gave an insight into the mystery of things. Among the best known is the legend of how the gods, terrified at Typhoios, fled to Egypt and disguised themselves as animals[3]. But the story which most completely typifies the ideas of this period is the fable of Teiresias. Homer, though aware of his blindness, makes no inquiry into the cause. Long before Homer's time there was a belief that it is unlucky to see two animals mating, especially serpents[4]. There was also an interest, certainly existing in post-Homeric times, in the relative intensity of love in man and in woman. So Teiresias, after seeing two huge serpents together, was first changed into a woman and seven years later was changed back into a man. Thus he experienced the passions of both sexes, and when summoned by Jupiter and Juno to decide which loved most, he pronounced in favour of the male. But in this latter age deities never hold communion with mortals

---

[1] *Homer and History*, chap. VIII. For a study of the full extent of Vergil's reputation, see Comparetti, *Vergilio nel medio aevo*.

[2] See W. H. Roscher, "Das von Kynanthropie handelnde Fragment des Marcellus von Side" in *Abhandlungen der philolog. histor. Classe der k. Sächs. Gesell. der Wissenschaften*, vol. XVII (1896), no. 3 (pp. 3–92), and Frazer's note, Paus. X, xxx, 1, *Transl.* vol. V, p. 381.

[3] Ovid, *Metam.* V, 325; Apoll. *Bibl.* I, vi, 3; Hyg. *Fab.* 152.

[4] For copious examples, see Frazer, note on Apoll. *Bibl.* III, vi, 7, Loeb Classics, vol. I, p. 365.

unless they leave behind some memory of their immeasureable superiority. So the goddess struck him with blindness and the god consoled him with the gift of prophecy[1].

Many other stories seem to have survived, because they offered a figurative explanation of familiar facts or objects: how the hyacinth and anemone came to grow[2]; how the aconite first sprang from the foam which Kerberos scattered, when dragged up from Hell[3]. But these aetiological myths are too plentiful and familiar to need discussing in detail, and besides they serve only to indicate the general tendency of the time and to help us to re-create the atmosphere. Can we not find direct evidence from narrative poems of action? Has not some "pre-Attic" poet represented a hero faced with a great task—it matters not what—involving a sense of the worthlessness and defencelessness of man, and overcoming this moral paralysis by wisdom, cunning and knowledge, as well as by skill and strength? It is one of the disappointments of literary history that some such development between the cessation of Homeric poetry and the rise of the Attic drama never took place or has not been preserved. One thinks of what Pindar might have accomplished, if his genius had not been attracted to a perhaps more facile and remunerative field. Even from the age of Perikles to that of Augustus we shall not find a complete realisation of the ideal. But from the age of Hesiod onwards we shall find innumerable *attempts* and *sketches*; and the study of these efforts will lead us to contemplate some of the most interesting and instructive aspects of human nature. Finally[4], this tendency will be traced down to man's ideas of the next world, in which epic and religious sentiments are merged into one. But in order to understand this development we must not overlook the meagre records still surviving of the old-fashioned Homericised epic. These relics preserve some hint of man's more conventional and less speculative efforts to rise superior to his misfortunes and retain some vision of perfection.

[1] Ovid, *Metam.* III, 316 ff.; Apoll. *Bibl.* III, vi, 7.
[2] Ovid, *Metam.* X, 162 ff., 560 ff.   [3] *Ibid.* VII, 406 ff.
[4] *Post*, chap. VII, and cf. vol. II, chap. XI.

v. *The* Homeric Cycle *and the* Theognis*; both productions illustrate the reflective and sentimental tendencies of the time.*

So we return to the question, were there no sustained narrative poems which can be taken to characterise this period? As is well known, a large and important cycle of narrative poems once existed, covering every phase of the Trojan war from its first inception in the minds of the gods, to the last adventure of the last chieftain, after his return to his native land, and it is now established with moderate certainty that all were produced subsequently to the *Iliad* and the *Odyssey*. The *Telegony* may have been composed by Eugammon of Kyrene as late as the mid-sixth century. Unhappily nothing of this great body of poetry is extant except in allusions, quotations and prose epitomes. But by collecting all that has been preserved by Proklos, Pausanias, Apollodoros, Athenaios, Eustathios and Hyginos, and summarised in *De Bello Trojano* of Dictys Cretensis and *De Excidio Trojae* of Dares, we can form some idea of their scope and range[1].

The most hurried glance over these fragments and abstracts will leave the reader with one unmistakeable impression: the episodes seem to be familiar. Even those readers who have no first hand knowledge of Greek mythology will recognise nearly every situation. This feature has already been noticed by Christ and by P. Gardner[2], and we need not dwell on it, except to observe the reason. These episodes have that sentimental or dramatic quality which inspires pictures, statues, poems or plays. Let the reader now return to the *Iliad*, and he will see at once that Homer has few or none of these *contrived* great moments. Which of his situations have caught the imagination of posterity? Most of the really great scenes do not appear to have invited imitation. Where, except in Homer himself,

---

[1] The epic cycle was composed of *Cypria, Aithiopis, Little Iliad, Iliou Persis, Returns, Telegony.* The latest book on the subject (T. W. Allen, *Homer, The Origins and the Transmission,* Oxford, 1925) contends that Dictys and Dares founded their abridgments on some old chronicle anterior to Homer, who lived c. 950–900 in Chios or Smyrna. The best *résumé* of the epic cycle will be found in Gruppe.

[2] W. Christ, *Gesch. d. Griech. Litt.* pp. 59 ff.; P. Gardner, *New Chapters in Greek Hist.* pp. 160 ff.

can you gather any idea of the Τειχοσκοπία, Διὸς ἀπάτη, or Aias's heroic stand against Hektor at the ships or the last fight between Hektor and Achilles, the climax of the whole epic? There is a similar contrast in medieval poetry. *Beowulf*, *Waltharius* and *Chanson de Roland* live only in themselves; the later romances of Arthur, Tristram, Lancelot and Siegfried have inspired hundreds of poems and pictures. We do not know what the original narratives were like, but in the surviving excerpts and chrestomathies, the characters have attracted so much notice because they have proved to be complex. They offer more contrasts to each other and suggest a greater variety of passions. The virtues of the warriors of the *Iliad* are pride of life, self-confidence and a high ideal of human power. These would inevitably be tarnished if the story had developed the more telling and dramatic situations of the later poems.

On the other hand, the *Odyssey*[1] has played a far bigger *rôle* in art than has the *Iliad*, because the poem does not confine itself to such simple effects, but begins to resemble the spirit of the Cyclic poets. The adventures open a wider field of speculation; the mere mention of a Kyklops or a lotus-eater starts one thinking. For instance, the memory of Skylla or of the Seirens, who seem to have originated in recollections of primitive magic, suggest philosophic ideas to Socrates[2], and Kirke's wiles, in the eyes of Porphyrios, symbolise the mystic circle of reincarnation from human to beast and then to superhuman[3]. The debates among the gods in the *Odyssey* are rather more philosophic than those in the *Iliad*, that is to say, the poet has probed a little more deeply into the origin of things. When two of the personalities meet, such as the disguised Odysseus and Eumaios over the body of the dog Argos, the poet's description is hardly more than an outline, a suggestion. We can each of us live the experience over in a hundred different ways. Above all, we get glimpses of the eternal struggle between goodness and evil. The episodes in the Homeric Cycle seem to be further developments of these *motifs*. The mysterious designs

---

[1] J. E. Harrison, *Myths of the Odyssey in Art and Literature*, 1882.

[2] *Memorabilia*, ii, vi, 31 ff.

[3] Ὅμηρος τὴν κύκλῳ περίοδον καὶ περιφορὰν παλιγγενεσίας Κίρκης ωσηγόρευκεν. Porph. p. 1050.

of the gods are examined with more penetration, or at any
rate revealed to a greater depth; the pregnancy of certain
situations is more fully realised. The problem of evil, which is
dimly recognised in the brutality of the Kyklopes, the be-
witchments of Kirke and the viciousness of the suitors, seems
now to be one of the leading themes. In fact Odysseus has
already become what he was to remain during the period of
the Attic drama, the villain of the piece. In the *Little Iliad*
he displays something of a Dorian's qualities, "disfiguring
himself,"[1] creeping into Ilion and there plotting with Helen
for the betrayal of the city. Dictys gives a most intriguing and
wholly un-Homeric account of the cunning devices by which
the Trojans were outdone and enmeshed before the Greeks consummated their final stratagem[2]. Nothing stimulates thought
fulness like the spectacle of imperfection, and in this study of
cross purposes, vicious tendencies, rivalries and the clash of
passions we discern the tastes of people who wish to understand things more than to do them.

It is surely no coincidence that the civilisation which produced or listened to the Cyclic poets should produce the
Theognis. This work has met in modern times with less than
its due measure of appreciation, because it lacks human interest,
and takes too much for granted. In fact the poet, probably
some successor to Hesiod, merely alludes to the episodes, as
if familiar to his audiences. One cannot resist the conclusion
that the contemporaries of the poet were already interested
in allegories of this kind and treasured earlier and more primitive versions, which our author was to supersede by a more
philosophical story, not uninfluenced by oriental doctrines[3].
Notice how the *Iliad* mentions only one harpy, who grazed
like a horse on the meadows near the ocean[4]. The *Odyssey*
speaks of them as storm spirits[5]; but the *Theognis* describes
them and gives them names and parentage[6]. Or consider the

---

[1] αἰκισάμενος ἑαυτόν, ΙΛΙΑΣ ΜΙΚΡΑ 1. Almost certainly mutilating himself in the way Herodotos so often records.

[2] *De Bello Trojano*, V, 9–11.

[3] Cf. *The Babylonian Epic of Creation*, transcription, translation and commentary, by S. Langdon, Oxford, 1923.

[4] *Il.* XVI, 150.   [5] *Od.* I, 241.   [6] ll. 265 ff.

character and position of Zeus. Poseidon, who in the *Iliad* is
no less than his brother though younger[1], and in the *Odyssey*
still dares to oppose him, is now hardly mentioned. The
victory of Kronos's youngest son is represented as complete
and the progressive stages of his triumph are marked by deep
cunning. He conquers the Titans by a crafty alliance; after
the victory he weds Metis, the spirit of counsel; by another
stratagem he gives birth to Athene, herself the mother of
children of guile (περίφρονα τέκνα). What wonder that he has
become less anthropomorphic, that he is more aloof, more
mysterious, more truly ἀγκυλομήτης, and that his deeper and
more secretive designs can no longer be fathomed by human
beings? Apollo[2] declares that no other immortals than himself,
much less any mortal, know the mind of Zeus, and that he,
the god of oracles, will never disclose more than the little
which human beings ought to know.

The allegory of creation, which the *Theognis* expounds, is
too well known to need recapitulating[3]. But the spirit which
gives significance and co-ordination to these myths and fables
is worth considering. It has the fervour and the sublimity of
an epic but an epic blended with philosophy. We have here
the European origin of a habit of thought which has found
expression in *Prometheus Vinctus*, *Divina Commedia*, *Paradise Lost*,
Faust, and many of Shelley's poems: the attempt to visualise the
conflict between Good and Evil. Ten centuries later, while
Marcus Aurelius believed in the unique and universal Intelligence expounded by Stoicism and Epiktetus denied that the
universe had any soul at all, Plutarch still clung to the doctrine
of conflict, finding confirmation in a kind of Zoroastrianism[4].
No poem could play a part in originating or transmitting such
grandiose conceptions, without that communicative and vital-
ising heat which emanates from the greatest ideas; and in this
sense the age may be said to have produced in the *Theognis*
an epic. But in other respects the poem falls short of the type.
It is too over-cast with thought. An epic need not deal

---

[1] *Il.* XIII, 354–5.   [2] *Hymn to Hermes*, ll. 541 ff.
[3] One of the best analyses is to be found in *Manuel d'Histoire de la Littérature Grecque*, par Mm. A. et M. Croiset.
[4] *Moralia, Isis and Osiris.*

exclusively nor even principally with human action. In fact we shall have occasion to discuss more than one narrative in which mortals figure only so far as they are raised above their own mortality. But an epic must deal with action, and that action must in some way reveal the possibility, the dream of human greatness. In the *Theognis* the poet is interested only so far in human nature as to remind us of its deterioration. Nor do the allegorical figures possess the reality and the intensity of Satan, or Sin and Death or God the Son going out to war in *Paradise Lost*. The Greek poet is dumbfounded at the vastness of the powers at war above us, and he cannot bring us back to thoughts of our own kind.

But yet the poem is immensely significant, because of its abstractions, and because Zeus, the most humanised and concrete of the figures, is infinitely remote from the species which worships him. Such transcendentalism is a sign that men were discovering unexpected depths and mysteries in their own nature. Just as the abridgments of the Cyclic poems seem to reveal new possibilities of emotionalism, so the *Theognis* might almost be termed an epic of uncertainty. We find corroboration of this view elsewhere. One of the *Homeric Epigrams*[1] declares that there are many things which a human being can fathom, but that nothing is so unfathomable as man. Hesiod computes that the best of all men is he who can unaided penetrate to the core of a situation and forecast its issue, while the worst is he who has no wisdom of his own, nor can avail himself of others'[2].

VI. *The practice of propounding and solving riddles is one of the most remarkable of the signs of these times. In its origin it is quite distinct from the cult of oracles, but was gradually merged into the study of the future.*

We have noticed that Homer[3] (and we shall notice later that Northern epics) cultivated a special and peculiar trust in Fate and that this cult seems to have developed along an independent line, and reached its full development in that era.

---

[1] Epig. v.   [2] *Works and Days*, 293-7.
[3] *Ante*, chap. III, §§ 2, 3; *post*, vol. II, chap. II, § 5.

In fact it becomes the chief moral resource of a warrior and could be taken as the characteristic sign of the Heroic Age. So now we shall find that the post-Homeric period—the transitional epoch between Achean and Periklean civilisation—was marked by a growing interest in riddles. At first such a suggestion seems almost frivolous, but we shall find that puzzles and enigmas become the most comprehensive form under which man then saw life and the most satisfying outlet for his emotions and aspirations. Some of the most exquisite and instructive touches of human nature are connected with what are in essence only conundrums.

A riddle—whether *Volksrätsel* or *Kunsträtsel*—is a story or description which has a hidden bearing on the hearer's knowledge or experience or affairs. It is his business to discover this bearing. Nowadays our methods of expression are so copious and simplified and our habits of thought so analytical that we do not easily realise how universal these stories or descriptions must formerly have been. In fact there was probably once a time when people thought almost entirely in symbols and pictures and when what we call an idea could be introduced into their consciousness only by some illustration or figure or even mummery. In those days the purpose of the parable or, as it soon came to be, the riddle, was to be clear, and if there was any mystification it arose because the thought conveyed was unfamiliar, or the ordinary mode of speech inadequate. Thus when the Samians found that their voluble harangue made no impression on the primitive Spartans, they at last resorted to the old pictorial way of speech, produced a bag, said it wanted meal, and their hearers at once understood[1]. Such primitive arts had one great advantage. If the symbol was well conceived, it excited the hearer's curiosity and com pelled him to work his way into the speaker's meaning, to follow his track of thought in order to arrive at his goal. When Themistokles wished to assert his claims to eminence over his rival, he told the fable of the Feast Day and the Day After the Feast, and so forced his listener to interpret the meaning and guess the connection[2]. In a word, the "parable,"

[1] Herod. iii, 46.   [2] Plut. *Themist.* 18.

"hard saying" or what Hesiod calls the αἶνος[1] was employed as the first means of enlarging the listener's mental vision, and of making him recognise new factors in the matter under consideration. But as men's interests generally run upon the same or similar lines and as experience showed that certain similes and illustrations were more suggestive and easily applied than others, there grew up and existed in circulation a stock of maxims, riddles and oracles familiar to all.

This proverbial wisdom may well have become the earliest material for didactic poetry. But the cult of riddling soon assumed another function. It not only induced a man to look closely and logically at what was in his mind, it also appealed to a different though kindred sentiment. As we have seen it exacted guesswork: it compelled the listener to draw an inference. Sometimes the inference was from the general to the particular, as when Athamas, banished from Boiotia, was told to settle in whatever place he was entertained by wild beasts (ὑπὸ ζώων ἀγρίων ξενισθῇ)[2]. Sometimes the inference is from the particular to the general, as when Temenos, Kresphontes and the two sons of Aristodemos, after dividing the Peloponnese, found each upon the altar on which he had sacrificed, a toad for Argos, a serpent for Lakedaimon, and a fox for Messenia, and the soothsayers had to guess the import of these three creatures with reference to the general prosperity of the three kingdoms[3]. In either case the riddle was like a brief abstract of what men of that time found experience to be: the discovery that events meant something other than at first appeared. In the *Contest of Homer and Hesiod* Homer declares that the sign of wisdom is

γιγνώσκειν τὰ παρόντ᾽ ὀρθῶς καιρῷ δ᾽ ἅμ᾽ ἕπεσθαι[4].

The poet might well speak of such clearsightedness as a rare virtue. Men's temperaments had become so many-sided that no situation was easy to judge, while behind all human

[1] *Works and Days*, 202.

[2] Apoll. *Bibl.* I, ix, 2. (He found wolves devouring the carcase of a sheep, which they left to him and fled.)

[3] Apoll. *Bibl.* II, viii, 4. (The toad implied masterly inactivity, the serpent aggressiveness and the fox diplomacy.)

[4] P. 321.

affairs men became increasingly conscious of the inscrutable designs of Zeus ἀγκυλομήτης. Thus the reading of a riddle was the counterpart to the reading of life, the search for what was concealed. It cannot be coincidence that riddles begin to be frequent and to develop in subtlety at a time when the hexameter poem of Xenophanes was warning men against taking appearances for the truth[1]. The men of Amathous once cut off the head of a certain Onesilos and fixed it over the gate of the city. As the brain and other tissues dissolved, a swarm of bees settled in the cavity, and filled it with honey[2]. Such was the caution and apprehensiveness of the time that the citizens at once regarded the portent as a riddle from Heaven and set about guessing the answer.

Thus the riddle becomes popular at a time when judgment and self-restraint are of the greatest importance, but before man has lost the picturesque and symbolic fashion of thought[3]. The taste may have been encouraged by the influence of Semitic Egypt. We have noticed the story of Greek gods fleeing into that country and becoming animals. Later, the migration was in the opposite direction. Between the seventh and sixth centuries, if not before, the Greeks became acquainted with the religious symbolism of the East. They learnt that the uncouth monsters painted on vases by Assyrian artists had always a mystical significance; that primitive rites, observances and legends were allegories of sin and purification. J. E. Harrison[4] has suggested that in this atmosphere the Homeric Seirens grew into the conception of bird-like daemons waiting to catch the soul of the mariner journeying over the ocean of life. At any rate we shall notice again and again how often the great issues of life and death are enveloped in enigmas and depend for their solution on guesswork which proves to be highly developed intuition. The popularity of the riddle represents the triumph of speculative thought over the poetry of action.

Such is certainly the case with the age of post-Homeric poetry. The riddles and periphrases to be found in the sur-

[1] Fragments of περὶ φύσιος in *Fragmenta Philosophorum Graecorum*, t. I, Mullach, Bibl. Didot.
[2] Herod. v, 114.   [3] *Post*, vol. II, chap. I, § I.
[4] *Myths of the Odyssey*, chap. v.

viving literature of this period are not numerous, but they are sufficiently typical to show that people of this period had reached the stage when they expected to be mystified and had acquired the habit of looking below the surface. Hesiod himself sometimes involves his thought in an enigma, such as the fable of the hawk and the nightingale[1], so that the reader or audience may be forced to get down to his true meaning by unwrapping the allegory; and he introduces his account of the Five Ages[2] with what must surely be a warning that there is more in the story than appears on the surface. The *Theognis*, with its symbolic names and tales of strange affinities and stranger genesis, must be intended as a complex allegory of human and cosmic destiny. Perhaps the peculiarities of poetic style are even more significant. We have noticed in discussing the *Iliad* that the imagination of the audiences, or at any rate of the poets, was caught by the sheer beauty or strength or agility of animals and natural phenomena—the observer being perhaps stirred by some recollection of the primitive quality once worshipped as *mana*—and this admiration found expression in similes. In the *Odyssey* this feature is still retained but the fancy of the poet shows signs of becoming allusive and enigmatical. In the *Iliad* there are a few circumlocutions and at least one attempt at a riddle[3]. In the *Odyssey* both types are more frequent. Oars are "wings of ships," ships are "horses of the sea." The celebrated wooden horse may, as Dr Leaf so ingeniously suggests, be a metaphor for a wooden tower with a projecting neck[4]. The sea itself is "unvintaged" ($\dot{a}\tau\rho\dot{v}\gamma\epsilon\tau\sigma$) and it requires just one second's almost unconscious guesswork before the explanation flashes across one's mind. The story of the district where an oar was taken for a winnowing fan is a fascinating circumlocution for complete ignorance of seafaring. They are even acquiring the habit of guessing the

[1] *Works and Days*, 202 ff.
[2] *Ibid.* 106 ff. λόγον ἐκκορυφώσω. I will tell over the main heads or points of the story.
[3] *Il.* XIX, 221–4.
[4] *Homer and History*, chap. I. Miss Harrison still maintains that the invention of Epeios was originally a "fertility horse," a ritual contrivance which may have been used as a military ambush. (*Mythology*, pp. 43 ff. in Our Debt to Greece and Rome Series.)

significance of names[1]. By the time that we reach Hesiod and
his successors the simile has practically disappeared and the
imaginations of the poets have become progressively more
enigmatical. What is the "hairless one," the "boneless one"
or "the hunter of deep sea prey"? Very possibly they were well
recognised periphrases, but they had once to be guessed; and
however familiar, they revive just for an instant the intuition
necessary to discover that a serpent, a cuttlefish, and a fisher-
man are indicated[2]. Or again, what is meant by "cutting the
withered from the green on the five branches"? Very possibly
this conceit was picked up from among the saws of husband-
men. But the listener or reader is none the less left to jump
to the conclusion that the poet is talking of paring one's nails.
Another such whimsey is found in the "riddle of the young
boys" (νέων παίδων αἴνιγμα)[3], where the answer depends on
remembering that those who go fishing might catch lice instead.

The "riddle of the young boys" was destined to mark the
hour of Homer's death, in that he could not guess the answer,
and it is noticeable that by this time the solution of riddles
begins to be bound up with the pronouncements of Fate. No
doubt an enigma gained piquancy by association with some
tragic issue, however far-fetched or old-fashioned. For instance,
there is a very ancient commonplace of folklore that the cause
of a wound could be its cure. The superstition is discarded by
Homer, but afterwards revived in connection with Telephos,
because Odysseus guessed that *auctor vulneris* meant the weapon
and not Achilles[4]. The reader will remember that before the
Sphinx took upon her to kill a man, she first made sure that
he could not guess her conundrums. In fact the more men
became accustomed to the unexpected in life and to the
enigmatical in thought and expression, the more they connected the two, till the study of the future became the study
of riddles.

We can trace the evolution of this sentiment quite clearly.

[1] *Od.* xix, 406 ff., *i.e.* the derivation of Odysseus's own name, cf. the
explanation of the word *Achilles* from ἀ-χείλη (Apoll. *Bibl.* iii, xiii, 6), or
derivation of Protesilaos, "quoniam primus ex omnibus perierat" (Hyg. ciii).
[2] *Catal. of Women*, l. 36; *Works and Days*, 524; *Contest of Homer and Hesiod*, 326.
[3] *Contest of Homer and Hesiod*, 326.   [4] Hyg. *Fab.* ci.

In Homer, as we have seen, a knowledge of the future was available to any living man who obtained the requisite insight into the language and movements of birds, whether granted by Zeus or communicated by serpents[1]. In fact, according to Herodotos[2], the first stationary oracle was established only because two black doves came from Thebes in Egypt and one alighted on the oak tree in Dodona and spoke with a human voice; and even down to the classical period the Aitolians with their neighbours the Acarnanians and Epirots had confidence only in doves and oak trees[3]. We have also seen that[4] those who acquired during their lifetime the power of reading the future were able to retain the faculty after death, and we learn in the *Returns*[5] that when Agamemnon and his followers were leaving the scene of the Trojan war, the ghost of Achilles disclosed what the future had in store for them. Being connected with the dead this stage of soothsaying is also connected with the earth and generally with night-time. Probably the cult of Delphi originated at this period, owing to the celebrated chasm in the ground, and the oracle was attributed, naturally enough, to Gaia[6], or according to one scholiast to night[7]. But there is no reason to suppose that the tenour of the oracular utterances, at this period, was not straightforward. We shall see in the next chapter how eagerly and trustfully men sought guidance from those who were buried, at any rate up till the Christian era. Plutarch suggests that just as the eye has the faculty of material sight so the mind has the faculty of spiritual sight: either will exercise this function if properly stimulated[8]. But long before the Attic period we discover traces of a fresh development. According to *Eumolpia*, a poem attributed to Mousaios[9], Gaia shared the oracle with Poseidon who, though god of the sea, had much to do with the ground. Eventually she resigned her portion to Themis, who transferred it to Apollo. Apollo subsequently

---

[1] *Ante*, chap. III, § 9.　　　　[2] II, 52 and 55.
[3] Paus. VII, xxi, 2.　　　　[4] *Ante*, chap. III, § 9.
[5] Proklos, ΝΟΣΤΟΙ I. Achilles's gift of prophecy probably arose out of his foreknowledge of his own death.
[6] Aesch. *Eum.* I ff.　　　　[7] On Pindar, *Pyth.* Argum.
[8] *De Defectu Oraculorum.*　　　　[9] Paus. X, v, 3.

gave Poseidon the island of Kalaureia off Troizen, in exchange
for his share, and so remained sole master of Delphi.

This peaceful intrusion, first of Themis and then of Apollo,
almost certainly marks the advent of the riddling oracle which
rivalled the mystic oracle and in the end apparently superseded
it. Tradition has handed down to us a wonderful collection of
baffling utterances, which apply to events after the Dorian
conquest and which grow more and more ironical and epigrammatic as time advances and men become more civilised.
Who will venture to maintain that all or even the greater
number were ever really uttered on the alleged occasions, either
at Delphi or elsewhere? No doubt oracles of some kind were
given, but the secret committed to some king or chieftain and
jealously guarded was not likely to have become almost immediately the common knowledge of his enemies, often of
another race, and sometimes dwelling in a distant country.
Besides, the utterances which have survived fit the events too
neatly and wittily with their enigmatical allusiveness to be
anything but epigrams created after the adventure. Sometimes
the story-teller seems half inclined to confess as much[1]. No
doubt the methods of oracle-mongery encouraged this development. At Pherai, for instance, the inquirer, after the proper
ritual, whispered his question, covered his ears, quitted the
precinct, and when at the proper distance uncovered them
and took the first sound that he heard as the god's answer[2].
The pointlessness of replies received in this fashion must have
immensely stimulated the passion for guessing and construing.
But if the traditional oracles which mark nearly every phase
of early Greek history are not genuine in the historical or
literal sense, they have that larger and more philosophical
truthfulness which represents the tendencies of an age. Take
as an example the story of the wars between Sparta and
Messenia. The fate of that interminable struggle seems at
times[3] to depend not on gallantry and endurance, but on
devising stratagems and on guessing enigmas. Men are waging

---

[1] *E.g.* Paus. x, x, 3. The oracle to the Spartan Phalanthos, that he would
win a country and a city when he experienced rain from a cloudless sky.
[2] Paus. VII, xxii, 3.   [3] Paus. IV, esp. xii, xiii.

war with their wits, so the gods are thought to be setting them puzzles to solve. Amongst others, the riddle about two coming out of their ambush and returning to their fate was found in the end to refer to the eyes of Ophioneus, which recovered their sight and then again became blind.

VII. *All these tendencies reach their culmination in Herodotos. He shows in how many ways men discarded their self-confidence in the presence of the gods; under how many guises they pictured the inscrutability and the deceptiveness of the divine powers; by what qualities man might retain a sense of security and worth.*

These and all the tendencies discussed in this chapter culminate in the work of Herodotos. We are now in the fifth century, and, of course, much has happened since the age of Hesiodic poetry. The so-called "Seven Sages" have established the study of philosophy and have even elaborated metaphysical doctrines. It need not be supposed that their cosmic theories and guesses at transcendentalism had gained general acceptance. But their daring speculations would not have been possible unless the whole Hellenic world had advanced and we shall notice that ideas similar to theirs are familiar to the "inquirer" from Halicarnassus. And yet it must not be forgotten that Herodotos closes one era rather than begins another. Longinus called him the most *homeric* of men[1]. He is the last of the logographers not the first of the historians. He is still possessed by the epic spirit of wonder and admiration, the primitive man's familiarity with and acceptance of the supernatural, the expectation of divine intervention and intense interest in human personality. So he is indispensable to our inquiry. He is the consummation of this civilisation which we have endeavoured to reconstruct out of fragments of poetry and scraps of folklore. Though the friend and contemporary of Sophokles, he represents the last and fullest effort to conquer fear and despondency in the old way before the coming of Euripides and Sokrates.

What aspects, then, of human nature interested the historian? What activities and talents had he the mind to appreciate?

[1] T. R. Glover, *Herod.* chap. XIII, 3.

What sort of curiosity was he trying to satisfy when he made
his inquiries and worked up his stories?[1] The question is not
difficult to answer. His tastes must have been like the tastes
of his audiences; an interest in the different means by which
other people solved the same difficulties and pursued the same
objects as their own—how they seek prosperity, suppress fear,
and elude death. As we read further we discover that these
games of hide and seek, as in the most primitive legends, are
constantly bringing men into contact with the gods. That is,
in fact, the secret charm of the spectacle. At the back of the
most curious and the best told stories, there is the suggestion
of interplay between the mortal and immortal. Sometimes, by
examining the burial rites and propitiatory customs of peoples
so different as the Egyptians and the Sarmatians, he directs
our attention to the ways by which men hope to control the
life of the spirit after death. Sometimes he reminds us of the
passion for life and happiness, as when he recounts how
Mykerinos, learning that he had only six years to live, collected all the lamps available and attempted to double his
allotted time by turning night into day[2]. But more often he is
interested in the struggle for power among the kingdoms of
the earth.

These ambitions and rivalries had opened a new and cloud-
laden horizon in man's outlook. The world had indeed changed
since the days of Homer. Armies are now so big and equipment is now so improved, and regal power is so firmly established, that there is no longer any question of needing a god
to nerve a warrior's arm. A monarch either possesses fleets
of triremes, like Polykrates, or hordes of hardy warriors like
Kyros, or well-drilled armies like Kroisos and Xerxes, enough
to work his will, or he does not dream of aiming at supremacy.
There existed a story that the ancient Aithiopians chose
the biggest and the strongest man of their nation to be their
king[3]. But the age which produced the three wonders of
Samos[4] had passed beyond the need of personal prowess. It

---

[1] For a full discussion from a quite different point of view see T. R. Glover,
Herodotus, 1924.
[2] Herod. II, 133.   [3] *Ibid.* III, 2.   [4] *Ibid.* III, 60.

is now guidance and direction and luck which these mighty
rulers desire. All through the literature and legends popular
in post-Homeric times we have noticed a growing reliance
on cunning and stratagems, and a growing conviction that
the purposes of the gods are far-reaching and obscure, but
must at all costs be ascertained. These ideas reach their final
stage in the policy and precautions which Herodotos attributes
to the oriental monarchs. The Greeks, who take note of their
pursuits and endeavours, also desire national prosperity, but
they have a horror of big empires which threaten their civic
existence. Thus from every motive they are bound to watch
the projects and ventures of these warlike rulers with hostile
eyes and anxious thoughts. They must already have begun
to realise as Cato long afterwards said of Eumenes, that "a
king is by nature an animal who lives on human flesh."[1] The
best way to lessen fear is to allay it with contempt; to invent
somehow a sense of superiority so that the consciousness of
weakness may not always be remembered. We have seen how
the Homeric Greeks staved off disquietude by believing that
the immortals lent them some portion of their divinity from
Olympos. The distant descendants of this civilisation can no
longer clothe themselves in such borrowed strength. They have
gradually learnt through the succeeding centuries to have more
reverence for the power and less trust in the friendship of these
incomprehensible deities. How are they now, in this latter age,
to satisfy their hate and keep up their courage? How can they
depreciate and belittle the warlike kingdoms which they dread?
By imagining that their enemies are in a false position in
relation to their gods.

At this point it is necessary to realise how the idea of god
had developed. Herodotos apparently does not mind recording
legends about the older spirit world[2]. At the same time he
seems to have caught something of the spirit of Ionic philosophy. He is so far persuaded that "the sole wisdom is to
know the thought which directs everything through all things;
it will and will not be called Zeus,"[3] that he believes one deity
to be supreme and sometimes alludes to this power as imper-

---

[1] Plut. *Cato*, VIII.   [2] *E.g.* I, 67–8, 167.   [3] Herakleitos, *Frags.* 12, 55.

sonal. But he does not therefore imagine that man's lot is any the happier because the divine powers have proved to be more complex. In his conception of man's position he follows further along the path already traced by the *Theognis* and the *Homeric Hymns*. In the *Iliad* mortals were regarded as the most wretched of all beings because their lives were so short. In the *Odyssey* the mania for plaguing themselves was recognised as added to the prospects of an early death. In the Hesiodic poems they are pitied yet more because virtue and peace are granted them only at the price of unremitting toil. But in Herodotos death is sometimes regarded as preferable to any kind of life, because the divine powers cannot bear the sight of human happiness[1]. Solon the wisest of all Athenians declared that the deity was by nature too jealous to suffer mortals to remain in peace, and that if one taste of felicity was granted, it was generally to embitter their fall[2]. So all he claimed for his countrymen was wisdom of a cautious and homely kind, which realises the risks of life and so precludes pride or even confidence[3]. The full change of sentiment is clearly revealed in the debate on whether Greece should be invaded[4]. Xerxes represents the old epic spirit; he recalls the memories of his ancestors and declares his resolve to equal their achievement and rival their fame. The warning of Artabanos, which occasioned that outburst, breathes the very spirit of the new era, especially when he justifies his anticipations: οὐ γὰρ ἐᾷ φρονέειν μέγα ὁ θεὸς ἄλλον ἢ ἑωυτόν[5].

Such a doctrine, which would have meant swift degeneracy in ancient and imperial Mykenai, was a source of strength to the more modern Greeks, surrounded by threats of invasion. In the hour of greatest danger the Lokrians drew profound comfort from the message that Xerxes was not a god but a mortal and therefore subject by birth to misfortune; in fact the greater the man the greater the disaster to which he was exposed[6]. But far subtler and more ingenious ways were discovered by which religious ideas could minister to the national courage and hatred. As we have seen, the great aggressive

---

[1] Herod. VII, 44–7.   [2] *Ibid.* I, 31–2.
[3] Plut. *Sol.* 27.   [4] Herod. VII, 10, 11.
[5] "For God allows none other but himself to have high thoughts," VII, 10.
[6] Herod. VII, 202.

monarchs outside Greece are represented as harassed by a sense of insecurity. The dream and hope of the greatest is that the gods would reveal the evil which they know must threaten them. Kyros, who was believed to be more than human[1], claimed that he enjoyed this privilege[2]. So they are pictured as constantly applying to the same gods as did the Greeks, for direction in their many schemes and enterprises. But in what spirit are they imagined to approach these mysterious and malignant powers? In much the same mood as if they were dealing with attendant councillors, whose foreknowledge was at the disposal of mortals. And how does the etherialised and secretive deity deal with such importunate and overweening inquirers? Sometimes he volunteers a communication, but more often he waits to be asked; in any case his utterance is a snare, for he baits the trap with riddles. With the *History* of Herodotos, the communications of the gods become not merely dark, they are actively misleading. Thus there was always one hope. However powerful the enemy, he might fling away his superiority through foolishness. An ambitious and headstrong ruler inquires the wisdom of venturing on some enterprise; the answer seems unmistakeably to promise success; he plunges into action, fails, and then discovers that the wording of the oracle admitted a quibble which he had never suspected.

> *Contain*
> *Your flux of laughter, Sir. You know this hope*
> *Is such a bait, it covers any hook*[3].

It is not suggested that these equivocal communications were really given on the occasions which Herodotos records. Like the earlier, mystifying type, they probably originated after the event, in response to the sentiment of the time[4]. In fact the quibbling oracle is but a new phase of an ancient conviction. We have noticed that at some very primitive and pre-Heroic period there was a belief or perhaps only a hope that magic could work immortality, and that at some post-Heroic period men's imaginations returned to this theme, and they pictured to themselves the impossibility of realising such a desire. If a mortal, in his overweening

---

[1] Herod. i, 204.   [2] *Ibid.* i, 209.
[3] *Volpone*, i, i.   [4] *E.g.* Herod. vi, 77; Paus. ii, xx, 4.

confidence, imagined that he had obtained this god-like
privilege, he would find that he had deceived himself; he had
overlooked some loophole by which death might enter. We
have not yet noticed how often disillusionment came with the
test of battle. The aspirant found that he had merely mis-
calculated his strength. Thus Kyknos was endowed with an
impenetrable skin, but he was throttled by his helmet thongs.
Kaineos, who by change of sex had somehow been rendered
invulnerable to the ordinary weapons of war, was buried
beneath the fir trees which the centaurs threw[1]. So that
Periklymenos might always elude danger, he was granted, by
Poseidon, the power of constantly changing his shape, but
was killed by a blow from Herakles's club, when in the form
of a fly[2], or shot by his bow when turned into an eagle[3].
Odysseus, in his old age, was troubled with mysterious
dreams. Being warned by the best soothsayers that he would
meet his death at the hands of his son, he closely guarded
Telemachos and was then unwittingly slain by Telegonos, a
stranger, but his own and Kirke's bastard son[4]. Such stories
suited an age which dreaded or despised the pretensions of the
individual warrior. The age of Herodotos dreaded or despised
the pretensions of organised monarchies. So the tradition of a
defective charm becomes the tale of a quibbling oracle. In
both types of legend, the downfall turns on a false impression,
an inability to foresee eventualities. Kleomenes is told that he
will conquer Argos; he invades the country, is defeated, and
then finds that the god meant a shrine of that name[5]. The
daughter of Polykrates sees her father raised on high, bathed
by Zeus and anointed by the sun, but this elevation befell him
only when his corpse was hung up exposed to the elements[6].
Thus the management of a kingdom becomes a game of wits.
The men of action, who are worth considering, are defended
from the ordinary accidents of mankind by their armies, their
fleets, and their wealth; but they have to relinquish these

[1] Apoll. *Epit.* I, 22.   [2] Schol. Apoll. Rod. *Argon.* I, 156.
[3] Ovid, *Metam.* XII, 549.   [4] *De Bello Trojano*, VI, 14, 15.
[5] Herod. VI, 76–80.
[6] *Ibid.* III, 124. (Polykrates suspected some snare as soon as he heard of
the dream.)

accessories and stand by their own intelligence, as soon as they
seek to know the will of Zeus or of Loxias. The type of man
most admired seems to have been such a one as Lichas̩ the
Spartan. His country was on the brink of disaster and the only
direction vouchsafed by the deity was a riddle which none
could interpret. In reality the source of divine help lay hidden
near at hand, but only Lichas had the wits to detect the
allusion and guess the enigma. Thus he became the saviour
of his country, καὶ συντυχίῃ χρησάμενος καὶ σοφίῃ[1].

Lichas may be taken as an example of the heroic type of
the age—the man who could put into action the qualities then
most admired. Polyeidos[2] is another illustration, almost exactly
similar. Both examples refer to an early time; Lichas is supposed to have lived during the wars of Sparta and Tegea while
the story of Polyeidos is told in connection with Minos and
Pasiphae. Those were the good old days when the paths of
wisdom were at any rate straightforward, even if obscure.
When once the truth was found, you knew your way. But it is
part of the purpose of Herodotos to show how complex the
latter age has become, how great is the need of wariness and
insight, and how often the inquirer's own wishes blind him
to his risks, especially if he is a potentate or a conqueror.
It seems as if prosperity and kingship disqualify men for
dealing with the gods and make them forget how subtle,
malignant, and grimly humorous the immortal powers had
become. As Epiktetos was to point out long afterwards, men
could not address an oracle with an open mind, and ask for
guidance as a wayfarer might inquire which of two roads he
should take[3]. The story of Kroisos is the classic example. The
prosperity of the great Lydian monarch is such that he believes
himself to be the happiest of men[4]. But he is conscious of his
dependency on oracles, so he devises a way of testing their
veracity and finds that Delphi is the most reliable[5]. He then
sets himself to win the favour of this shrine by profuse offerings[6]
and in return he is told nothing but the truth. Yet the truth

[1] Herod. i, 68.   [2] Apoll. *Bibl.* iii, iii, 2.
[3] *Discourses*, ii, 7.   [4] Herod. i, 34.
[5] *Ibid.* i, 47.   [6] *Ibid.* i, 50.

is his undoing. Before venturing to attack the Persians he
receives two oracles. One is merely equivocal and the monarch
jumps to the obvious and misleading conclusion, because it
gratifies his overweening confidence[1]. The other contains a
riddle which he does not even suspect, so little is he accustomed
to think or to examine[2]. So he falls. Yet he does not disappear
from the stage. Now that he is of no account, popular sentiment
endows him with just those qualities which he lacked in the
day of his greatness. He typifies the men who are wise, though
weak. Kyros, even at the height of his first triumph, reflecting
that nothing human is secure, had spared his victim's life and
had attached him to his person[3], and Kroisos had declared
"as the gods have made me thy slave, I think it fitting to tell
thee, if I discern anything more than others."[4] So throughout
the remainder of his captive life he becomes the seer[5].

It need not be supposed that all men took so enlightened a
view of the part which intelligence might play in the affairs
of this world. The many hazards and chances of those troubled
times revived the soldier's confidence in the omnipotence of
Fate. This conviction was bound to be strengthened when men
began to observe how irretrievable a single error in judgment
might now become. Besides when they saw that neither prayers
nor pity could stave off the consequences of ambition many
must have come to the conclusion that after all our lives are
in the hands of an impersonal power. Zeus himself is represented as so convinced of this truth that when he heard of the
oracle of Proteus that Thetis's son should be greater than his
sire, he abstained from the goddess, though burning with love[6];
and when Kroisos reproached the Delphic oracle for its deceptions, he was answered that Loxias οὐκ οἷός τε ἐγίνετο παρα-
γαγεῖν μοίρας[7]. Herodotos himself probably believed much
more firmly in divine justice than in this blind power, but whatever the creed of the author or of his audiences, they must

---

[1] Herod. I, 53.   [2] Ibid. I, 55. For solution, see I, 91.
[3] Ibid. I, 86.   [4] Ibid. I, 89.
[5] E.g. ibid. I, 88 ff., 155, 207. The life of Astyages teaches a similar lesson.
I, 107–13, 120.
[6] Surely not an early myth. Chief source is Ovid, Metam. XI, 22, and the
other sources (see Frazer, Apoll. Epit. II, 67) are all late.
[7] Herod. I, 91.

equally have realised that the greatness of a man depended on his caution and clear-sightedness. So we may conclude that by the fifth century the age of Intelligence was fully established, and that Herodotos is the first wholehearted exponent of cleverness and subtlety. Never were the arts and contrivances of the ingenious more admired than at this time. We are told of the secret methods by which men learnt to communicate with each other[1]; of their ways of impressing their ideas on their listeners[2]. We hear much of the traps which human beings laid for each other's weaknesses[3]. Best of all, we are told the story of yet another riddle of the sort which brings out the core of folly and wisdom however disguised. When Darios invaded Skythia, his enemies sent him a bird, a mouse, a frog and five arrows without a word of explanation. The king, possessed by his lust for conquest, at once jumps to the conclusion that these symbols signify surrender, and he readily finds ingenious arguments to support his theory. Gobryas, who realises the dangers of the expedition, is unprejudiced enough to give his imagination free play. So he divines the true import of each object and concludes that the message is one of defiance[4].

VIII. *Relations of the warrior hero to the intellectual hero. Position of the* Odyssey *between the two ideals.*

The existence and currency of these tales prove that the older epic ideal had not merely lapsed, but had been replaced by something more intellectual and complex, and that the transition was complete before the age of Perikles. But we must not suppose that Homeric ways of thinking had entirely disappeared. Herodotos describes the warrior-class of Egypt, for whom it was unlawful to practise any craft and who studied nothing but the arts of war and handed them on from generation to generation, and he wonders whether it was from this source that the Greek states had derived so similar an ideal[5]. At any rate Plutarch tells us that Pyrrhos devoted the whole

---

[1] Herod. I, 123; V, 34. [2] *Ibid.* I, 27, 71, 126, 141.
[3] *Ibid.* II, 121; IV, 3, 110–17. [4] *Ibid.* IV, 131–2.
[5] *Ibid.* II, 166–7.

of his intellect to the study of war, holding such to be the only pursuit fit for a king[1]. Assuredly the spirit of the ancient Acheans must have lingered among some of the men of this type. There was a persistent legend that the gods fought on the side of the Greeks at Marathon and Salamis; that the Delphic god, aided by national heroes, drove the Gauls from his sanctuary, and that Poseidon helped to rout the Persians at Mantineia. Even when Alaric approached Athens, he is supposed to have seen Athene and Achilles in arms on the wall[2]; and it was Demeter who really slew Pyrrhos at Argos[3]. Wherever there are men of action, there lingers something of the spirit of Homer. Some more recent tales are even more remarkable. We are told that Alexander the Great was once so incensed against a member of his bodyguard named Lysimachos that he shut him up in a lion's den. The condemned man overcame the beast, whereupon the monarch, filled with recollections of the feats of Herakles, not only laid aside his anger but honoured him as among the noblest of his Macedonians. At the death of his master, the hero reigned as king over those Thrakian tribes bordering on Macedonia[4]. The earlier wars of Rome must have retained much of the spirit of an Homeric battle. Tullus Aufidius and Gaius Marcius used to challenge each other to "mortal combat" when their armies met. Flaminius was found dead at Trasimene surrounded by the corpses of the bravest of both sides[5]. Pyrrhos was challenged on a battlefield by one of the Mamertines splendidly armed and won the battle by killing him with a single blow[6]. Clovis slew Alaric in single combat at the battle of Poictiers[7]. Pausanias[8] has also preserved a tale which breathes the very spirit of the old world epics. According to an apocryphal legend, one of the crew of Odysseus was stoned to death at Temesa and haunted the land. At the bidding of the Pythian oracle they erected a temple to the avenging spirit and every year offered up the fairest maid of Temesa. One day Euthymos, visiting the country at the time of this annual rite, saw the

---

[1] *Pyrrh*. VIII.   [2] Paus. VIII, x, 9; x, xxiii, 2.   [3] *Ibid*. I, xiii, 8.
[4] *Ibid*. I, ix, 5.   [5] Plut. *Vit. Fab. Max*. 3.   [6] Plut. *Vit. Pyrrh*. 24.
[7] Gibbon, *Decline and Fall*, chap. XXXVIII.   [8] Paus. VI, vii, 7.

victim, fell in love with her, donned his armour and worsted
the spirit, who plunged into the sea and disappeared. Rarely
will you find such promising material for a tale of human
greatness and enterprise superimposed on a tradition of human
sacrifice and a haunting goblin.

So the old ideal of courage and strength and the old dream
of anthropomorphic gods must still have persisted, but not in
the forefront of civilisation. They had dropped behind in the
march of ideas; they were no longer in touch with literature
and thought. Herodotos, in representing the progressive attitude, had probably absorbed the teaching of Xenophanes,
whose utterances sometimes read like a direct attack on the
mythic past. Wisdom, says the philosopher, is "high above the
strength of men and the swiftness of horses,"[1] and Demokritos
adds, "the beauty of the body is an advantage worthy of an
animal if Reason does not elevate it." Herodotos develops
this idea among the practical affairs and adventures of men.
He represents the gods as being just as remorseless and as
implacable as of old, and just as divinely endowed with the
excellences to which men aspire. But in this latter age the
valued qualities are wisdom, foreknowledge, penetration, self-
control, and self-knowledge. A mortal gifted with these virtues
may win the friendship of the immortals or may even for a
space outwit them, as Amasis contrived to do, in dealing with
the men of Barka[2]. But for the most part they realise neither
their own weakness nor the power of the deity. Yet those who
could live up to this ideal were enabled to make their way
fearlessly and successfully through the world. For one thing
they understood that the gods however envious were no longer
impulsive or capricious, and so they could be reckoned with.
When Pyrrhos invaded Lakedaimon without a declaration of
war Mandrokleides was able to face the crisis with the courage
which comes from insight. "If you are a god," he said, "we
shall not be harmed by you, for we have done no wrong. If
you are a man you may meet with one stronger than yourself."[3]
Besides, clearheadedness and ingenuity had become essential

---

[1] Mullach, *Fragmenta Philosophorum Graec.* t. I, pp. 330–82, Bibl. Didot.
[2] Herod. IV, 200.   [3] Plut. *Vit. Pyrrh.* 26.

to civilisation. Another anecdote from Plutarch will illustrate this truth. Human sacrifice appears to have been still possible so late in Greek history that even in the life of Pelopidas men were still hesitating for or against the superstition. Theokritos the prophet has the wits and the insight to solve the difficulty and as it were to humanise his age. Before the battle of Leuktra the Theban general dreamt that the "daughters of Skedasos," whose tombs stood on the plain, appeared and demanded the sacrifice of a "red maiden." While the staff debated on the right course, some quoting the example of Agamemnon and Iphigeneia, a beautiful filly, either a roan or a chestnut, escaped from its tether and galloped up to the tent. Only Theokritos was quick-witted enough to seize the opportunity[1]. In fact, if oracles retained their hold on men's imagination, it must have been because they also appealed to their intelligence. No doubt there were then many who felt strongly the reverence and mystery to which Dr Glover alludes[2]. On the other hand, there must have been many capable of the kind of disbelief expressed later by Oenomaus[3], Cicero[4], and Voltaire[5]. But many a sceptic must have been won over to believe in utterances, which needed his quick-wittedness to become truths.

On returning, after this review, to the *Odyssey*, one cannot help feeling that the germs of these tendencies are already to be found in that poem, and that the story of Odysseus reminds the reader almost as much of the post-Homeric epoch as of the *Iliad*. We note an unmistakeable step towards monotheism, as Zeus is now supreme and no longer even looks for opposition, except from Poseidon[6], and Poseidon has lost caste. He is associated with the uncouth and retrograde Kyklopes; his feud with Odysseus is ignoble, and his petty vindictiveness is frustrated. If this god of bulls, horses and the sea represents the spread of Minoan influence, his effacement must accompany the advent of new domination. The old type of augury still exists, but the poets are beginning to cultivate the kind of

[1] Plut. *Vit. Pelop.* XXI.   [2] *Herod.* chap. VIII, 2.
[3] *Frags.*   [4] *De Divin.*
[5] *Opinion* added to Fontenelle's *Hist. des Oracles.*
[6] *Od.* I, 69; XII, 128.

phraseology which resembles inverted riddles. The old race of heroes still exists, yet they seem to be more heavily afflicted. Even Menelaos in the midst of his wealth speaks of his sorrows[1]. Yet they are almost replaced by a newer generation which seems to be more like the Iron Age described by Hesiod. They are undisciplined, quarrelsome, self-seeking and, above all, purblind[2]. As a consequence, they are more in the power of the gods whom they do not understand. One thinks of how the suitors were bedewed with sleep and distorted with laughter[3]. Telemachos was so unused to the older type of hero that when his father appeared in his natural complexion and figure the youth thought that a god was mocking him[4]. Great value is put on cleverness. Helen can imitate the voices of the heroes' wives outside the horse of wood[5]. Telemachos recognises that horses would be useless in Ithaka[6]. Odysseus notes that it would be fatal to kill the Kyklops, as no man could move the rock at the entrance[7], and he can frustrate the Seirens only by an ingenious device[8]. Eumaios dwells on the arts of conversation[9]. Whereas there is but one hurried allusion to Autolykos in the *Iliad*[10], his thievishness is fully described in the *Odyssey*[11], though these attributes have no bearing on the context, except so far as he is an ancestor of Odysseus. Besides, one of the few apocrypha to the *Odyssey* deals with an exploit of this resourceful and felonious progenitor. The auxiliary gods, though now so completely subjected to Zeus, are further removed from human beings. They no longer suffer an immortal openly to love a mortal[12]. We have already[13] discussed what seems to be the one exception, the relations between Athene and Odysseus, but it might here be noted that even this deity is no longer simply a goddess of war, but begins to resemble the Hesiodic picture. As the Olympians begin to withdraw from the world, their place begins to be taken by monsters.

---

[1] *Od.* IV, 75–112.

[2] *Ibid.* X, 28–55 (Hippotades's bag of the winds); XII, 340–65 (slaying of oxen of the sun); XVIII, 405 ff.; XIX, 1–13 (suitors).

[3] *Ibid.* II, 413 ff.; XX, 345 ff. [4] *Ibid.* XVI, 172–200.

[5] *Ibid.* IV, 265–89. [6] *Ibid.* IV, 593–619.

[7] *Ibid.* IX, 287. [8] *Ibid.* XII, 165–200.

[9] *Ibid.* XV, 389–402. [10] *Il.* X, 267.

[11] *Od.* XIX, 396 ff. [12] *Ibid.* V, 118–44. [13] *Ante*, chap. IV, § 6.

Pausanias remarked that though giants are not even mentioned in the *Iliad*, they are vividly described in the *Odyssey*:
for instance the Laistrygones[1]. This teratology is, as we have
seen[2], a feature of the post-Homeric Age.

The tendency of poetic thought can also be traced in the
aspects and appearances of heroes. In the *Iliad* there is no
talk of tarnishing the outward glory of a warrior. Even after
a wound, a god is likely to render the man more beautiful.
This sense of grandeur survives in the *Odyssey* but a less dignified
tone has begun to make itself felt. There is the story of how
the hero of the poem disguises himself to enter Troy, and of
his appearance as an old man and a beggar. In the *Little
Iliad* we are told that he actually mutilated himself (αἰκισάμενος). In Herodotos we have several versions of this trick,
especially the device by which Peisistratos[3] entered Athens or
Zopyros betrayed Babylon[4]. We have also noticed that the
heroes of the *Iliad* are singularly free from crime, but that
in the poetry which survives in abridgments and has presumably undergone the influence of the post-Homeric ages,
the warriors sometimes stoop to fraud or meanness, and that
Odysseus is often represented as the hero of such underhand
victories; almost as the villain of the piece. Such is certainly
not his character in the *Odyssey*; but may not the tide of thought
have just begun to turn in that direction? Would the Odysseus
of the *Iliad* have sought for poison, which Ilos refused him
"for he feared the gods"?[5] In Dictys Cretensis no place is
left for such scruples. Philoktetes challenges Paris to a duel of
archery and kills him with the Herculean arrows which were
poisoned[6].

---

[1] Paus. VIII, xxix, 2.
[2] *Ante*, § 4.
[3] Herod. I, 59.
[4] *Ibid*. III, 154.
[5] *Od*. I, 253 ff.
[6] *De Bello Trojano*, IV, 19.

CHAPTER VII

MAN'S ADVENTURE INTO THE NEXT WORLD

IN the foregoing chapter we traced a phase in the history of doubt and perplexity. It seemed as if the shifting races of Greece had begun to find that the traditions of the Heroic Age were too simple, if not too childish, for their imitation. The poetry of Homer may have been more than enough for certain cults, and the whole population, without regard to creed, sect or class, may for all we know have still found in the epics something which gave free rein to their imagination. But as human beings began to lead more varied and probably less purely contentious lives, as they continued to migrate, multiply, colonise, project and exchange both commodities and ideas, they must have discovered in themselves much that was beyond Homer's ken. We have based these conclusions on the fragments of literature which have come down to us from the post-Homeric Ages—oracles, legends, myths, and stories which originated in forgotten rites and were preserved to illustrate more modern emotions and curiosities. We see through them that man, as usual, was creating fresh dangers and difficulties, which found expression, from Hesiod to Herodotos, in a growing sense of insecurity and a growing desire for enlightenment. Did this state of mind produce no artistic creation in which strength and comfort could be found? Did man resign himself to speculation and the study of his own weakness or did he not, as heretofore, imagine some new type of hero capable of overcoming these new difficulties?

We have looked for an answer along conventional lines, that is to say, in such works as the *Theognis*, the abridgments of the Cyclic poets and the *History* of Herodotos, and we have found that man does not seem to have become more materialistic. He seems have become more acutely conscious of the mysterious forces within and around him, and less and less certain about the purposes of the gods and the tendencies of his own nature. Under such conditions, tales of battle and adventure could not give a full outlet for man's spiritual ambitions. The old-fashioned epic was bound to emphasise his insufficiency and blindness. As a result, we have been able to form a better idea of man's needs than of his ways of satisfying them. We must look further afield for the picture of positive virtues—the qualities to face this world and at the same time to fathom the abysses beyond it. We shall find our material among burial rites and eschatological doctrines and we shall be able therein to trace a source of inspiration which endured to the end of the Classical Age.

1. *Primitive beliefs and practices with regard to the burial of the dead. The hope of extracting knowledge of the future. The persistency of this hope. How the quest of foreknowledge develops the epic spirit.*

To look for an epic of this world in the contemplation of the next, seems at first sight to be too paradoxical to be seriously considered. Yet there is nothing in the subject to discredit such a search. The epic spirit is not confined to martial themes; it seeks an outlet wherever the true greatness of man can be portrayed in action, and if we find that the study of the dead mirrors the encouragement and energy needed by the living then we have, if not an epic, at least epic sentiments.

At the very outset of our inquiry we find that man's ideas of the next world have not developed along the easiest and most obvious lines. Nothing, it is agreed, is more natural than to expect a future life; even the prehistoric Casci, to quote Ennius[1], held that belief. But nothing is more natural than to think of life as breath and the power of growth and to imagine that after death the spirit returned to the wind, the streams and to vegetation. Even down to historical times human beings were killed so that their life might pass into the land, and bodies may originally have been buried for that reason, especially as mortals were sometimes supposed to have sprung from the soil. But human beings did not long remain contented with this, the simplest creed. Just as woods, rocks, streams and even trees and pools were haunted, each by its separate daemon,

[1] Cic. *Tusc.* I. 12.

so each life-spirit was soon expected to stay near its former haunts: the village where the man had once lived and the place where his corpse had been interred. Then we find that these surmises brought perplexity or doubt into man's rudimentary speculations; some believing that the souls of the dead were diffused into creation, others convinced that they lurked somewhere near the living. Thus the ancient Egyptians once believed that the soul—or *ba*—flitted about its burial place like a human-headed bird. As we shall see, men seem to have had, at an early period, the stronger motives for hoping, and so believing, that the disembodied spirits were within reach. So they supposed that ghosts naturally required the same things as they sought when embedded in the human frame—nourishment, ornaments and dominion—and still cherished the same hatreds or distrusts—especially against strangers and the rivalry of the rising generation. So ancestor worship probably originated.

We have become so familiar with the later presentations of Hades and Niflher, that we are inclined to forget how profoundly this other earlier cult has influenced human sentiments. From the time of the tombs at Mykenai, Tiryns and Orchomenos to those of the two Roman cemeteries discovered near Carthage, "departed spirits" seem to have been fed with sacrifices or libations at their graves. The *Iliad* twice speaks of embalming as a recognised custom[1] and Plutarch[2] records that the bones of Theseus were discovered by Kimon and solemnly interred in Athens. The persistence of burial customs, even while cremation was also practised, has been proved beyond reasonable doubt. It remains, now, to show how this cult of the dead contained one of man's earliest dreams of greatness. It was not only that the spirit great in life continued to be great in death, and that the ingrained energy or passion still clung to any fragment or relic of the once vigorous body. Men actually came to believe that the greatest obstacle to wisdom and foresight and the chief cause of irresolution and despondency were dissipated by the process of death.

Even at the present time, despite our analytical habits of

[1] *Il.* vii, 83; xvi, 456.   [2] *Thes.* 36.

thought, we find it natural to talk as if the experiences of the present (such as joy or sorrow) were really entities, independent of human beings: and we are even more inclined to regard the future not as a succession of undefined events, but as a veil about to disclose what already exists. In early days, before races had yet learnt to anatomise their own minds, this fiction was a genuine belief. People were really convinced, as they prepared to invade their neighbours' territory, that a battle was already there, waiting somewhere for them, and on the stricken field victory or death was expecting their arrival. In fact, warriors of old, before drawing the sword, sometimes tried to discover whether ultimate victory or defeat was signified by the presence of a deity. But a glimpse of the unseen world was not easy to obtain. Biarke[1] had to look through Hrut's arm akimbo, in the hope of so gaining second sight, before he could expect to catch a glimpse of Othin. Venus had to dissipate the cloud which darkens all mortal vision before Aeneas could discern the Achean deities engaged in overthrowing Troy[2]. For it was the living flesh which darkened the eyes of the spirit. The body was bound down to the world of things which you can touch and feel, and so the spirit within the body had to suffer the same limitations. But there was another sphere—the world of thought—which consisted of things not near enough in time and place to make their presence felt to mortal senses. Even during lifetime the mind could escape for a while into visionary surroundings— for dreams appear as pictures—and the ghost of Patroklos, though merely breath and outline ($\psi\upsilon\chi\dot{\eta}$ $\kappa\alpha\dot{\iota}$ $\epsilon\ddot{\iota}\delta\omega\lambda\upsilon\nu$), could yet speak to Achilles in the shadowy union made possible by sleep[3]. When Sigrun heard that the dead Helgi had been riding near his own burial mound, she made ready a bed so that she could visit him there and be united in sleep[4]. No wonder sleep and death were supposed to be twins who fulfilled the same function of divesting thought[5]. Thus death was now seen to bring both loss and gain. The spirit lost touch

---

[1] Saxo, *Gesta Danorum*, II, xxi[a], p. 106.　　[2] *Aen.* II, 604.

[3] *Il.* XXIII.　　　　　　[4] *Helgakvitha Hundingsbana*, II, 39–50.

[5] *Il.* XVI, 672; *Theog.* 758; Paus. V, xviii, 1 (chest of Cypselus); Clement, *Misc.* IV, 22; Herakl. *frag.* 26.

with substance and material. In fact burial gifts, as found in the Mykenaian tombs, needed only to be the flattened copies of this world's goods, preserving merely their outline in the thinnest gold-leaf, and the models of food and of the dead man's possessions, which used to accompany the corpse in Egyptian burials, were replaced by painted figures before the Fifth Dynasty. The substance was found to decay, but the form or semblance, which transcends the sense of touch, but appeals to thought, was believed to be less perishable. On the other hand, the soul became a part of the unseen world, and blended in some way with the past and the future.

Thus the dead were believed to possess the knowledge which all men of all ages have most ardently desired. When once they were quit of the body, they were free to acquire insight into the invisible events which gather round us, ready to declare themselves. Such a creed must have come to the living with the promise of almost endless power. No wonder they tried to court the attendance of this or that ancestor by offering all the inducements which experience or primitive reasoning had taught them to be the most effectual. So they preserved and guarded the body which he had once loved and to which possibly he might still in some magic fashion be attached; so they offered food and drink, especially blood which contained the energy of life and with its warm deep colours and mysterious evanescence seemed more akin to the spiritual than to the earthly. Finally the inquirer would come as near as possible towards meeting the ghostly councillor half way, in the shadowy no-man's land of sleep[1]. This belief continued to satisfy men in the age of reason. When Plutarch consoled Apollonios on the death of his son, he reminded him that the spirit, released from the encumbrance and obscurity of the body, is free to pursue the search for Truth without impediment[2], and argues that the mind is just as able to look forward into the future as backward onto the province of the memory, except so far as perplexed and retarded by the flesh[3].

From the very first, the cult of the dead must have appealed

---

[1] Herod. IV, 172; *Aen.* VII, 88. Frazer, *The Golden Bough*, pt II. *Taboos and Perils of the Soul*, chap. II, § 2.   [2] *Moralia.*   [3] *De Defectu Oraculorum.*

to the imaginative side in man's nature, and have enabled him to look beyond the present. It is, then, no wonder that the ancient world was unwilling to relinquish its observances. Sulla is said to have asserted in his *Memoirs* that dreams were more worthy of belief than any other kind of supernatural communication[1]. Cicero is supposed to have been influenced by this means to side with Octavius after the murder of Julius Caesar[2], and the νεκυομαντεῖα of "meus amicus Appius" to which he alludes[3] was probably a rite for evoking the dead. Plutarch tells the story of Elysios as though the ψυχομαντεῖον was still a usual practice[4]. Lucan represents Pompeius resorting to a witch and contriving that a corpse should be summoned from Hades and interrogated, as if necromancy were a practice worthy of his hero[5]. The procedure of the "Cave of Trophonios" reads to us like an impudent fraud, yet it is solemnly recorded by Pausanias[6], and his description certainly reads like a visit to a tomb. St Augustin protests "nec anima mea unquam responsa quaesivit umbrarum"[7] as if such were in his day a usual custom.

Mankind might well be pardoned for clinging to this belief. Besides learning to see life through the eyes of spirits, unobscured by the flesh, could not each mortal hope one day to become himself a spirit and indulge to the full this passion for knowledge and this desire to serve his clan, while at the same time he enjoyed after death a vast increase of homage and influence? Long after the belief in Hades was established, warriors were known to return to earth to warn their fellows, as Achilles warned Agamemnon[8]. And then the worship of chthonic deities must have advanced civilisation in other ways. Spirits who foretell the future and bestow the gift of second sight are not to be managed by fools or cowards. There must have been unwilling spirits to cajole or compel, angry spirits to placate, and furtive or elusive deities who were difficult to find. Such exigencies must have taxed to the utmost the resources and ingenuity of the age, and have compelled men

---

[1] Plut. *Vit. Lucull.* 23. [2] Plut. *Vit. Cic.* 49.
[3] *Tusc.* I, chap. 16, § 37. [4] *Moralia.*
[5] *Phars.* VI, 413. [6] Paus. IX, xxxix, 4, 5.
[7] *Confess.* X, 35. [8] *Ante*, chap. V, § 6.

to revise and enlarge their ritual, and borrow from other countries; if Greeks, probably from Egypt and the Chaldees. Besides, whatever the original mood in which the living approached the dead, the cult must eventually have been filled with terrors. We have already noticed in several connections that mankind seems always to be haunted by fear, and that one of the ever-recurring problems of culture is to put this dread into a form which can be encountered and overcome. So the horrors of the unknown, and of the supernatural, as well as the loathsomeness which accompanies the signs of death, were associated with the worship of the "departed." The Etruscans seem to have believed that all ghosts were malevolent, and to have transmitted their fears to the Romans. An old inscription runs "mortuus nec ad deos nec ad homines acceptus est."[1] We still have an abstract of the epic of Asmund[2]. This prince formed so close an attachment with Aswid, the son of Biorn, that the two vowed not to be parted even in death. Soon after Aswid died, and was buried with his horse and dog, and Asmund, true to his oath, took up his abode in the same barrow as the corpse. Not long afterwards some Swedes broke into the tomb and what was their horror when they found themselves encountered by a wild-eyed, unkempt figure, ghastly pale, reeking with the loathsome corruption of the grave, his face covered with blood and his left ear torn from his head. When the intruders had recovered from their terror, and had gathered round this apparition, he persuaded them that he was still a living man, like themselves, and then proceeded to reveal the secrets of the tomb; how the spirit of Aswid was enabled by infernal power (Stygium numen) to mount up at night into the cavern; how it devoured the horse and the hound and then turned upon the former friend, mangling his cheeks and tearing off his ear. Thus, in the solitude and darkness of the cavern, amid the stench and decay of a charnel house, Asmund had been forced to wrestle for his life with a loathsome ghoul; and bore tokens of this ghastly contact in his deathlike pallor. But in spite of its dehumanised ferocity,

[1] Corp. Insc. Lat. I, 818; G. Boissier, *La Rel. Rom.* v, § 1.
[2] Saxo, *Historia Danorum*, v, xliv a, b, pp. 243–6.

the *monstrifer* was no match for the human being and Asmund had conquered.

Other stories, equally gruesome, must have arisen at this stage of culture, and must then have been attached to the later idea of Hades, and so have been made to illustrate another phase of religious sentiment. For example, Odysseus digs a trench and performs the appropriate sacrifices, so that the spirits creep up from the earth to drink the blood. Yet not till the end of the episode, in a passage indisputably added by a later hand, does he fear that Persephone will send up the Gorgon from Hades[1], though a terrifying apparition of some sort would be more suitable to the primitive ritual, and to the mood of the inquirer performing it[2]. The tales illustrating human cunning and resourcefulness in constraining reluctant spirits followed the same course of development. For we have, in these cults of necromancy and ancestor worship, the kind of material out of which the intellectual epic takes its rise. The hero who would know the secrets of the dead needs the utmost fortitude and ingenuity; he must be prepared to face the most terrific adventures; and the prize which he wins is not merely fame or territory or prisoners, but insight and foreknowledge. Above all, even though the inquirer recognises the menace of supernatural danger, he also recognises that such danger can be overcome. These ghosts with their weird power are in origin only human. Even while yet on earth he will find that he can master their terrors, if his courage is equal to the test.

The disadvantages of ancestor worship and of burial cults in a n age of conquest. Rise of the belief in a special abode for g ods and for spirits divorced from the body. New ideas on the unsubstantiality of the spirit. The older beliefs do not disappear.

These cults must have arisen and flourished in a fairly settled period, when the succession to the kingship was moderately assured and the living could count on the paternal, or at any rate the friendly sentiments of the dead. Possibly we can here divine another aspect of the Golden Age of which we have already caught glimpses elsewhere. But when dynasties

[1] *Od.* XI, 634.   [2] *Ibid.* XI, 42–3.

were rising and falling, the risk of offending these spirits must have been too great. Besides, the first care of every invader must have been to sever the defenders from the help of their ancestors, by destroying or desecrating their barrows and burial grounds. Even if there had been no strategic reasons for abolishing cemeteries, a conqueror would not willingly face the prospect of occupying a land haunted by the vengeful ghosts of the former possessors. Nor would he often find much comfort when he looked within his own house. Many an adventurer, who had conquered a kingdom, must then have gone on to fight his kinsmen or children for its possession. Many a young chieftain, in those stormy times, would have trembled if he thought that the outraged ghost of his predecessor still had power to harm.

Even those warriors who were not conscious of having incurred the enmity of the dead would find it inconvenient to worship them. There must have been many warriors like Diomed or Beowulf who lacked established kingdoms and who constantly changed their abode in search of honour and wealth. Some were little better than outlaws[1]. As is well known, they tended to gather round themselves a following of young men as ambitious and unfortunate as themselves, bound only by personal allegiance and the prospect of reward[2]. Ancestor worship was impossible under such a system. A warrior might still be proud of his forebears; he might wish to benefit by their prestige and reputation; he might even believe that they were divine. But how could he bring in the sons of other warriors, born in different countries and under different auspices, to share their influence? How could Achilles thus admit Patroklos, Hygelac Beowulf or Jonathan David? Moreover, as the *comitatus* again and again proved its worth in battle, hereditary kings must have tended more and more to invite strangers within their gates. As the palaces became gradually, like Arthur's or Olaf's court, a rallying-point for warriors, the bonds of even the oldest and proudest families must have weakened.

---

[1] *Ante*, chap. II, § 7.
[2] For the *comitatus* see *ante*, chap. II, § 2; *post*, vol. II, chap. I, § 2.

So there were many reasons why the cult of the dead, which had once proved a source of pride and encouragement, now became a cause of fear, and it is intensely interesting to know how the newer age conquered these obsessions and created out of them others which restored their confidence. They needed, above all things, the conviction that a human being once killed was done with; so they persuaded themselves that the spirit which had left the body flitted away to some ghostly abode far from the haunts of the living. It is most probable that this doctrine was independently reached in different countries and at different times by a similar train of thought, as often as an invader needed release from the importunities of the dead. The religion of a conquering race must generally have prepared them for some such conclusion. As often as a series of migrations or wars brings to the front a so-called "heroic age," it also establishes a breed of warrior gods and goddesses who inhabit some mountain or island or enchanted land. This new dynasty, like their worshippers, has first to conquer the former powers, and as daemons, frost-giants, ogres or Titans cannot be annihilated, being immortal, they must be overwhelmed and imprisoned. So there arises the idea of a dungeon for the dispossessed; some kind of durance in which the irreconcileable powers of the old world are kept from interfering with the new rulers of heaven and earth. It seems unlikely that Tartaros or Niflher, any more than Olympos or Valhal, was originally imagined to be open to the spirits of human beings. But the primitive mind works by analogy, and having once agreed that abodes exist both for the conquering and the conquered deities, they would readily grant that others attached thereto await the ghosts of human beings.

Apart from expediency, these beliefs were congenial to the materialism of the Heroic Ages. Men who placed such enormous value on the joys of this life and who expected to find the fullest self-realisation in earthly possessions and achievements, would naturally be inclined to regard the disembodied spirit as futile. Besides, once granted that the soul had got to leave the activities and pleasures of the flesh, and be banished to an unknown land, there was some consolation in assuring one's self that it was now a thing of naught, incapable of human powers, however loath to leave them. It suited the mood of a warrior to expect nothing from the world to come. So the great Achilles declares the creed of the warrior caste

ἦ ῥά τίς ἐστι, καὶ εἰν ᾿Αίδαο δόμοισι,
ψυχὴ καὶ εἴδωλον, ἀτὰρ φρένες οὐκ ἔνι πάμπαν[1],

and the poet of the *Odyssey* speaks of bodiless spirits as heads without human vigour (ἀμενηνὰ κάρηνα)[2]: compares them to a dream[3] or to twittering, squeaking bats in a dark cave[4].

One imagines that from the first these doctrines must have caused great searchings of heart. How many warriors succeeded in regarding their personality as eventually evaporated into a mangled corpse and a gibbering will o' the wisp? Those who could not realise the annihilation of self had to face the prospect of a journey through subterranean regions into an unexplored world controlled by unfamiliar powers. So, as we have seen, the more ancient rites and beliefs were never wholly abandoned. It seems likely that a tomb or burial ground and a corpse embalmed against corruption brought with them some assurance of possession and permanence. There was a suggestion of reality and peacefulness about a body reposing its weight on a site familiar to it. At least so St Augustine found many centuries later[5]. But the man who believed in Hades had nothing to look forward to but danger, exile and the strangeness which primitive men hate.

But yet these discouraging phantasies persisted, and for long periods became part of the established creed. As we have seen, the conditions of warfare imposed some such beliefs. So we must now trace the steps by which warriors rendered the prospect of Hades acceptable. They overcame their repugnance by a process of thought which we have already studied in other connections. They associated their fears and hopes with what they knew of their gods. They pictured their ultimate abode as being connected with those of the immortals; so that the terrors or consolations of death could be envisaged under the same guises as were their deities. In fact they came to believe

---

[1] *Il.* XXIII, 103–4.   [2] *Od.* XI, 29.   [3] *Ibid.* XI, 222.
[4] *Ibid.* XXIV, 6–10.   [5] *Civ. Dei*, XIX, 12.

that their own dead sometimes experienced the same fate—whether for good or for evil—as the victorious or conquered gods. They surrounded these remote kingdoms with impassable barriers, such as the brazen wall round Tartaros, or the river Slith, filled with swords and daggers, guarding Nastrand, in order to make clear the inhospitality of the region. Finally they employed a ritual which should act as a passport through all these obstacles to the permanent abode behind them. By the time that the *Odyssey* had assumed its present form they also believed in a special guide to lead the ghosts direct to this mysterious world.

III. *The funeral pyre, its origin and significance. Probably employed in the first place to ensure the severance of soul from body, it becomes the means by which men conjecture the possibility of a second more glorious existence.*

Of all these features, the ritual probably developed first and should now claim our attention. Much evidence still survives of the funeral customs of both Greeks and Romans; we know something of their preparations and initiations both before and immediately after death. But when we come to follow any clue or to trace any distinct line of development, we find that the influence of the Orphic or Dionysiac mysteries[1] generally prevents us from penetrating further backward into the labyrinths of time. Perhaps there was very little to investigate before those elaborate rites took possession of the imagination. At any rate one of the most noticeable features of primitive burial was the obligation to call upon the dead man by name. Odysseus specially states that he thrice addressed each of those who were killed by the Kikones[2]. Another obligation was to wash the corpse before proceeding further with the rites[3]. Pliny, in *Naturalis Historia*, explains that both observances were necessary in order to be sure that the soul had really left the body[4]. But when speaking of any Heroic Age we naturally think of the funeral pyre. This truly epic rite never seems to have become universal[5], and it has been suggested that the

---

[1] See *post*, § 7; vol. II, chap. IX, § 1.   [2] *Od.* IX, 65.
[3] *E.g. Sigrdrifumol*, 34.   [4] *Apud* Serv. on *Aen.* VI, 218, 325.
[5] Rohde, *Psyche*.

practice was originally adopted when a buried corpse ran the risk of desecration. Such may sometimes have been the case; but apart from times of very distant or rapidly moving warfare there were many other ways of obviating that danger. The Skythians who led a nomad life among the northern wilds, and frustrated the Persian invasion by flight, yet preserved their burial grounds by keeping their location a profound secret[1]. Prokopius tells us that certain northern tribes of the Franks, as well as Frisians, Angles and Britons, used to ferry their dead to a dangerous and remote shore on the west coast of the island of Brittia and that certain families of fishermen were employed to discharge that office[2]. Servius records that the inhabitants of the district round Syene used to convey their dead to one of two almost inaccessible islands in the midst of a marsh[3], and it is noticeable that Odysseus has to seek a distant and inaccessible place, indicated by a goddess, before he can gain access to the dead. So it seems difficult to believe that the fear of desecration was the only or chief motive for destroying the corpses of the dead. On the other hand, the funeral pyre rendered any further connection between the spirit and the body impossible; and it seems in the first place to have been used, as were the lustrations and the invocations, to ensure the irrevocable flight of the soul.

Why were the warriors of epic poetry so apprehensive that the corpse might still harbour or attract the breath of life? We have seen why they found a belief in Hades so necessary, but why could not the ψυχὴ καὶ εἴδωλον flit away as soon as the body had been killed? These fears must have arisen in some pre-epic time when they not only believed that each body and spirit were ordained to journey together for an appointed span of time, but also held that any violent and premature severance crippled and mutilated this partnership, but could not annihilate it. The life clung to the corpse however broken, as in the case of Dido[4]. War must once have been regarded as something unnatural, and death in battle as a plague which

---

[1] Herod. IV, 46, 127.

[2] *Bell. Goth.* IV, 20. See remarkable passage by Gibbon, *Decline and Fall*, chap. XXXVIII.

[3] *Aen.* VI, 154.　　　　　　　[4] *Ibid.* IV, 696–9.

cut short the career of a chieftain before his time. Those who
died of pestilence in the Achean camp seem to have been
burnt, no less than those who died of wounds[1]. Kalamos may
still have been influenced by some such thought of untimeliness
and not by a desire to imitate "Indian philosophers." He
found himself dying of an internal disorder in the prime of
life, so he had a pyre lighted and after riding up, pouring a
libation, offering a lock of hair, and performing the ancient
sacrifices, he allowed himself to be burnt[2]. Possibly warriors
may at one time have claimed to know by omen or intimation
whether their approaching death was fated or premature, or
perhaps they may have begun by thinking that all young
men who perished on the field of battle should be burnt.
But in any case the funeral pyre was for the βιαιοθάνατοι.

These conjectures are worth making, because if they strike
anywhere near the truth, they help us to appreciate the
grandiose idea which man gradually built onto this practice.
We have mentioned that men came eventually to believe that
mortals might even hope to join the gods as companions in
immortality. There are a few hints of this possibility in Homer.
The Lykia to which Sarpedon was borne by sleep and death
was perhaps some allusion to a land of light[3]. Menelaos is
promised immortality in the Elysian Fields because he is the
husband of Helen and so allied to Zeus[4]. When we look forward to the post-Homeric Age we find Hesiod declaring that
Zeus has withdrawn all that remained of the old heroic breed
to live with him[5]. Dieterich[6] has collected many examples of
the same belief in later literature. The funeral pyre seems
gradually to have become, at any rate in the imaginary realm
of poetry, the passport to this immortality. In sloughing the
dross of earth could not the spirit become divine?[7] No doubt
the ghosts of ordinary mortals hovered vainly above ground
like the wraith of the serpent described in the *Catalogue of
Women*[8], until finally liberated by the pyre, to flit to Hades.
Surely some warriors were descended almost directly from

[1] *Il.* I.   [2] Plut. *Alex.* 69.   [3] A. Dieterich, *Nekyia*, I, I.
[4] *Ibid.* and *Od.* IV, 563.   [5] *Works and Days*, 166 ff.   [6] *Op. cit.*
[7] Jamblichus, *De Mysteriis*, v, 12. *The Golden Bough*, Adonis, Attis, Osiris,
Bk I, chap. VII, §3.   [8] 68 B, ll. 46 ff.

deities, and their spirits would regain their inherited divinity
when released from the flesh. One remembers particularly the
end of Herakles. He mounted the pyre and Poias was induced
to set it alight. Then λέγεται νέφος ὑποστὰν μετὰ βροντῆς
αὐτὸν εἰς οὐρανὸν ἀνάπεμψαι[1].

iv. *In this Hades-literature men gratified the longing for communion with the dead. Then the love of adventure and the
admiration for resourcefulness and self-restraint, especially in
the story of Gorm's voyages. Then the desire to know the
future or even to rectify the present.*

When endeavouring to reconstruct the aspirations and
ambitions of the past, it is inevitable that we should put the
utmost value upon each single piece of evidence.We are dealing
with the fragments and relics of a literature, so like the traveller
who surveys the ruins of the Acropolis at sunset, or stands near
the lion gate of Mykenai glancing now at the Cyclopean
walls and now at the strip of sea visible far away below, we
must make the most of what is left to us. In this spirit we have
seen how the dreary doctrine of Hades, and the rites of the
horrificum bustum[2], might yet offer the possibility of a second and
more glorious existence. We have now to see how the same
thought might render this life more full of hope and enterprise.

In the first place, however expedient it might be to imagine
that the dead were far removed from the living, all men
worth the name have felt a desire to see again their former
comrades and kindred. So they devised means of communication. The Getai, who were, according to Herodotos[3],
ἀνδρηιόταται καὶ δικαιόταται, believed that those slain in
battle went direct to Salmoxis, and once every four years they
sent a messenger thither by flinging him in the air and letting
him fall on their spear points. If he died immediately, he was
accepted by the god. In Italy curses were inscribed on lead
and placed in tombs apparently in the expectation that the
dead man would take them down to the lower world[4]. Joinville

---

[1] Apoll. *Bibl.* ii, vii, 7.   [2] Lucr. iii, 906.
[3] Herod. iv, 94-6.
[4] Conway, R. S., *Italian Dialects*; Pauly-Wissowa, *Real-Encyclopaedie*,
Art. "Devotiones."

relates how the Saracens buried alive a sergeant so that he might perform a similar mission. Saxo[1] records a sublime action of a warrior filled with this desire. When Harald I of Denmark was treacherously murdered in the battle against the Swedes, his enemy Ring stopped fighting, and spent half a day searching till he found the corpse. He then procured the royal Danish chariot and harnessed to it one of his own horses richly caparisoned, so that the dead king might reach Tartaros before the others, and might petition Pluto to give rest to the warriors of both sides when they arrived. Having delivered his last message to the departing spirit, the corpse and chariot were duly placed on a pyre heaped with precious spoils, and the ashes were afterwards transferred to Leire. The greatest hero of the *Iliad*[2] and the greatest of the *Odyssey*[3] are alike vouchsafed communion with the dead. Both passages are among the noblest in Homer, but neither derives its grandeur from what the warrior learnt of the future or of the nether world. The inspiration arises from the thought of love and friendship, ten times more precious because of separation, and also from the feeling that death, the greatest of all Homer's enemies, has for once, in a certain measure, been overcome.

The living were not content to send messengers to Hades by the short and certain road of death. They liked to imagine that it was possible to find their way there while still alive. So the desire to break through the barrier of death was blended with the love of adventure. Sometimes the journey thither was pictured as a furious ride. Hermódr rode nine nights through dark and precipitous valleys till he came to the river Gjöll with its thatch of glittering gold and found that he had reached the *helvegr*[4]. When Helgi communed with Sigrun near his burial mound, he told her that he would have to ride his bay charger through the sky, far into the west to the "wind-helm's bridges."[5] But more often Hades was reached by a long sea voyage. So Skyld started on his last journey[6]. Odysseus had to sail to Kimmeria. Claudian conjectured

[1] Saxo, VIII, lxxviii[b], pp. 390–91.   [2] *Il.* XXIII, 100 ff.
[3] *Od.* XI.   [4] *I.e.* the *Hell-way*, *Gylfaginning*, XLIX.
[5] *Helgakvitha Hundingsbana*, II, 48.   [6] *Beowulf*, 26 ff.

that the kingdom was somewhere on the coasts of Gaul[1]. St Brandan found it on an island in an uncharted sea[2]. Sometimes we find that a band of heroic adventurers set out for a long sea voyage, generally in search of treasure, and after encountering every hardship, especially famine and shipwreck, they finally reach a chain of islands, or a stretch of broken mainland. Everything in this domain is mysterious or terrible, and the audience or reader soon realises that the explorers have reached the abode of the dead.

The two stories connected with Gorm's voyages[3] are the best examples of this type. The hero sets out with three hundred adventurers and Thorkill for guide. After many hardships they reach *ulterior Byarmia* where a giant offers them every hospitality. At the bidding of their guide they resist all the *blandimenta uisus illecebraeque gule* offered them, except four, who yield to temptation of the senses, and the rest are conveyed across a river which separates the world of men from the world of monsters. They find themselves approaching a dreary looking dilapidated town, guarded by ferocious dogs who are pacified by a horn smeared with fat. On entering they are greeted by a foul stench and by dismal cries. They find themselves in a vast hall filled with every kind of obscenity and offensiveness, the floor crawling with snakes, the doorposts black with soot and the walls daubed with filth. Pale gibbering ghosts are huddled on iron seats which form a kind of theatre. Through a gap in the rocky wall they catch a glimpse of four giants lying crippled for ever by Thor's fury. As in the former experience they are subjected to temptation. A treasure is offered them, and when some few cannot keep their hands off the spoil a wild shriek arises, the whole cavern rocks, the ghosts fall upon the intruders, and barely twenty of the king's party escape. Soon after, Thorkill led another party in search of Utgarda-Loki. As before they suffer untold hardships and reach a land of perpetual twilight. Two giants, with horn noses, refuse to guide the travellers unless Thorkill could tell them three truths. The explorer succeeded, and after following

---

[1] *In Ruf.* I, 122. [2] *Post*, vol. II, chap. XI, § 3.
[3] Saxo, VIII, lxxxv b, p. 420.

their many directions, the band finally crossed a stream and entered a cave. There lay Utgarda-Loki, loaded with ponderous chains. The whole rock dungeon reeked, and when Thorkill ventured to break off one of the hairs of his chin, thick as a cornel spear, the stench nearly overcame the whole party. Their return was beset by snakes and daemons whose stings and poisonous slaver, together with the stench, slew all but five.

It will be noticed that the heroes of the adventures are not merely men of action, they are exposed to insidious temptations; they find themselves in a world for which they are totally unprepared; courage is necessary, but courage is not enough. Besides, the narrator takes but a moderate interest in the immortals who undergo the truly loathsome horrors of that stinking, slimy cavern. In fact, his conception of the next world is extremely vague[1]. He is chiefly concerned with the human and earthly virtues of the explorers. This attitude may be partly due to the age in which Saxo wrote[2], but it also follows from the tone inherent in this type of story. The legend of Gorm's voyages belongs partly to the tales which glorify man's spirit of enterprise, but partly to those which inculcate the need of wariness and foresight, and emphasise the unexpectedness and mystery of supernatural things. Very special difficulties beset the adventurer who penetrated to the next world. Because bidden to put up his sword and warned that what he saw were mere outlines and apparitions[3], he was not therefore free from danger. We have already suggested that tales illustrating the elusiveness or double-dealing of spirits in the days of ancestor worship may have been transferred to those who adventured into Hades. According to one obscure fragment of legend, Rhampsinitos goes down and plays dice with Demeter, and as the game is about equal, he receives a scarf of gold work[4]. There is a quaint *fabliau* telling how St Peter played chess with the devil for captive souls. Besides, it always needed a traveller of unusual watchfulness and sagacity to deal with beings of another nature than his own. If he tasted the food which they offered him, he would become

[1] See Rydberg, *Teutonic Mythology*, Engl. trans. R. B. Anderson, 1889.
[2] *Post*, vol. II, chap. III, § 4.
[3] Apoll.*Bibl.*II, v, 12; Bacch.*Epinic.*v, 7; *Aen.*VI, 290.   [4] Herod.II, 122.

like them and never return. When Theseus and Peirithoos found their way thither, Hades induced them to sit on the chair of forgetfulness: ᾧ προσφυέντες σπείραις δρακόντων κατείχοντο[1]. So the entry into the land of shadows was something more than a human feat. In yet another type of story, as we have seen in both of Gorm's voyages, the adventurer availed himself of superhuman guidance. Folklore has preserved tales of how a man or a woman appears to the privileged mortal, often bearing some flower, and conducts him along a road, over a river, through sunny fields into a dim mysterious land till they come to a walled enclosure which cannot be entered without some ritual or magic. As in battle epics, the achievement of the human being is due to the alliance of a superhuman.

After picturing mortals sufficiently favoured and accomplished to penetrate into the forbidden land and return in safety, the next step was to imagine the use which they could make of their opportunity. As in the days of ancestor worship they seek wisdom and foreknowledge, or else they actually presume to outrage the laws of death, and rescue some human being who cannot be spared from the upper world. Thus Dionysos entered Hades to recover his mother Semele, Orpheus sought Eurydike, Keres went there for Proserpine, Theseus for Peirithoos, Herakles for Alkestis, Hermódr for Baldr; Hippolytos effected an entrance at the wish of Diana, the so-called Virbius Adonis at the wish of Venus, and Herakles again at the bidding of Eurystheus. Protesilaos returned to console Laodameia, Kastor and Pollux were believed to alternate between death and life (*alterna morte redeuntes*[2]); Odysseus and Aeneas sought guidance for the future, each at the turning-point of his enterprise. The origin of these stories is obscure. Some appear to be very ancient nature myths which were preserved and recast, after their early significance had been forgotten. Some may have sprung up in response to the post-Homeric ideal of human greatness. Whatever their sources, one cannot help concluding that a great body of romantic and imaginative literature has been lost. We still

[1] Apoll. *Epit.* I, 24. According to some versions Theseus was afterwards rescued by Herakles.
[2] Hyginus.

possess some tales retold with inimitable art and feeling by Vergil or Ovid, but we can only guess at the part which they all once played in enlarging the sense of victory and achievement.

Their disappearance is not difficult to explain. The epics of the Heroic Age have regained their position and stand between us and this second growth of narrative poetry. Such heroes as Achilles, Hektor, Aias, Beowulf, Biarke, Walther, Siegfried found enough to do in their own world of adventure and warfare. Living men and monsters provided all the opportunity necessary to develop their ideal of the perfect hero. Such was the materialistic tone of every Heroic Age, and even after this enthusiasm had diminished, succeeding poets and storytellers found it difficult to escape from such mighty models. The *Odyssey* is a striking example. It contains the best early surviving account of intercourse with ghosts, and yet that experience lacks fullness and significance, because the hero had already, in the upper world, undergone the kind of trials and adventures which were at other times to be associated with the land of the dead. He is tempted with magic food which has power to change his nature; he faces superhuman powers which can be eluded only by cunning or witchcraft; he reaches among the Phaiakians a land and a city which have something of the Olympian calm and prosperity of the immortals. So Beowulf dives down a deep pool teaming with exhalations and overhung with sinister growths. One thinks of the Alkyonian lake. This latter was so terrible in its depth that when Dionysos plunged through its waters, it was to enter Hell and fetch Semele[1]. But at the bottom of Grendel's pool there is only a subterranean cave and its formidable occupant has not yet been relegated to Tartaros.

v. *The intellectual hero again. Hades becomes the brief abstract of this world's problems, and so the proper field for his adventures. Development of the idea through the* Theognis, *the Mysteries, Plato, and the* Somnium Scipionis. *Hades as the presentiment of our moral weaknesses and fears.*

Apart from these questions of artistic propriety and the influence of poetic schools, there was another and far deeper

[1] Paus. II, xxxvii, 5.

reason why the earlier tales of infernal adventures and discoveries did not develop or were afterwards discarded. As we
have seen, from the days of ancestor worship the inquirer must
have been actuated by curiosity and a desire for foreknowledge.
But by the time this theme had developed all its mystery and
terror, the adventurer himself had become something more.
Saxo seems to have realised as much when he depicted the
character of Gorm. His words are explicit: "Hic enim, nouum
audacie genus complexus, hereditarium fortitudinis spiritum
scrutande rerum nature uestigiis quam armis excolere maluit,
utque alios regum ardor bellicus, ita ipsum cognoscendorum
mirabilium, quecumque uel experimento deprehensa uel
rumore uulgata fuerant, praecordialis stimulabat auiditas."[1]
He was the kind of man who used his strength, skill and courage
to learn more about life. Such an ideal is comparatively easy
to visualise amid the pursuits and perplexities of actual life,
and we have caught many glimpses of the type in the descriptions and anecdotes of Herodotos. But no character is
more difficult to develop in narrative poetry. The audience
expect to be thrilled by his adventures, to be possessed by
hatred or even by horror at the thought of his enemies, and at
the same time they wish to look out on the world through his
discerning eyes, and to see life more clearly and intelligently
than they did before. Action must be combined with thought
and wisdom with emotion. As far as we can judge, the Hades
legends current after the Dorian invasion did not fulfil these
conditions. They seem to have been too realistic and to have
relied too much on the older heroic appeal.

In other words the intellectual hero was now the ideal, and
if he was to live in the imagination of posterity he must be
confronted with intellectual adventures, that is to say, with
crises and experiences which are the brief abstract and simplification of earthly problems. It is a common experience in our
own day suddenly to light upon the perfect expression of
some intricate mood or idea in a chance tone or tint or per-
spective. For instance, from the dust and trouble of a railway
carriage, the traveller speeding through steep valleys may

[1] Saxo, VIII, lxxxv[b], p. 420.

suddenly view, among the skyey mountain rocks above him, a secluded fold of a snowfield touched with the morning sun. The train flies on, but just for a moment he enjoys the intense realisation of remoteness, silence and purity. His impression is so vivid, because it is so simple. The vision, however fleeting, displays in uncontaminated fullness something which life generally obscures and blends with countless other disturbing elements. Men gradually learnt to look for some such clearness and singleness when they thought of the next world. After all, what could be more natural? From the very first the spirit was supposed to shed the disabilities and obscurities of its own flesh. In this later stage of development the whole shadow world is supposed to be purged of the transitory accretions of this muddled and disconcerting existence. Hades exercises the direct and powerful appeal of objectively conceived ideas.

It should be noticed in the first place how the Tartaros of the *Theognis*[1] became the centre and symbol of all that was primitive and uncivilised, and how later poets[2] added the horrors of darkness, eclipse, earthquakes, and the powers of discord and vengeance, and even supposed that the rivers of Acheron and Styx must have flowed through Hades because they seemed so gloomy and forbidding. It is not to be supposed that people expected to find in the next world all these picturesque terrors. It is more likely that they found in the thought of Tartaros the artistic outlet for all that harassed and oppressed them. In the earlier versions, men did not themselves expect to join the imprisoned gods in their torture chambers. If any of mortal breed were to be found therein, they were the monsters of crime, the special enemies of both gods and men like Tityos who attempted to rape Latona and so was first shot down by her children and then punished καὶ μετὰ θάνατον[3], or Tantalos who betrayed the mysteries of the gods and shared ambrosia with mortals[4].

At a later stage these shadowy subterranean lands were

[1] 664 ff.
[2] *E.g.* Aesch. *Eum.* 72 ff.; Ovid, *Metam.* VII, 179; IV, 434; V, 357; also the many examples collected by Dieterich, *Nekyia*, and Frazer's graphic note on the rivers Suliotike and Styx, *Transl. of Paus.*
[3] Apoll. *Bibl.* I, iv, 1.   [4] *Ibid. Epit.* II, 1.

pictured as the background on which purely human qualities stood out in silhouette. It is impossible to trace the consecutive steps of this next development, because all our evidence comes from relatively late sources. We can only say that the cult of Hades probably became more and more a study and a consolation, as existence became more and more perplexing and full of surprises. We have traced the growing fondness for riddles from Hesiod to Herodotos[1]. Hades was in some sort the collective answer to all that these riddles implied. But as such an answer required philosophy and imagination, reason and emotion, analysis and intuition, symbolism and realism, it came late in the history of culture.

Perhaps the next unmistakeable landmark is the influence of the Eleusinian mysteries, the Pythagoreans and the Orphics[2]. According to the well-known myth of Dionysos Zagreus[3], men were endowed with a double nature, and the great problem of life was to cherish the divine spirit and to burn out the sinful, earthly nature which clung to it, so that man could eventually rejoin the god-like element. As so profound and mystic a purification could not be accomplished within the short and uncertain orbit of one's life on earth, the process of atonement became associated with experiences after death. Pythagoras began by teaching that the soul, having left one shell, had to change into another, and by this system of transmigration had to live through the whole scale of animal and human lives, each existence involving its special purgation. The growth of this belief marks more clearly than any material change how completely civilisation had altered its course. In Homer men found in animals the exemplification of that ferocity and perseverance (the prehistoric *mana*) which they themselves admired. In the age of Pythagoras at least one sect discovered in these same creatures the soul of some fellow-mortal doing penance for the stain contracted in some former existence. This belief was far too crude to retain its hold for long. As men gradually developed a higher ideal of human

---

[1] *Ante*, chap. VI, § 6.

[2] See Glover, *Studies in Vergil*, chap. X, § II, with ample bibliography in footnotes.

[3] For quotations, see Cornford, *Greek Religious Thought*, v (b).

dignity and a clearer idea of the divine essence, they must also have grown more and more dissatisfied with the doctrine of metempsychosis. From whatever motives, no man could endure for long to recognise the voice of a dear friend in the howls of a beaten dog[1]. So they must have been ready to lend an ear to the teaching of the Orphics, and so came to believe that this cycle of reincarnation was varied by penalties in Hades. Thus the ideas of the next world were expanded to contain the profoundest aspirations of this one. The incomplete and degrading afflictions of this earth could hardly lead to reunion with God, but the purgations and atonements of Hades might ensure such a consummation.

Plato is the first surviving author who realised how graphically death could represent the most serious preoccupations of life. In the *Gorgias*[2] and in the *Phaedo*[3] he seems to be examining the means by which we hope that virtue and nobility will be renewed and reinforced on earth; he shows that suffering is the only true purifier, but above all, that our chief problem is to see the soul as it really is, to disentangle its nature from the many corporeal wrappings and accessories of this life, which disguise us from ourselves; and again that true happiness consists in freedom from the prejudices and intellectual limitations of the body. So he describes our spiritual experiences and transformations after death, but he is careful to insist that his description is only a tale ($\mu\hat{v}\theta o\varsigma$), not such as a sensible man would insist on taking literally[4]. Plato's best study of the next world is the vision of Er[5]. The philosopher again warns his hearers that this is no story of the kind that Odysseus told to Alkinoos ($o\vec{v} \ \mu\acute{e}v\tau o\iota \ ^{\prime}A\lambda\kappa\acute{\iota}v o\upsilon \ \gamma\epsilon \ \dot{a}\pi\acute{o}\lambda o\gamma o\nu \ \dot{\epsilon}\rho\hat{\omega}$), but such as puts things clearly to the reason. We are reminded again, in the person of Ardiaios the Great, of the penalties which the utterly depraved must undergo as an example to the rest, but the true problem of life is allegorised as something far more subtle. Er is wafted to a distant region from which he can

---

[1] See epigram by Xenophanes, quoted by Diog. Laert. VIII, 36, and by Glover, *Conflict of Religions*.
[2] 523.   [3] P. 110.   [4] P. 114.
[5] *Rep.* x, 614. A good *résumé* by R. S. Conway, "The Growth of the Underworld," in *New Studies of a Great Inheritance*.

behold the earth and the stars, and he is initiated into the secrets of Fate. He learns what no earthbound drama or poem could teach him, that the tragedies of life do not arise from the destiny which some ironic deity imposes, but from the choice which we ourselves make. The disembodied spirits have samples of lives put before them, and if they are not free, within certain limits, to choose their next career on earth, it is because they have no insight into the essence of good and evil, cannot distinguish appearances from reality, and are swayed more by their passions than by their reason.

These three sketches leave the reader with the satisfying sense of having grasped a truth in its simplest form. The more imaginative may even feel that they have themselves penetrated into a magic region, and are bringing back a treasure unobtainable on earth. Nor need this land seem less enchanted, because it is the world of pure reason. Yet no admirer can fail to mark one defect. The allegories lack a hero. Only in the case of Er, as in the case of Bishop Salvius[1], who fell into a like trance fourteen centuries later, do we feel that the character of the man may possibly have had something to do with what he was permitted to see. Plato tells us that he was a brave man, though unlike Odysseus, and one wonders whether his previous career, or perhaps his connection with the Teuton sky-god[2], had not in some way entitled him to the supernatural experience which was granted. Such is the real secret of Hades-literature. The problem is not only to invent an allegory of life, but to create a character worthy to overcome all that stands between us and the truth. He must show us how to face the horrors which we associate with death and wickedness and he must bring back as his guerdon an insight into the mysteries of existence. The vision of Er is a mere hint at these possibilities.

We find much more than a hint in the vision which has come down to us as the *Somnium Scipionis*, attached to Cicero's *Respublica*. The hero is the great Publius Cornelius Scipio while still a young man, at the threshold of his brilliant career. His ancestor, Scipio Africanus, appears to him while his spirit is

---

[1] Greg. de Tours, *Hist. Frank.* VII, 1.
[2] A. B. Cook, *Zeus*, vol. II, pp. 109–14.

released from the body in sleep, and the hero that was instructs the hero that is to be. The revelation is worthy of them both. We see, in the first place, how high an ideal of manhood is propounded. The purpose of the creator has found its noblest and most complete expression in the *concilia coetusque hominum quae civitates appellantur*[1], and the men who guide and ward these city states are the true heroes of the Roman world. So they are endowed with something more than human fortitude. Their qualities are *lumen animi, ingenii, consiliique* and their virtues are *iustitia et pietas*. In fact, they are to be regarded as something even greater than the ministers of God's will. Their origin is celestial; they are emanations of the divine essence; their life on earth is merely a *munus humanum assignatum a deo*[2]. Scipio lends a ready ear to this doctrine of divine origin, which his ancestor comes from the immortals to expound. He realises that his patriotism is the will of God working through him. He resolves to keep this sacred aspiration unsullied by any baser passion, such as the old-fashioned epic desire for fame, so that his spirit may more completely reunite with the heavenly essence from which it sprang.

The influence of Platonism is easily recognised in this conception of the future, and as both the Scipios were really interested in Greek philosophy during their lifetime, it was fitting that their views on death and eternity should also come from the same source. Yet these few pages of succinct and earnest argument contain much more than metaphysical speculation. While seeming to prove that life is but death and death is the door to the true life, this discourse is yet a call to a career of activity and self-devotion. Its other-worldliness is consummated by deeds. So the *Somnium* surpasses the three myths of Plato, in that it establishes an ideal of heroism. But the Roman visionary falls short in one respect. His revelation is not only a simplification of life. It is a medal which has no reverse. He has shut his eyes to the terrors of death and of the spirit world.

At first we may think that these terrors did not exist, for a movement against thanatophobia seems to become noticeable

---

[1] Chap. IV   [2] Chap. VII.

towards the end of the Periklean Age. The death of Sokrates is quoted more than once to show the calmness with which death should be faced. Aristophanes[1] ridicules the conventional terrors of Hades in the public theatre as if he expected many to laugh with him. Polybios[2] declares that the superstition was invented to terrorise the uneducated. Lucretius[3] in a celebrated passage proves the folly of dreading death. In the *Somnium* itself, the younger Scipio alludes once to his alarm[4] and once to his anxious uncertainty[5], but only to show how soon these unworthy apprehensions were banished. Cicero wrote a whole book to urge the unwisdom of dreading the end of life[6]. Servius[7] argued quite seriously against the existence of Hades, for geographical reasons, and maintained that what Aeneas saw was an allegory of life on this earth. Epiktetos[8] insisted that death meant a return to the elements and not a journey to the terrors of Hell. Marcus Aurelius[9] had the noblest conception of death, which he held to be merely a respite from dependence on the senses and from servitude to the impulses, an intermission from the distractions of physical life. Was this attitude gradually becoming universal among men of culture? At first such a deduction seems inevitable, and yet we find so many who continue to talk as if Hades really existed. Surely it is something more than a literary turn of phrase when Aischylos imagines

εἰς ἀναύγητον μολεῖν
῎Αιδην κνεφαῖά τ' ἀμφὶ Ταρτάρου βάθη[10].

Pindar alludes to the judgment of the dead[11] and describes Elysium. Kephalos confesses that in youth he scoffed at the terrors of the next world, but that old age brought back misgivings lest there might be some truth in it[12]. Cicero speaks contemptuously of those who still believed *poetarum et pictorum portenta*[13]. Yet he has to admit that a shudder went through

[1] Arist. *Frogs.*
[2] Polyb. vi, 56.
[3] Luc. iii, esp. ll. 791–1023.
[4] ii.
[5] *Ibid.* v.
[6] *Tusc. Disp.* i.
[7] On *Aen.* vi, 134.
[8] Epikt. iii, 13.
[9] M. Aur. vi, 28.
[10] *Prom.* 1028–9.
[11] *Olymp.* ii, 53.
[12] *Repub.* i, 330 d.
[13] *Tusc. Disp.* i, 10, 11.

the theatre when the ghost of Polydoros described the gloomy wilderness which he had just left[1]. Vergil's poetry bears witness to a lifelong interest in Hades[2]. Horace and Tibullus were not ashamed to describe the Elysian Fields filled with music and poetry, and Hades with its gloomy rivers and house of torture[3]. Seneca filled his plays with visions of Hell[4]. Juvenal ends his description of a street accident with the picture of the victim not merely a corpse, but sitting disconsolately on the banks of the Styx[5]. We notice two distinct ideas in these allusions. On the one hand there are the systems of pains and purifications, influenced by Dionysos and Orphism (such as Plato described), on the other hand there are unmistakeable appeals to the sense of horror and fear. But the two sentiments are akin and seem to merge into one when confronted with the rationalism of the unbelievers. Were there, then, two irreconcileably opposed attitudes to the problem of death? Was all this imagery a genuine obsession or a literary conventionality?

To answer that question it must be remembered that we are dealing with a civilisation founded on art. That is to say, people did not so much cultivate what is real, as what implies reality. They judged the truth of anything by the impression which it produced. After all, this method is the more truly intellectual. Which requires the greater mental effort—to ascertain what rain has fallen, or having learnt that there is a depression over the Atlantic and another on the south-west coast of Ireland, to foretell that it will rain in Scotland and the west of England? Yet such is the function of the artist. Given the circumstances, he predicts how a man would stand, or act or speak or think, and shows that the interest of the imagined episode lies in its implications: its power to impress us as a study of cause and effect. We may still endeavour to cultivate this receptivity when we contemplate a picture; but

---

[1] *Tusc. Disp.* I, 36.

[2] *Culex*, ll. 212 ff.; *Georg.* I, 36–9; IV, 219–27, 467.

[3] Hor. *Odes*, III, 13, 14; Tib. I, iii, 57 ff.

[4] *H. F.* 86–99, 548–618, 662–863; *Oed.* 160–70, 582–618; *Ag.* 1–27, 750–74; *H. Oet.* 1061–89; *Thy.* 1–121; *Med.* 740–9; *Oct.* 965–9.

[5] III, 265.

we no longer rely on intuition when assimilating ideas. The ancients were less ready to recognise the dividing line between fact and fiction; they were more accustomed to appeal to the reason through the imagination; to blend facts with fables and thought with emotion. Of course this habit of mind did not pass unchallenged. As men became capable of abstract reasoning, some of them felt the inadequacy of visualising ideas, and became analytical. Such were the philosophers who lost the power of seeing thought in pictures, and so despised the arts of the imagination[1]. Vergil may himself have fallen into this error, in youth[2]. Yet even with the most extreme, scientific methods were not so pervasive as now. Even Plato, who protested against pure literature, nevertheless found it convenient to embody an abstract idea in a myth. Even Thoukydides, who insisted on historical accuracy, yet indulged in epigrammatic and picturesque speech-making. Even now it is impossible to view the relics of classical art in congenial surroundings, say at Athens, Rome or Naples, without feeling the universality of their appeal.

So it was with the idea of Hades during the Greek and Roman classical ages. The contrast between the sceptics and the believers could not have been so deep as it at first appeared. Many of the artistically minded must still have clung to the superstition, because the idea gave shape and dignity to the terrors of life. Lucretius was not far from the truth when he declared

Atque ea nimirum quaecumque Acherunte profundo
Prodita sunt esse, in vita sunt omnia nobis[3].

But he hardly realised the significance of his own pronouncement. Being himself one of the materialists, he could rationalise the tortures of Tantalos, Tityos, and Sisyphos[4] only so far as they reflected the exact suffering of people on earth. In reality, Hades came to typify the vague, more mysterious troubles of life. If Lucretius ever gained any insight into its significance, it was when he explained the symbolism of the Danaai[5]. Every

---

[1] See *post*, vol. II, chap. IX, §§ 2, 3.
[2] *Katalepton*, VII.   [3] III, 978.
[4] *Ibid.* 980–1002.   [5] *Ibid.* 1003–10.

human being who has reached a certain stage of civilisation is at some time haunted by a consciousness of futility, the dread of darkness or stagnation, the shrinking before tremendous heights and impenetrable depths, or the fear of storms and precipices. Or it may be the sense of mental insecurity; the apprehension of false dreams or yet again of the measureless potency of evil. It is an immense relief to give definite shape and place to these elusive and treacherous misgivings; to drive them out of one's consciousness by visualising them in Hades. It was the only hope of really looking such moral plagues in the face. So we find that the idea of death brings with it much more than an artistic background. It suggests the dark secrets of life, the sources of decay, crime, disease, terror and destruction. It challenges the investigation of all that makes our existence hideous and defective. It draws attention to what is worst as well as what is best in life. When once men have begun, through this glass, to visualise their afflictions, they will also look for a hero who can brave them.

So we reach the last stage of the tendency vaguely indicated by the character of Gorm. Men have at last discovered all that the idea of Hades can imply. This atmosphere seems to have been created some time about the age of Perikles and to have endured throughout Greek and Roman civilisation, till by contact with Christianity it grew into something far deeper and more varied[1]. During that long period poets were able to enlarge their emotional appeal by alluding to this second imaginary world of real joys and sorrows. We notice them again and again experimenting with the kind of adventurer who might be suited to reveal all that was hidden beneath the ground. On the whole Herakles and Orpheus seem to have attracted most admiration, the one for the heroism with which he devoted his god-given strength; the other for the persuasive power of his art and the mysteries which he divulged. Either might have come to typify the pagan victory of man over death, if that feat had not been achieved by Aeneas.

[1] *Post*, vol. ii, chap. xi.

CHAPTER VIII

THE EPIC SCOPE OF THE *AENEID*

THE world has long ago made up its mind on the scope and purpose of the *Aeneid*. In it Vergil aimed at showing that the empire of Augustus was connected with the mythical past by an unbroken chain of human endeavour and divine interposition. So he retold the story of its inception, casting an Homeric glamour over the earliest traditions, interweaving threads of Italian folklore and Greek scholarship, discovering the will of heaven and the emergence of Roman religious ceremonial at every crisis of the story, and looking forward through ages of heroic warfare to the grandeur of the consummation. The hero of the poem, the founder of the Roman nation, is meant to be worthy of this destiny. He is no mere chieftain of the warrior caste, satisfied with earthly honour. Fate exacts from him the most rigorous allegiance to his high mission. His arduous career of battle and adventure is also a moral-pilgrimage in which he gradually becomes perfect in the duties of public service[1]. Boissier goes even further: "Sa personnalité s'efface devant ces grands intérêts; il obéit malgré ses repugnances et s'immole aux ordres du ciel."[2]

1. *We see the character of Aeneas only in outline; but we can distinguish certain features which show how the figure was meant to develop. In particular we note his perseverance and the self-conquest of his emotions, especially pity.*

Is this the whole Aeneas? As we have seen in other epics, a hero is not known only by his deeds of arms. He has another, more intimate nature, often at variance with his public achievements. While in pursuit of his quest with all its traditional difficulties, he encounters other obstacles in his own thoughts, and these belong to the age of the poet. So Aeneas, while

[1] See Warde-Fowler, *The Religious Experience of the Roman People*, chap. xviii.
[2] *La Relig. Rom.* iv, § 2.

exploring the Mediterranean of Homer, and fighting the battles of prehistoric Latium, was also facing the problems of Augustan Rome. This aspect of his character has often been disputed. Apart from the *pietas* which steadily develops with every step of his career, and gradually becomes his chief title to the high office of first Roman Father, he is sometimes thought to have no other qualities. In fact many lovers of Vergil confess that for these reasons he does not appeal to them.

One would be tempted to take this view and to look no further for any half-developed meaning in his character, were it not for the words of Suetonius[1]: "egerat cum Vario, prius-quam Italia decederet, ut si quid sibi accidisset, Aeneida combureret; at is ita facturum se pernegarat; igitur in extrema valetudine assidue scrinia desideravit, crematurus ipse." Men do not thus wish to destroy their life-work, because it lacks its last revision; least of all when they have just realised that nothing else of themselves will survive. The Romans, almost as much as the Egyptians, cherished a passion for the im-mortality which monuments confer, and Vergil must have realised that the *Aeneid*, even as he left it, was indeed a monu-ment. After eleven years of concentrated and brilliantly suc-cessful labour, he cannot have been blind to the merits which others were recognising. If he really gave this order, and if his mind was sane, he must have felt that the poem, even in its apparently finished state, was essentially incomplete, that it needed the addition of something without which its intention would be mistaken, and its spirit misinterpreted.

There is no particular reason to doubt Vergil's sanity or Suetonius's truthfulness, and the more we study the character of Aeneas, the more it appears not so much weakly conceived as incompletely developed. The artist has not had time to make clear all that he meant to convey. Yet if the reader will consider the lines on which the hero is conceived, he will realise how vast and inspiring a part Aeneas was intended to play, and how profoundly he was to have illustrated the moving forces of the Vergilian era.

In the first place Aeneas must give proof of a virtue on which

[1] *Vita Vergilii.*

the *Iliad* did not greatly insist, but which was essentially
Roman, and distinguished all the great men of the later
Republic, Catiline and Clodius, no less than Cato and Brutus
—tenacity and indomitable resolution. It is noticeable that he
does not suffer the kind of reverses which befall Hektor, or
Aias, or even Odysseus—mere setbacks in the heat of battle
or dangers which were too thrilling to crush the heart. His
trials are those which sap the mind. During the burning of
Troy he has to witness, without sharing, not only the downfall
of all that he most reverenced, but also the particularly
poignant agony of the two who least deserved their fate,
Priam and Kassandra. He seems to realise that his own life
is sacred, but even after the sack of the town he is obliged to
witness, as he thinks, the overwhelming destruction of all his
followers on the sea. When he at last reaches the promised
land, he does not come as an invader. He humbly petitions
a vacant site on which to establish an abode for his gods and
a township for his followers. It is the least that he could ask,
but the powers of evil raise up the hardy Italian tribes against
him, and the stranger who has hardly gained a foothold is
faced with a new and disastrous war.

Though Aeneas knows himself to be the chosen vassal of
Olympos, he is not spared his share of dejection and discouragement as a mortal. He seems to have too sensitive and
apprehensive a temperament for a man of action. At every
crisis of his fate his imagination leaps forward and envisages
the threatened disaster in all its terrors. One thinks of Julius
Caesar meditating on suicide before Mutina or exclaiming
"alea jacta est" when he crossed the Rubicon. Even in moments
of calm, a sense of hardship, almost of desolation, seems to
be secretly preying on his mind[1]. A warrior who suffers so
keenly, who takes so little pleasure in his own prowess, must
be endowed with other than Homeric qualities before he can
achieve that which will raise him to the stars. In the discharge
of his high mission he must be able to conquer the misgivings
and apprehensions which beset the more modern mind.

Such is the first enemy which the Roman epic hero has to

[1] *E.g.* I, 49, 403, 459; II, 657; III, 493; V, 687; VIII, 18.

overcome; but there is a more subtle and elusive adversary—
his own disposition to pity. It is told[1] of Scipio Africanus that
after he had brought himself to capture Carthage and raze it
to the ground, he walked over the smoking ruins, shedding tears
and murmuring ἔσσεται ἦμαρ ὅτ᾽ ἄν ποτ᾽ ὀλώλῃ Ἴλιος ἱρή. In
the same way Aeneas has to suffer for every experience which
leads him further along the path of destiny. His sympathy is
stronger than his love of victory. Once when fighting Mezentius,
young Lausus dashed between them and received his spear
thrust through his own body. Even in this tense moment
Aeneas is seized with pity as soon as he sees the blood welling
up into his victim's bosom, and watches his colour fade into
the ghastly pallor of death. He pauses to think of the splendid
young life that he has cut short, and for a moment he half
believes that it is his own Ascanius[2]. The severest trial of his
humanity befalls him at Carthage. Vergil's intention is quite
clear. The episode of Dido was introduced in the first place
to supply a legendary and romantic origin to the later historical
feud between Carthage and Rome, and secondly to show that
the founder of the Roman nation was no mere Herakles to
accomplish heroic tasks and then fall uxoriously under the
sway of an Omphale. It must be remembered that ever since
Catullus addressed his love poems to Clodia, eroticism had
ceased to be a pose and had become a fine art. We need not
take too seriously all those amatory flames which burn in the
pages of Horace, Propertius and Tibullus, but this was certainly
one of those epochs during which culture and concupiscence
seem to pull in the same yoke more evenly than the two ill-
paired steeds in Plato's dialogue. At any rate Augustus regarded
the tone of society as too dangerous to be treated with in-
dulgence, so the hero of the *Aeneid*, who typifies the virtues
most needed in this later era, is exposed at Carthage to the
allurements of ease and luxury. As the whole adventure is
narrated in epic fashion, looming in gigantic outline through
the mists of antiquity, Jupiter himself forbids the liaison and
orders the stranger to depart[3]. But the Trojan chieftain is
spared no bitterness that his finer nature might inflict on him.

[1] Polybius.   [2] *Aen.* x, 821 ff.   —   [3] *Ibid.* IV, 220 ff.

He has already surrendered himself to the pleasures of designing and founding a new state, and has assumed a gorgeous Tyrian robe, the token of kingship, all the more precious because Dido's own hands had wrought it[1]. Yet it costs him less to renounce all this felicity than to break the heart of the woman who had ensnared him. The character of Dido is not idealised. She is at heart a kind of Medea, one who consorted with witches, almost herself a wise woman, who usurps the functions of a haruspex[2], and all through the adventure she retains a vein of savagery, and of impulsive, barbaric vengefulness. Yet Vergil has exhausted every resource of art and genius to stir the feelings of compassion in the breast of any honourable man. He portrays her as beautiful, heroic, devoted, loyal, generous and unfortunate. There is only one thing at fault in her conduct: she does not understand the destiny and character of Aeneas. What she loves in him are the attributes of the old world epic hero—his beauty, his prowess and his divine descent[3]. She imagines that she can win and hold her lover for ever, and when she has discovered her mistake, she gives herself up to an excess of passionate despair that can end only in death. Aeneas has to endure her infinitely pathetic supplications[4], then her withering scorn[5], then her utter abasement of spirit, which he knows will turn to fury[6]. As Vergil cannot possibly have intended the future founder of the Roman state to appear, in Dr T. E. Page's phrase, "as a man... *contemptible*," he must have wished to portray him as sorely tried and beset. To judge by the sympathy and insight with which her agony is unfolded, he must have intended this desertion to be the hardest of all his superman's trials. Professor Conway[7] has convincingly argued that the poet is asserting a woman's right to be treated, not as Augustus and most other Romans of that age did treat her, but as an equal, as a human being. But, whatever his own view, Aeneas need not be supposed to suffer less because there was a conflict between humanity and the will of the gods.

[1] *Aen.* IV, 259 ff.   [2] *Ibid.* 60–4.   [3] *Ibid.* 11–12.
[4] *Ibid.* 305.   [5] *Ibid.* 365–87.   [6] *Ibid.* 412–38.
[7] "The Place of Dido in History," *New Studies of a Great Inheritance.*

II. *Like most other literary compositions subsequent to the Attic drama, the* Aeneid *develops its characters in speeches. The speeches are highly expressive in the case of other characters, but not so in the case of Aeneas. The springs of the hero's character are not revealed.*

It may be objected that so many individual touches could not have been given to the character unless it had been depicted in detail. The portrait stands out completed, full length, with the personality and much more with the weaknesses fully developed. And yet not altogether so. We are never vouchsafed more than a glimpse into the springs of moral and heroic energy which overcome this human frailty. Let the reader recall how Hektor nerved himself to face Achilles[1], or Satan to take vengeance on Heaven[2], and he will realise how much Vergil has left undone in the portraiture of his hero. In a poem abounding in great speeches, hardly a single characteristically noble utterance is put into the mouth of the chief character. These omissions are all the more surprising because Vergil was unmistakeably influenced by the Attic drama. It has often been noticed that the great tragedies are in some respects like a series of debates or even assizes in which every character is given the chance of developing his point of view and of explaining or defending his conduct. In fact, many of the great set speeches read like appeals to win the sympathy of the spectators. Vergil has unquestionably adopted this method, and intended to follow it throughout the composition of his poem. At the very outset Juno appears, as it were, on the stage and fully explains the motives for her hostility[3]. As the story advances, and the number of *dramatis personae* increases, each is enabled to appeal to the reader and to enlist his sympathy. Besides the tragic figure of Dido, Helenus, Andromache, Palinurus, Deiphobus, Anchises, Beroe (inspired by Juno to be the mouthpiece of the Trojan women) and even Charon have something arresting to say, something that opens up vistas of thought and gives a glimpse into the forces which stir human emotions. When the Trojans have

---

[1] *Il.* XXII, 99 ff.   [2] *Paradise Lost*, IV, 32 ff.   [3] *Aen.* I, 34 ff.

reached Italy and Vergil begins "the mightier half" of his epic, no student can help remembering with pleasure how vigorously human the characters appear[1]. Why have Nisus and Euryalus[2] always fascinated the imagination of posterity? The adventure on which these two boys enter is, unlike the raiding enterprise of Diomed and Odysseus[3], a ruinous failure. Everyone concerned with them suffers, and they themselves throw away their lives because they cannot resist the pleasure of murdering sleeping men and then neglect the most obvious precautions. Yet the episode more than justifies itself because the participants say their say. We look beneath their actions, to their motives and aspirations. Only one conspicuous figure fails to discharge this, the special function of all narrative poetry—Aeneas himself.

Vergil has accomplished what we might call the earlier stages of his hero's portraiture. In Book I Aeneas dwells upon his endless reverses and disappointments[4]. Books II and III, though put into the mouth of Aeneas, are more particularly Vergil's revelation of himself in narrative, so we should not expect his spokesman to put too much of himself into his narration. Yet, as we have seen, Aeneas is still allowed to disclose his apprehensiveness, his pity, and his intense love for his father[5]. But as the poem advances further, this tendency to self-revelation becomes weaker and weaker. We are told all that we need know about his actions; how attentively he listened to prophets and oracles, how faithfully he paid the required homage to every place visited by a god, how firmly he could control his anger or sorrow, and yet how invincible an adversary he proved to be in battle. But we do not learn anything of the greatness of soul which carried him through his gigantic enterprise. We do not know with what feelings he first set foot in Italy, nor what thoughts were uppermost when he returned from his embassy to Evander and found his camp beset and all but stormed by the Italians. We are not told what inward promptings led him to demand a duel with

---

[1] *E.g. Aen.* VII, 293, 473; VIII, 560; XI, 336; XII, 632, 676.
[2] *Ibid.* IX.   [3] Δολώνεια, *Il.* X.
[4] *E.g.* 94, 198, 372, 405.   [5] *E.g.* II, 657; III, 708.

Turnus, nor how he braced himself for the final encounter.
All we know of his attitude to Dido are the two constrained
and embarrassed apologies that he makes, the one in Carthage
and the other when they meet in Hades[1]. We are told *obnixus
curam sub corde premebat,* that he was *magnoque animum labefactus
amore,* and *magno persensit pectore curas*[2]. Yet we learn nothing
more of this passion and pity, nor what it cost him to overcome them.

III. *Vergil lived in an age of disillusionment and satiety; to make
his hero really live, the poet would have to show how these
depressing influences were overcome. Instead of some such
intimate study we have a great "structural" achievement, more
suggestive of architecture than of literature. Yet in some respects
Book VI does not conform to this spirit.*

Are we to suppose that Vergil would let his minor characters
plead their own cause with such fire and eloquence and yet
be content to leave his hero a mere lay figure, a form without
a soul, like the shadow which Juno fashioned out of a swelling
cloud[3]? For it is this lack of greatheartedness and fervour which
renders Aeneas so unattractive, and forces the reader to conclude that the poem itself is not an epic. We obtain glimpses
of his mind only in moments of discouragement and perplexity,
at the beginning of his enterprise, or when attending to some
religious observance, or when delivering a rather conventional
exhortation to his followers or his son. Thus we see only the
surface of his character and not the volcanic energy beneath.
Would this lack of insight, this suggestion of unreality, have
been made good if Vergil had lived another three years?
There is no knowing what genius may achieve, but such a
consummation is unlikely. It seems more probable that the
qualities which Aeneas was intended to possess could never
have found free play in the wars of Italy or while wandering
among the coasts and islands of the Mediterranean.

To make this contention clear, let us glance at what appears
to have been the chief moral problem of this epoch. Why does
Vergil, in a poem of action, picture life as full of illusions,

[1] *Aen.* IV, 333; VI, 456.   [2] *Ibid.* IV, 332, 395, 448.
[3] *Ibid.* X, 636–42.

wasted effort and unsatisfied desires? This melancholy may
partly have arisen from his temperament; but it must also have
been the result of the *taedium et displicentia sui*[1] which took
possession of his age. The feeling of changefulness and futility,
which we have already noticed in the age of Herodotos[2], had
been handed on to the Romans and assimilated as part of
Hellenic culture. But the events of the later Republic, cul-
minating in seven consecutive civil wars, afforded other than
literary reasons for believing in the decadence of mankind or
in the prevalence of Evil. Perhaps the most damning piece of
evidence against the humanism of the period is to be found in
the famous lines of Lucretius on the Roman noble[3] and in the
sheer fact that the author of those lines should have taken
refuge from his age in a philosophic poem. Servius Sulpicius,
in a letter to Cicero, tells of a voyage from Asia Minor, and
how he viewed the towns which *quodam tempore florentissima
fuerunt, nunc prostrata et diruta ante oculos iacent*[4]. Thus from the
evidence of his own eyes he almost echoes the words of Herodotos: τὰ γὰρ τὸ πάλαι (sc. ἄστεα) μεγάλα ἦν, τὰ πολλὰ ἀστῶν
σμικρὰ γέγονε[5]. Cicero himself was almost as despondent about
the uncertainty and unsubstantiality of knowledge[6]. Livy declared that his chief inducement for burying himself in historical
research was the prospect of averting his gaze *a conspectu
malorum, quae nostra tot per annos vidit aetas*. He then goes on to
explain that what causes his melancholy is not so much any
national disaster, as the slow decline of morals and civilisation
until the Empire had reached *haec tempora quibus nec vitia nostra
nec remedia pati possumus*[7]. Many other examples of Roman
pessimism could be given. In fact there seems little doubt that
the average intelligent Roman of Vergil's day must have felt
instinctively, even if he could not give very clear reasons,
that his world was nearing its end. Most seem to have staved
off the thought, either by contemplating the military and

---

[1] Sen. *De Tranq. Animi*, II, 13.   [2] *Ante*, chap. VI, § 7.
[3] Luc. III, 1053–67, see also IV, 1133 ff. Matthew Arnold's paraphrase in
Obermann Once More should be compared.
[4] *Ad Fam.* IV, 5.   [5] Herod. I, 5.
[6] *Academ.* I, 12; Paraphrase, Byron, *Childe Harold*, IV, xiii.
[7] *Praefatio*.

political greatness of the city under the early emperors, or by displaying the facilities and resources which their commanding position gave them. Such is the significance of their buildings. Roman architecture is not like Renaissance architecture. It speaks of difficulties overcome and of powers concentrated at one man's will. It reminds its organisers of all that they could control; of the wealth, the labour, the knowledge at their command. Latin literature bears testimony to this passion for constructing, but the student of Roman civilisation will be more convinced after a glance at the ruins on the Palatine, the space covered by the aggregation of the Roman *fora*; the foundations of the *Palazzo di Tiberio* at Capri; or even the architecture of a mere provincial township like Pompei. The human beings who planned and those who afterwards admired these structures on their completion must have experienced a renewed confidence in energy, co-operation and resourcefulness such as no literature can give. In this respect Roman architecture is perhaps the most significant phenomenon of that time.

Vergil seems to have felt to the full the need of these assurances, and to have sought distraction and encouragement in contemplating achievement. Now the Roman Empire was, or then seemed to be, the greatest work ever achieved. Quite apart from the decay of manners or humanism or the sense of satiety, the defence and administration of those vast territories seemed to be the most sustained and concerted effort of which any nation could boast. No doubt Vergil had many other reasons for choosing what cannot have been an altogether congenial theme, but whatever the other public or private inducements, the Roman Empire must of itself have appealed to Vergil as the most lasting of all structures and therefore as a source of comfort worthy to be developed by a poet. So the *Aeneid* has the kind of excellence which we expect from buildings. In fact one of the greatest living exponents of Vergil has defended its structure and design on those grounds[1]. But whereas architecture expresses completed victory, literature

[1] J. W. Mackail, *Virgil and his Meaning to the World of To-day*, 1925 (Our Debt to Greece and Rome).

expresses growth and effort and especially the moral and emotional states of mind through which men pass while pursuing their heart's desires. So the poet of such an age and of such a theme could not shut his eyes to the failures, misgivings and despondencies of his time, from which architecture was hailed as an escape.

It was, perhaps, the chief artistic problem of the *Aeneid* to first express and then combat this spirit of disappointment and helplessness in a story of martial victory and homeric heroism. As we have already seen the poem is not in this respect a complete success. The poet seems to have realised that his hero was no longer of the old epic type and he has therefore avoided the boastfulness, intensity, and self-confidence of the pure man of action. He has moreover endowed Aeneas with the special Roman virtue of *pietas*, and has shown how his career might symbolise the growth of national greatness under the uninterrupted guidance of destiny. He has associated his memory with the structural grandeur and durability of the Roman Empire. But the poet has not shown whether his hero had the one other virtue most needed at that time: the wisdom and the moral courage wherewith to conquer his despondency. In fact, Aeneas was really called upon to play the part of an intellectual hero. We suggest that Vergil realised these possibilities but found his material too intractable. At any rate he showed that some such ideas were in his mind when he wrote the sixth book.

IV. *Vergil succeeds in filling Hades with all that depresses and dejects in this world, so that Aeneas encounters the causes of Augustan pessimism. Then his hero is enabled to visualise the ideas and hopes which heal this melancholy, and he leaves Hades not only comforted but inspired for action.*

The man who studies death has to face the last and deepest humiliation to which human nature is subjected. His contemplation begins by recognising the collapse of all purely mundane hopes and merits, and any comfort or inspiration which he derives therefrom can be acquired only by first accepting this abasement. Vergil has used this opportunity to the full. We have already noticed the artistic difficulty of giving appropriate speeches to a character whose spirit and actions were at variance. But here there was not the same need for self-explanation. The scene itself is sufficiently impressive without the warrior's thoughts, and automatically creates the atmosphere of brooding and introspection so suitable to the Augustan Age. The adventurer's original motive is the immemorial desire to break through the barriers of death, and we need not stop to discuss the ritual by which he placates the chthonic deities and specially prepares himself for the ordeal, perhaps as if it were the initiation into some mystery. For our present purpose it is more important to notice that Aeneas has to encounter in an enlarged and simplified form all that renders this world terrible or disheartening.

In the first place Hades is the kingdom of shadows, silence and illusion, and Vergil expends some of his finest and most eloquent poetry to enforce an idea of its blankness and unsubstantiality[1]. It is like groping through a dim wood. But to the ancient mind forests, especially at night time, were the abode of hidden dangers[2], and as soon as Aeneas becomes aware of his surroundings he finds himself to be in the presence of all that we fear in real life. Dr J. W. Mackail has suggested that Vergil had in mind some Minoan labyrinth of which the underground passages and chambers, and perhaps some upright masses of masonry, still existed at Cumae. He adds that the palaces of Dis are astonishingly like the palace of Knossos[3]. But little has been discovered on that excavated mound near Candia to suggest the allegory of human infirmities and perils which the hero has to encounter.   First the actual afflictions and affections which lead to death—grief, care, disease, old age, hunger, toil and war—then the obsessions and illusions which render existence vain or hideous, such as lying dreams or the imagined forms of superhuman monsters. Lucretius[4] records the superstition that the *di manes* hovered by the Gate of Orcus, eager to suck men into Hades. Vergil does not ignore these "vulgar errors," for no fantasy which terrifies is really vain.

[1] *Aen.* VI, 268–72.
[2] *Post*, vol. II, chap. I, § 4.
[3] *Classical Studies*, 1925.
[4] Luc. VI, 762–6.

But he gives them their proper place, and so the hero of the *Aeneid* undergoes his ordeal of fear. Aeneas then follows his guide to the waters of Acheron. Here a more insidious trial awaits him. On the banks of the river some of the true miseries of life are displayed in all their nakedness. He notices first among the strangely assorted army of the newly dead that the majority are broken destinies; boys, unmarried girls and others who never fulfilled their being[1]. He realises that though the promises and pleasures of existence are past, its desires remain: and above all that most of those before him have not only failed in life but in death also. Aeneas had himself newly performed the last rites to Misenus, and no doubt both he and his comrades had experienced something of the old epic satisfaction that they had assured their fellow-traveller a speedy and certain journey to his last home. But the hero has now to realise the reverse of the medal. The observance of that rite means an added terror to life: the fear of missing these benefits through mischance or the carelessness of survivors. So strong is the old unsatisfied desire for rest that they stretch out their hands in yearning for the farther shore[2].

It is still the land of shows, sleep and night. In fact warlike intruders, such as Herakles, Theseus and Peirithoos, never found anything else. If Aeneas is privileged to penetrate beyond and to learn the deeper truths, it is because he is the more modern hero, armed with virtue and wisdom[3]. So he crosses the Styx and enters into the permanent abodes of the dead. At this stage Vergil only alludes to the dispositions of Hades, apparently assuming that such details are too well known to need recapitulating. But Servius, who must still have been in touch with the traditions, tells us that rather like the Hades of Plato, the region was contained by nine circles[4]. This classification serves only to distinguish and emphasise the disappointments and disillusionments of life. First he meets those who died in early childhood; then those who have suffered the death penalty unjustly, because they could not defend themselves; then the suicides; then those who died of love. All are still

---

[1] *Aen.* VI, 295–312.   [2] *Ibid.* 313–83.
[3] *Ibid.* 390–410.   [4] On l. 426.

haunted by the desires which they have never been able to gratify. Even those in the fifth circle, who died in war, suffer from their loss of power and energy[1]. Up to this point Aeneas has reviewed those who never fully possessed themselves. He finds little here to terrify or overawe, but much to fill him with perplexity and despair. "Even in our ashes live their wonted fires"—such a thought may well bring you peace when considering the dead from your own vantage point on earth, even if in a churchyard. But the same sentiment works very differently if you imagine yourself in Hades, in the world of broken threads and thwarted self-realisation, and look backward across the Styx to the memories of your former existence and to the events which brought you to this state of ineffectiveness and unsubstantiality. No other literary device can expose so clearly and ruthlessly the false values of life. And what is the truth which Aeneas can visualise so much more clearly in Hades than elsewhere? Such complex surroundings cannot easily be reduced to a formula, but surely this favourite of heaven and of destiny must at this point have felt the unreality of everything except regrets.

By such skilful and artistic devices Vergil had brought his hero to face the despondency and disillusionment of the Augustan world without shedding his epic dignity. The poet had then to show how Aeneas could triumph over these melancholy impressions and return from Hades comforted and encouraged. So his gaze is now directed to those who followed the law of their being to its utmost realisation. The single path diverges into two directions[2]. On the left he catches sight of Tartaros which imprisons not only the ancient offenders of lore and legend, but the more modern offenders against civilisation; all who gave themselves up whole-heartedly to evil and carried through their fell purposes to the end— *ausi omnes immane nefas, ausoque potiti*[3]. Plato had already suggested some such fate for the utterly wicked, and the doctrine may have been a common feature in other eschatological systems, so the explorer needed only to be reminded that such a place existed. Yet even that glance added

---

[1] *Aen.* VI, 492–3, 534.   [2] *Ibid.* 540.   [3] *Ibid.* 624.

something to his vision of human wretchedness, since he learns
that the types of crime with their punishments were too
numerous to be told[1]. So with his guide he turns to the right
and begins his initiation into the triumph over Evil. First he
contemplates the heroes of old time (*nati melioribus annis*) who
recall the bronze and silver ages described by Hesiod[2]. No
doubt the thought of these honoured spirits does something
to efface the recollection of so much wickedness and disillusionment. But such comfort is available to any student of
old-fashioned literature, and can be gained without a journey
to the lower world. Aeneas was to acquire a deeper insight
into the springs of life. So Anchises reveals the Platonic doctrine
of the divine origin of the soul, and the initiate learns that the
longings and passions, which seemed so remorselessly to torment
the departed spirit, are only the relics of its bodily nature. This
revelation is followed by another even more comforting. As the
souls are immortal and came from God to enter into earthly
existence, through the gate of birth, it is certain that they will
go that way again, and Anchises shows him the crowds already
drinking the waters of Lethe, so that they may forget the
miseries of earth, and be willing to return to the upper air.
Who are these spirits who, after a thousand years' preparation,
are ready again to become mortal? The answer is not quite
clear, but apparently Norden is right in explaining that the
very best and the very worst remain for ever in Elysium and
Tartaros, while the others, after a thousand years purification
of varying intensity, are restored to life[3]. They already, in
this vision, bear the εἴδωλα of their future existences[4]. Servius
remarks that the sixth book is full of philosophical theology
and the wisdom of the Egyptians, and Vergil apparently felt
that much could be left to his readers' knowledge of these
sources. We can still trace the influence of Plato and Pythagoras
and Poseidonius[5], and other obscurities probably seemed far
less puzzling to readers familiar with the Dionysiac and Orphic
mysteries.

[1] *Aen.* VI, 625–7.   [2] *Works and Days.*
[3] Norden, E., *P. Vergilius Maro, Aeneis VI*, Einleitung C.
[4] *Ibid.* D. 9.   [5] *Ibid. passim.*

So Vergil seems to have been confident that his presentment will readily be accepted and he hastens on to apply it to history. Aeneas is allowed to foresee what spirits are destined to become Roman heroes and to carry on his own work by their faith and fortitude. The vision has been justly praised by every lover of Vergil and its place in the structure of the poem has often been explained. Yet the reader of whatever epoch who has shared Aeneas's doubts and perplexities at man's uncertain and unequal destinies, but is not, like him, preoccupied by the prospect of his descendants, can look further than Roman history. Anchises is revealing the continual rejuvenation of the world. The inquirer has been led gradually to turn his back on the miseries and failures of life and by the help of philosophy and mystic teaching he has learnt to look forward to what is best in the nature and fortunes of men. The death which was the end of the old epic life is shown to be the source and strength of the new. In fact man has conquered the sense of decadence and failure by realising that the human spirit never dies and is capable of endless regenerations. It seems that some such study of philosophy really was the solution to the pessimism of the age. Vergil resolved to devote the declining years of his life to such pursuits[1]. Horace actually lived long enough to do so[2]. But Aeneas finds in these lucubrations the mainspring and inspiration of action.

As is well known[3], Vergil produced this impression by blending popular legends with systems of philosophy, and we need only note in conclusion that the effect is unique. A character created in literature is generally valued in so far as it enlarges our mental horizon and gives scope or form to our thoughts, impulses and ideas. The character of Aeneas does even more. It enables the imagination to look back over hundreds of years and to realise in a flash the many contributory efforts of brain and will which at last united in this serene and considered attitude to life and death. Thus the modern reader can face his own problems with the detached and tranquil gaze of the ancient Roman. Such is one of the privileges which literature

---

[1] Donatus, *Vit. Verg.* XIII.   [2] *Epp.* I, i, 10 and *passim*.
[3] *E.g.* Norden, E., *Aen. VI*, Einleitung *passim*.

confers: the student who seeks insight will also find the right mood in which to exercise it. Above all he will be convinced of the permanence and continuity of the human spirit. He will find that the many convergent tendencies which led through Homer, Hesiod, Herodotos, Plato and Vergil to this achievement, were again active in medieval Europe, and, despite the differences of age and of environment, brought men by similar steps to a like consummation.

The inquiry into this second, more complex stage is the subject of the following volume.

INDEX

TO PROPER NAMES AND TOPICS NOT ADEQUATELY INDICATED IN THE CONTENTS

Academica, 213 n.

Acarnanians, 159

Achan, 59

Achean warrior, 21 (human grandeur), 51 (true heroes of the *Iliad*), 83 (believe in the gods they revile), 101 (how represented in *Odyssey*), 121 (origin), 123 (assimilated poetry of conquered race?). *See* Homeric

Acheron, 196, 217

Achilleion, 44

Achilles, 19 (equipment), 34 (egoism), 35 (grief), 36 ff. (slays Kyknos), 43 (adventurer), 44 ff. (legend of early death), 48 (ruthlessness), 60 (human sacrifice), 68 (divine honours), 73 (does not fear ghosts), 78 (illuminated by flame), 82 (prayers), 84 (reveals his soul to Thetis), 87 (conquered by Fate), 92 ff. (treatment of Hektor's corpse), 93 (compared to a lion), 102 (miseries of serfdom), 117 (admires Odysseus), 159 (discloses future), 170, 183, 185 (Homeric idea of ghosts), 194

Adam, 82 ff.

Ad Familiares, 213 n.

Adrastos, 140

Aeneas 3, 24 (horses of), 68 (divine honours), 69 (destiny), 144, 178, 193, 204, 205 ff. (character), 211 ff. (defects of portraiture), 215, 218, 220

Aeneid, 114 n., 205 ff.

aeroplane, 26

Aeschere, 42 n.

Agamemnon, 18, 19, 21 (character and indifference to insult), 37, 59 (compared to Zeus), 71

Agelaos, 98

ἀγκυλομήτης, 71, 133, 152, 156

Aiakeidai, 68

Aiakos, 43

Aias, 3, 77, 80, 82 (prayers), 101, 150, 194, 207

aigis, 61

Aigisthos, 53, 103

αἶνος, 155

Aiolia, 135

Aiolos, 61

Αἶσα, 65

Aischylos, 159 n., 201

Aison, 143

Aithiopians, kingdom of, 115, 162

Aithiopis, 41 n., 149 n.

Aitolians, 159 (oracles)

Alaric, 170

Alexander the Great, 16, 170

Alkestis, 193

Alkinoos, palace of, 96

Alkyone, 145

Alkyonian lake, 194

Allegory, an, 7

Allen, T. W., 120 n.

Alpine scenery, 4

Althaia, 65

Amasis, 92, 171

Amathous, 156

ἀμενηνὰ κάρηνα, 185

Amphiaraos, 93

Amphinomos, 53, 102

Amphitryon, 44

ἀνάλκιδα θυμόν, 86 n.

Ancestor worship, 68, 70

Anchises, 24, 210, 220

anchorites, 8

Andromache, 40, 48, 49, 53, 84, 100, 210

Androphagoi, 117

anger, effects of, 36

Antilochos, 41

Antinoos, 102

Aphrodite, 18, 74 (origin)

Apollo, 10, 43 (guilty of homicide), 66, 74 (origin and attributes), 79, 80, 87 (kills Patroklos), 88 (forsakes Hektor), 93 (pleads for Hektor's corpse), 144, 152 (*Theognis*), 159 ff. (oracles)

CAMBRIDGE: PRINTED BY W. LEWIS, M.A., AT THE UNIVERSITY PRESS